Greta Gerwig's
Barbie

Greta Gerwig's
Barbie

Popular Culture, Cinema, and Gender

Edited by Hilary Radner
and Rebecca Stringer

BLOOMSBURY ACADEMIC
LONDON · NEW YORK · OXFORD · NEW DELHI · SYDNEY

BLOOMSBURY ACADEMIC
Bloomsbury Publishing Plc, 50 Bedford Square, London, WC1B 3DP, UK
Bloomsbury Publishing Inc, 1359 Broadway, New York, NY 10018, USA
Bloomsbury Publishing Ireland, 29 Earlsfort Terrace, Dublin 2, D02 AY28, Ireland

BLOOMSBURY, BLOOMSBURY ACADEMIC and the Diana logo are trademarks of
Bloomsbury Publishing Plc

First published in Great Britain 2026

Cover design: Ben Anslow
Cover image: *Barbie* (2023), dir. Greta Gerwig (© Warner Bros./Photofest)

A catalogue record for this book is available from the British Library.

A catalog record for this book is available from the Library of Congress.

ISBN: HB: 978-1-3505-2395-1
       PB: 978-1-3505-2396-8
       ePDF: 978-1-3505-2398-2
       eBook: 978-1-3505-2397-5

Typeset by RefineCatch Limited, Bungay, Suffolk
Printed and bound in India

For product safety related questions contact productsafety@bloomsbury.com.

To find out more about our authors and books visit www.bloomsbury.com
and sign up for our newsletters.

We dedicate this volume to our parents who are no longer with us, without whom we would not have become the women we are today.

Contents

Figures

Contributors

Melis Behlil is Professor at the Radio, Television, and Cinema Department at Kadir Has University, Istanbul, Turkey. She has been Visiting Scholar at Massachusetts Institute of Technology, Cambridge, US, a Research Associate at Stockholm University, Sweden, and a founding member of European Network for Cinema and Media Studies (NECS). Her three-year funded project titled "Positioning the Spectator in Cinematic Virtual Reality" was completed in 2025 and she serves as the country coordinator for the Horizon project "REBOOT: Reviving, Boosting, Optimising and Transforming European Film Competitiveness." She has published extensively on the contemporary Turkish film and television industry, as well as transnational Hollywood.

Pamela Church Gibson, formerly Reader in Cultural and Historical Studies at the London College of Fashion, University of the Arts London, UK, where she initiated an MA program in Film and Fashion in 2008, is now lecturing at Central Saint Martins. She has an international reputation as a scholar in the field of film and fashion, an area of research that she inaugurated and defined. She has published extensively on film, fashion, gender, costume, and heritage, and has co-edited six books and edited a seventh. A second edition of her monograph *Fashion and Celebrity Culture* is forthcoming from Bloomsbury Academic.

Seán Cubitt is Honorary Professorial Fellow at the University of Melbourne, Australia. His publications include *The Cinema Effect* (2005), *EcoMedia* (2015), *The Practice of Light* (2014), *Finite Media: Environmental Implications of Digital Technologies* (2017), *Anecdotal Evidence: Ecocritique from Hollywood to the*

Mass Image (2020), and two volumes of a trilogy on aesthetic politics, *Truth* (2023) and *Good* (2025). Co-editor of *Ecocinema: Theory and Practice 2* (2022), his research focuses on ecopolitical aesthetics and the history and philosophy of media.

Michael DeAngelis is Professor in the Department of Media and Popular Culture at DePaul University, Chicago, US. He is the author of *Gay Fandom and Crossover Stardom: James Dean, Mel Gibson, and Keanu Reeves* (2001) and *Rx Hollywood: Cinema and Therapy in the 1960s* (2017). He edited and contributed to the volume *Reading the Bromance: Homosocial Relationships in Film and Television* (2014). His essays appear in journals including *Camera Obscura*, *Cultural Critique*, and *Celebrity Studies*, and his work on queerness has appeared in book chapters on Robert Stigwood, Todd Haynes, Tom Cruise, and Russell Crowe.

Frédéric Dichtel is a PhD candidate at the University of Otago, Dunedin, New Zealand. The title of his doctoral research project is: "'He aha ai?'—'Nā te mea!' Ka taea e te mātai wetereo whakatairite me te mātai whakapapa reo te whakamārama ngā whakatakotoranga e kotiti ana i ngā ture wetereo?" ["'Why?'—'Because!' Can linguistic typology and historical linguistics explain the origin of some irregularities of Māori grammar?"]

Alex Dickie is a researcher at the Research Institute for Languages and Cultures of Asia at Mahidol University, Bangkok, Thailand. He holds an MA from the University of Otago, Dunedin, New Zealand and a PhD from the University of Auckland, Australia. His thesis, titled "Transnational Antipodean Auteurism: Australian and New Zealand National Cinema, Hollywood, and Film Style," grew out of his research interests in cinema as art and artifact, film genre studies, cinephilia, and auteurism. He is currently conducting a Worldwide Universities Network-supported research project on Muslim minority filmmakers in Thailand.

Ruken Doğu Erdede is a PhD candidate in Communication Studies at Kadir Has University, Istanbul, Turkey. She was a researcher on the project titled

"Women on Screen and Behind the Camera: A Contemporary Outlook of Representation and Labor of Women in Film and TV Industries in Turkey (2017–2021)." Currently, she is a researcher for REBOOT, a Horizon Europe project focused on the European film industry.

Suzanne Ferriss is Emeritus Professor at Nova Southeastern University, Davie, US. She has published extensively on literature, theory, film, and cultural studies. Notable publications include volumes on the cultural study of fashion, *On Fashion* (1994) and *Footnotes: On Shoes* (2001), both co-edited with Shari Benstock, and on chick culture: *Chick Lit: The New Woman's Fiction* (2005) and *Chick Flicks: Contemporary Women at the Movies* (2008), both co-edited with Mallory Young. She edited *The Bloomsbury Handbook to Sofia Coppola* (2023) and authored both *The Cinema of Sofia Coppola: Fashion, Culture, Celebrity* (2021) and the BFI Film Classics volume on *Lost in Translation* (2025).

Alistair Fox is Emeritus Professor at the University of Otago, Dunedin, New Zealand. In addition to his own scholarly publications, which include ten monographs, the most recent of which is *Melodrama, Masculinity and International Art Cinema* (2023), he has translated four books, as well as numerous articles and book chapters, from French into English, notably *Totally Truffaut* (Anne Gillain, 2021).

Bruce Isaacs is Associate Professor in Film Studies at the University of Sydney, Australia. His work focuses on the intersection of technologies of production, aesthetic styles, and modes of representation in classical and contemporary Hollywood. He is the author three books, most recently *The Art of Pure Cinema: Hitchcock and His Imitators* (2020). He is also the co-creator of the popular podcast, FILM Versus FILM (https://filmversusfilm.podbean.com/).

Claire Perkins is Senior Lecturer in the School of Media, Film and Journalism at Monash University, Melbourne, Australia. She is the author of *American Smart Cinema* (2012) and co-editor of several collections including *Indie Reframed: Women's Filmmaking and Contemporary American Independent Cinema* (2016) and *Independent Women: From Film to Television* (2021). With

Constantine Verevis, she also edits the "Screen Serialities" series for Edinburgh University Press.

Hilary Radner is Emeritus Professor of Film and Media Studies, University of Otago, Dunedin, New Zealand. Author of three monographs addressing the formation of contemporary feminine identity, *Shopping Around: Consumer Culture and the Pursuit of Pleasure* (1995), *Neo-Feminist Cinema: Girly Films, Chick Flicks and Consumer Culture* (2011), and *The New Woman's Film: Femme-centric Movies for Smart Chicks* (2017), her recent publications include *Raymond Bellour: Cinema and the Moving Image* (2018) and a special issue of the *Journal of New Zealand Studies*, "Art and Aotearoa New Zealand: Cultures, Controversies and Histories," co-edited with Edward Hanfling and Mark Stocker (NS38, September 2024).

Thomas Schatz is Mary Gibbs Jones Centennial Chair Emeritus of the Department of Radio-Television-Film at the University of Texas at Austin, US. His publications include *Hollywood Genres: Formulas, Filmmaking, and the Studio System* (1981), *The Genius of the System: Hollywood Filmmaking in the Studio Era* (1988), *Boom and Bust: American Cinema in the 1940s* (1997), and *Power Surge: Conglomerate Hollywood and the Studio System's Last Hurrah* (2026), and articles in the *New York Times*, the *Los Angeles Times*, *Premiere*, *The Nation*, *Film Comment*, *Film Quarterly*, and *Cineaste*. His history of Universal Pictures for Routledge's Hollywood Centenary series is currently in progress.

Geneviève Sellier is Emeritus Professor of Cinema Studies, Bordeaux Montaigne University, Pessac, France. A specialist in cinema and gender studies, her publications include *Jean Grémillon: Le cinéma est à vous* (1989), *La Drôle de guerre des sexes du cinéma français (1930–1956)* with Noël Burch (1996), *La Nouvelle Vague: Un cinéma au masculin singulier* (2005), *Masculine Singular: French New Wave Cinema*, trans. Kristin Ross (2008), *Le Cinéma au prisme des rapports de sexe* (2009), *The Battle of the Sexes in French Cinema*, trans. Peter Graham (2014), *Le Cinéma des midinettes: Cinémonde, ses "potineuses" et ses "potineurs" (1946–1967)*, (2023), and *Le Culte de l'auteur* (2024).

Sarah E. S. Sinwell is Associate Professor and Director of Graduate Studies in the Department of Film and Media Arts at the University of Utah, Salt Lake City, US. She is an award-winning researcher and has published essays in *Alphaville, Flow, Journal of Cinema and Media Studies, Jump Cut, MAI JOURNAL, New Review of Film and Television Studies, The Projector, Queer Studies in Media & Popular Culture, Refractory*, and *Women's Studies Quarterly*. Her research investigates the intersections between contemporary American independent cinema and new media platforms. Her book *Indie Cinema Online* (2020) redefines independent cinema in an era of media convergence.

Amy Skjerseth is Assistant Professor of Popular Music at the University of California, Riverside, US. Her scholarship focuses on intersections of music, media, material culture, and technology. She is currently working on two books: "Instrumental Presets: The Visible Past of Music Technology" and "The Feminist Wall of Sound." Her work has appeared in *Spectator, [in]Transition: Journal of Videographic Film & Moving Image Studies, Film Criticism, animation: an interdisciplinary journal, The Radio Journal: International Studies in Broadcast and Audio Media, Music, Sound, and the Moving Image*, and *Journal of Popular Music Studies*, among other venues.

Rebecca Stringer is Associate Professor in the Sociology, Gender Studies and Criminology Programme at the University of Otago, Dunedin, New Zealand. Her research explores gender and victimhood in theory, politics, and culture, and history of victimology. She is the author of *Knowing Victims: Feminism, Agency and Victim Politics in Neoliberal Times* (2014), and co-editor, with Hilary Radner, of *Feminism at the Movies: Understanding Gender in Contemporary Popular Cinema* (2011). Her work has appeared in journals such as *Feminist Legal Studies, Crime Media Culture, SubStance: A Review of Theory and Literary Criticism, New Zealand Sociology*, and *The Australian Feminist Law Journal*.

Patricia White is Director of the Aydelotte Foundation, Centennial Chair in Film and Media Studies, and Coordinator of Gender and Sexuality Studies at Swarthmore College, US. Her books include the BFI Film Classics volume on *Rebecca* (2021), *Women's Cinema/World Cinema: Projecting Contemporary Feminisms* (2015), *Uninvited: Classical Hollywood Cinema and Lesbian Representability* (1999), and, with Timothy Corrigan, *The Film Experience* (2020). Her current project is "Horizons of Women's Cinema: US Indie Women's Filmmakeing in the World." She is a member of the *Camera Obscura* editorial collective and serves on the boards of *Film Quarterly* and Women Make Movies.

Dylan Young is a PhD candidate at the University of Liverpool, UK on the topic of "Musical Continuity Across Disney's Transmedia Expansion of *Star Wars*," supervised by Giles Hooper and Lindsay Carter. His research focuses on popular culture's understanding of a franchise's music.

Alexandre Zamboni is a freelance fashion scholar and curator. He holds a BA in Fashion Design from Università Iuav di Venezia, Italy and an MA in Fashion Studies from Stockholm University, Sweden. Taking a feminist perspective, his MA thesis investigated the celebrity personas of the so-called Insta-girls, the new supermodels of the digital age. He is currently co-authoring a book with Pamela Church Gibson exploring the relations between fashion and celebrity in contemporary culture.

Acknowledgments

This volume evolved over many months of conversations with feminists around the corner and around the world, from as far away as France and Turkey. I myself would like to thank Audrey Mitchell whose invitation to contribute to a Forum on "Barbenheimer," published in the *Australasian Journal of American Studies* 43, no. 1 (2024), prompted me to look more closely at this new iteration of the woman's film, a genre that has preoccupied me for several decades. I would also like to express my gratitude to Veidehi Hans at Bloomsbury Academic who encouraged me to pursue a project on Greta Gerwig's *Barbie* when it was just a vague idea, noted hurriedly on a piece of paper. Veidehi and later Rex Cleaver, also at Bloomsbury, have been patient and consistent sources of information and encouragement over the several years of the project's incubation and emergence.

Rebecca Stringer, closer at hand in Dunedin, co-editor on the volume and comrade-in-arms, has provided good cheer and feminist companionship since she joined the project in late 2023, as well as expertise in contemporary gender theory. We owe a big shout out to our friends who attended our workshop screening of *Barbie* in May 2024: Bridie, Maeve, Wesley, Mark, and Charlotte. Their discussions served to point us in the right direction. Further down the line, the volume contributors have kept us going even when the going got tough. Their insights and perspicacity, the diversity of their approaches, have been a constant source of inspiration. We also wish to signal our appreciation to those scholars who read our proposal and the first draft of the manuscript, whose expert advice added significantly to our critical understanding of the film. These kinds of reviews are a crucial dimension of contemporary scholarship that rarely receives recognition, something of which we are both very aware.

Back in Dunedin, Frédéric Dichtel has proven himself yet again to be the right arm that every editor seeks to have by her side, while Jon Cox and Hayden Stephens were ever generous in sharing their expertise, providing much-needed technical support, as well as their insights about the movie. Jon Cox, in particular, was ever patient with what he called the "pink" Barbie-generated atmosphere of our shared workspace. Without the assistance of Sarah McGaughran, our very enthusiastic research assistant, who joined us in the final stages of preparing the manuscript, the project may never have seen the light of day.

Finally, we wish to thank our partners in life Alistair Fox and Brian Roper for their understanding, support, and forbearance in the long and, at times, rocky, but always rewarding, journey of discovery and consolidation that has produced this volume.

Hilary Radner
Dunedin, 2025

Foreword

HILARY RADNER

"If you love Barbie . . . This movie is for you . . . If you hate Barbie . . . This movie is for you."[1]

BARBIE MAIN TRAILER

One of the most striking aspects of Greta Gerwig's *Barbie* was the divisive response it elicited when it hit big screens around the world. Veteran French feminist film scholar Geneviève Sellier remarked in an online review of the film: "Here is an over-the-top instance of Hollywood's ability to reclaim even political and ideological advances that seem, at first sight, to run counter to its capitalist goals."[2] She asks us to consider the logic behind the film's production by "a capitalist company (Mattel) that for fifty years has been producing Barbie dolls, representing the most alienating feminine stereotype in consumer society, [which is facing] declining sales due to feminist criticism"—a situation that the film (funded in large part by Mattel) was designed to remedy. *Barbie*, for feminists such as Sellier, is a prime example of what Andi Zeisler has described in detail as "Marketplace Feminism."[3] And yet, Richard Brody—iconic cinephile and film reviewer, writing for the *New Yorker*—opines that *Barbie* is "a film that's energized throughout by a sense of artistic freedom and uninhibited creative passion greater than what Gerwig has brought to even her previous projects made outside the ostensible constraints of studio filmmaking." He argues that *Barbie* "is a film of the politics of culture and, by extension, of the need for a creative rebellion to reëstrange the familiar for the sake of social change."[4]

Brody was one of the many critics who repined against the judgments delivered by the 2024 Academy Awards. He highlighted, in addition to the poor reception of *Barbie*, the failure of Lily Gladstone to win an Oscar for her performance in Martin Scorsese's *Killers of the Flower Moon* (2023).[5] The Oscar awards, as well as Brody's response, underscores the splintered and diffuse identities that comprise today's cinema audience. The decisions of the Academy routinely, and increasingly, over the years, spark controversy, testifying to the fragmented nature of audiences and to the state of media industries, currently in flux.

To address the complexity of this film and the diversity of opinion that it has produced, this volume has drawn together a set of chapters from an international cohort of scholars covering four broadly defined fields. Part One deals with the cultural context of the film, with chapters by Thomas Schatz, Patricia White, and Pamela Church Gibson (with Alexandre Zamboni). Part Two comprises a discussion of the "Greta Gerwig touch" (her identity and style as a director), with Alex Dickie on the contemporary auteur, Claire Perkins on *Barbie* and the "smart chick flick," and Suzanne Ferriss on self-fashioning in the films of Greta Gerwig, with a focus on *Barbie*. Part Three addresses issues surrounding the contemporary conceptualization of identity as a disputed and fragmented cultural terrain with Sarah Sinwell on queer identities in *Barbie*; Amy Skjerseth and Dylan Young on music and the articulation of gender as a binary structure offset by a yearning for fluidity; and Melis Behlil and Ruken Doğu Erdede on the politics of gender and the reception of *Barbie* beyond audiences located in the Global North, notably Turkey. This section concludes with Michael DeAngelis's discussion of Ryan Gosling's star persona—its relations to "Ken" and the contemporary crisis of masculinity.

The fourth and final part characterizes the polemics and debates that have arisen around the film. Geneviève Sellier explores the bifurcated reception of the film among French feminists, observing that "*Barbie* attests to the fact that the issue is no longer the denunciation or the defense of feminism . . . but a debate on the nature of the kind of feminism that the film illustrates."[6] Bruce Isaacs contests the implicit racial and cultural biases that he sees the film presenting under the guise of arguing for reform. Rebecca Stringer, drawing on the theories of Guy Debord, Roland Barthes, and McKenzie Wark, demonstrates how Debord's strategy of "détournement" (often discussed in the Anglophone world as "culture jamming") has become a form of what Barthes described as inoculation in the 1950s, or in Wark's words "détournement détourné" (re-routing re-routed, or culture jamming jammed). Seán Cubitt raises the ecological issues underpinning the cultural values displayed by *Barbie*, despite (or, perhaps because of) the ironic and satirical bent of its discourse. He argues that the film appears to undermine contemporary social norms while masking their most invidious consequences in terms of ecological and human exploitation.

Topics addressed include: the contemporary auteur director; white American girlhood on film and in novels; the "smart film"; self-fashioning and consumer culture; queer identities; popular music and film; the dichotomization of gender; politics and reception studies; the global audience; star studies; the ambiguities of contemporary feminism; the politics of race, class, and gender; "culture jamming"; fashion and celebrity; contemporary ecological issues—as these relate to *Barbie* as an off-brand event film, emerging in what is perhaps the end of an era in which the most prominent forms of the woman's film were the girl-lead teen-blockbuster.

The breadth of topics covered in this volume mirrors the complexity of this deceptively simple "fable." As a female coming-of-age narrative, *Barbie* cannot avoid engaging with the contradictions and controversies that mark contemporary feminism, particularly in its relations to consumerism and neo-liberalism.[7] The success of this film raises an important question: was *Barbie* a spectacular one-off, or does it portend a reorientation of the whole cinema industry, the effects of which may not be apparent for several years? Cumulatively, then, the chapters included in this volume offer a detailed and nuanced perspective on a historically significant, benchmark film, produced, and distributed, by an industry in crisis—the brainchild of a contemporary director whose star is on the rise.

Introduction
"Barbie Land," Contextualizing Greta Gerwig's Barbie

HILARY RADNER

The editors of this volume live in a small, geographically isolated, university town called Dunedin in the south of New Zealand's South Island Te Waipounamu. When I told a friend that we were editing a volume on Greta Gerwig's *Barbie*, she said: "I thought that was all over. You don't hear anything about Barbie now." In fact, Barbie is everywhere in our town, from dolls in the Night n' Day (a local convenience store) to the decorations on battery-powered toothbrushes in the supermarket; she appeared in a Christmas parade last year as a float the size of a tiny house, and about as mobile; in December 2024, a local clothing store, geared toward students and the skateboard contingent, featured pink Birkenstocks. Even the Dunedin Public Art Gallery includes in its permanent collection a 1992 mixed-media work, by noted Aotearoa New Zealand artist Judy Darragh, titled "The Birth of Barbie".

Over the past months, the internet has not ceased announcing academic activities on the topic: podcasts, blog entries, articles, special issues of a journal, competing edited volumes, monographs on the director, at least one conference—the bibliography continues to grow. The *Neuron Daily*, an online

Figure 0.1 *A depiction of Barbie parodying the traditions of European art by Aotearoa feminist artist Judy Darragh. (Judy Darragh, "Birth of Barbie," 1992, mixed media, 1000mm h x 874 mm w x 195mm d.) Courtesy Judy Darragh/Dunedin Public Art Gallery, Dunedin, New Zealand.*

newsletter, reports: "Open AI and Mattel are making AI toys." Grant Harvey in the *Neuron* speculates that Mattel might produce what he calls a "Barbie DreamChat Companion . . . A Barbie that speaks multiple languages . . ." She "remembers your fashion choices . . ." and is "basically the friend every 8-year-old (and . . . 28-year-old) dreams of."[1] "Barbie" as a cultural icon has penetrated every dimension of contemporary life, including the halls of academe. Greta Gerwig's blockbuster film *Barbie* speaks to this phenomenon while actively participating in it, arguably aggrandizing Barbie's influence and, by extension, that of Mattel.

The chapters grouped here focus on the film and its director, seeking to elucidate the meta-commentary on contemporary culture that she provides. The director of *Barbie*, Greta Gerwig, developed her craft within American independent cinema in what director Nicole Holofcener calls the "little movie,"[2] independent films produced for a fraction of the cost of a blockbuster. These low-budget productions often took advantage of new developments in digital technology and distribution. Film scholar Yannis Tzioumakis notes that "mumblecore," a low-budget, very loose film style and genre associated with the first two decades of the twenty-first century, through which Gerwig initially launched her career, "was particularly known for its non-theatrical distribution, becoming known for their makers' creative use of video platforms and on-demand services."[3]

Barbie, in contrast, is a big movie, with a budget of over $100 million. As a Hollywood movie, it also draws on the tradition of popular films directed at a female audience financed by the Big Six conglomerates, the major international corporations controlling current Hollywood.[4] Building on the formulas and strategies of late-twentieth-century popular films directed at a female audience, *Barbie* (dir. Greta Gerwig, 2023) succeeded in capturing the complexity and contradictions of contemporary femininity, or, more specifically, neo-liberal feminism,[5] which is caught between feminism and consumerism. Speaking to women across a number of generations, from Baby Boomer to Gen Z, the film posed questions rather than serving up answers, offering current cinema at its most vital and most controversial. The purpose of this volume, then, is to depict the map of contemporary society offered by a film that records a story that captured a wide and diverse audience, whose enthusiastic response made it the top-grossing movie of 2023, an unprecedented feat for a film targeting primarily a female audience and helmed by a woman.[6]

Using a light touch, the film gratified the audience's need for a fun, smart, and entertaining fairy tale—a trip to fantasyland in which desires were fulfilled and simultaneously reexamined—or rather, questioned. What emerged was a general perplexity about the state of women and men today, in which

Stereotypical Barbie, or "Barbie Margot," as played by Margot Robbie, functions as a generative absence, her quest for identity revealing at the film's conclusion not an answer, but a question: "What was I made for?"

Barbie and the woman's film

Greta Gerwig's *Barbie* was an unprecedented success with audiences—it topped the worldwide box office in 2023 when it was released and was the all-time highest grossing film directed or co-directed by a woman.[7] Notwithstanding, it was snubbed at the 2024 Oscars despite favorable reviews from notable reviewers such as David Fear in *Rolling Stone* and Richard Brody of the *New Yorker*.[8] The divided views that the academy awards generated were reproduced in the varied reception of the film in different national contexts as described by Melis Behlil and Ruken Doğu Erdede in Chapter 9.[9] *Barbie's* reception, then, underscores the viability of what many call neo-liberalism or neo-feminism, while highlighting the denigrated position still accorded the woman's film.[10]

Barbie emerges out of a long history of films for women within the Hollywood context, many of which were traditionally distributed globally. At the same time, the film contradicts the cinema industry's expectations about *femme fare*, as it is called. Hollywood's current relationship with its female audiences arguably began in the second decade of the twentieth century, when the industry sought to attract upper- and middle-class female audiences with a view to making cinema respectable.[11] Considered the primary tastemakers in the decades that followed during the studio era, Hollywood produced a steady stream of films directed at the female audience featuring women stars, while typically remaining produced, written, and directed by men, with notable exceptions such as the director Dorothy Arzner.[12]

With the collapse of the studio system, a cohort of ever younger male audiences became the primary demographic target, beginning in the 1970s with New Hollywood and continuing during the period of conglomerate dominance.[13] The reasons for this shift were diverse, but a principal factor was that women by and large preferred to stay home, watching the screen narratives created by television in its various avatars, including broadcasting, cable, and streaming.[14] In the later twentieth century, the film industry made sporadic attempts to woo the female viewer. *Titanic* (1997), directed by James Cameron, a "commercial auteur," in Tim Corrigan's terms,[15] topped the 1998 box office but also took home a record number of Oscars. Gaylyn Studlar and Kevin S. Sandler point out: "*Titanic* represents the zenith of a self-conscious industrial attempt to woo female cinemagoers without simultaneously alienating its key male demographic in the process."[16]

Twenty-five years later, *Barbie* again attempted to surmount this same challenge. "The Hollywood film industry in 2023 was in serious disarray," in the view of Thomas Schatz, a perspective he elaborates in Chapter 1.[17] With the industry in crisis, its equilibrium disrupted by the rise of the streaming giants, in particular, Netflix and Disney,[18] *Barbie* (2023) constitutes a marked departure from that earlier model predicated on the importance of the male audience, which had continued to inform Hollywood's choice despite the success of *Titanic*, a film that deliberately targeted both male and female audiences. The increasing importance of streaming to the distribution of narrow-cast films had done nothing to discourage the widely accepted view that women preferred the home screen to the movie theater.

Titanic commenced with a premise designed to appeal to a male audience, not unlike *Oppenheimer* (dir. Christopher Nolan, 2023), a film often pitted against *Barbie* as the top movie of 2023, as Behlil and Erdede highlight in Chapter 9. Both *Titanic* and *Oppenheimer* focused on historical events designed to intrigue the male audience. *Barbie*, in contrast, helmed by director Greta Gerwig, associated with independent cinema and women-centered films, was unabashedly geared toward the female audience from the outset. The male audience appeared almost an afterthought; the film also, however, unexpectedly attracted a significant number of male viewers, with Ryan Gosling in the role of "Ken" garnering a distinct number of followers.[19] One fan, a university student, proclaimed: "I feel as through Ryan embraces me as a human being. He is more than a man crush, he's everything,"[20] echoing memes that appear under the "literally me" rubric,[21] a phenomenon explored in some depth by Michael DeAngelis in Chapter 10.[22] To the astonishment of many, in November of 2023, the *Barbie* audience was reported as "66.2 percent female . . . with 74.6

percent under the age of 29 . . .," meaning that it included a male audience of over 30%, most of whom were under 25. In contrast, *Oppenheimer* "had an audience that was 70.7 percent male with 52.9 percent over 30 years old."[23] The *Oppenheimer* audience, then, tended to be largely male, with more than half its viewers over 30.

Barbie's exceptionalism and affinities

Barbie is an exception in the history of films for women. Despite its appeal to the male audience, and its affinities with the "girly film," to borrow from Charlotte Brunsdon's discussion of films like *Pretty Woman* (dir. Garry Marshall, 1990)—films that combined an emphasis on consumerism and what is known as a neo-liberal feminism,[24] *Barbie's* performance in its category—its genre—is unprecedented. To give a sense of scale, *Pretty Woman* had an all-time worldwide box office of $463,406,268. *Barbie* reached $1,447,038,421.[25] *Barbie* topped the worldwide box office in 2023 and enjoyed a budget of "roughly $145 million," according to the *New York Times*, in comparison with *Pretty Woman's* $14 million (roughly the equivalent of about $36.7 million today).[26] *Barbie* has much in common with the girly film, characterized by a focus on shopping and, to a lesser degree, heterosexual romance, with significant variations, all of which were very much in line with what has been called neo-feminism, or, more generally in the past decade, neo-liberal feminism. Most importantly, as in *Barbie*, the film's protagonist was a woman at the center of her universe in which her own self-fulfillment was her primary concern.

Pretty Woman arguably inaugurated a renaissance of mid-tiered films for women—films that were neither "little movies" nor blockbusters in terms of budget. This cycle continued until the relative failure of *Sex and the City 2* (dir. Michael King, 2010) marked its end. The demise of the "girly film" genre, targeting a female audience and focused on romance and fashion, coincided with the near disappearance of the mid-tiered film as a whole, as pointed out by Alex Dickie in Chapter 4.[27] To some degree, streaming and independent low budget films continued the tradition of the woman's film and saw the development of the "smart chick" film, with which *Barbie* also had much in common, as signaled by Claire Perkins in Chapter 5.[28] The waning of the girly film, however, also coincided with an increasing paucity of films for the female audience designed for theatrical release.[29] Hollywood did develop various groupings of films that, to some degree, suggested an increasing recognition of the female audience. Film franchises addressing females under 25, such as *The Twilight Saga* (2008–12), *The Hunger Games* (2012–14),[30] *Divergent* (2014–16), all based on successful novels, mimicking the more successful franchises appealing to males under 25, also appealed to a lesser degree to females over 25.[31]

The success of *Wonder Woman* (2017), an extension of a preexisting franchise, directed by Patty Jenkins, with a 56-percent female audience in the United States, intimated that women might be able to look forward to their own superhero films starring women as well as girls;[32] however, with a worldwide box office of $822,963,408, it ranked only tenth in ticket sales.[33] Furthermore, it was unable, at least in part due to the COVID-19 pandemic, to produce a successful franchise. With Gal Gadot, the film's star, moving into more mature roles, the fate of the franchise remains uncertain.[34] It is also worth noting that *Barbie*'s box office was far below the top box offices of pre-pandemic films such as *Avatar* (dir. James Cameron, 2009) with a worldwide box office of $2,923,706,026, the top worldwide grossing film of all time, to date.[35] Perhaps even more significantly, the Chinese production *Ne Zha 2* (dir. Jiaozi, 2025), an animated film and the second in a series, released at the end of January 2025, is currently the worldwide top grossing film of 2025 at $2,000,814,256, perhaps constituting a more potent indicator of a future trend in which Hollywood no longer dominates the world's screens.[36]

While *Barbie* differed from its *femme fare* precursors and was significantly more successful, it was not part of a franchise, but it did have Mattel. It was not just a girly film; it was also about "toys," linking it to other successful event films targeting the family audience.[37] The successful *Toy Story* franchise featured Barbie in *Toy Story 2* (dir. John Lasseter, 1999) in a small role and she was given a more significant role in *Toy Story 3* (dir. Lee Unkrich, 2010). Many in *Barbie*'s audience would have grown up watching these films, meaning that it also followed a pattern of successful event films based on toys and video games, usually animated. *Barbie* was also, in many ways, a fairy tale, a story that takes place in a land far, far away, underlining that it also had much in common with Disney's successes for the female audience, such as *Frozen* (dir. Chris Buck and Jennifer Lee, 2013) that, like *Barbie*, introduced songs that would later become popular as stand-alone creations.

"Stereotypical Barbie": A central character without depth

Gerwig's fairy story offers an unlikely heroine in "Stereotypical Barbie"—incarnated by Margot Robbie, or "Barbie Margot," as she is called in the film's script, a character that has less appeal, and perhaps less notoriety than the "supporting" characters that surround her, such as Ken, Gloria, and Weird Barbie.

In the film's opening sequence, *Barbie*'s "female" narrator (Helen Mirren) proclaims: "Barbie is all these women. And all these women are Barbie." The camera glides over an array of beaming women and girls, all of whom have more in common with "Stereotypical Barbie" than does the film's audience. All are a credit to the dental profession, not a hair out of place, resplendent in their spotless outfits, which reflect the diversity of their represented activities. All conform to the impossible physical norms displayed by "Barbie Margot"; the Barbie cohort offers a sense of perfection that can only be achieved temporarily—with the help of physical trainers, makeup artists, experienced lighting technicians, hairdressers, fashion stylists, costume designers, etc., a veritable team of professionals—and, thus, undermines the claims to universality made by Mirren's voice-over. Mirren herself makes this point indirectly near the film's conclusion when Barbie Margot remarks tearfully, "I'm . . . not . . . pretty . . . anymore . . . Not Stereotypical Barbie pretty." Mirren comments: "*Note to the filmmakers, Margot Robbie is the wrong person to cast if you want to make this point.*" Barbie Margot is marked out de facto by her position as a celebrity and the star of the movie such that she incarnates a "stereotype" against which all women will be considered inadequate.

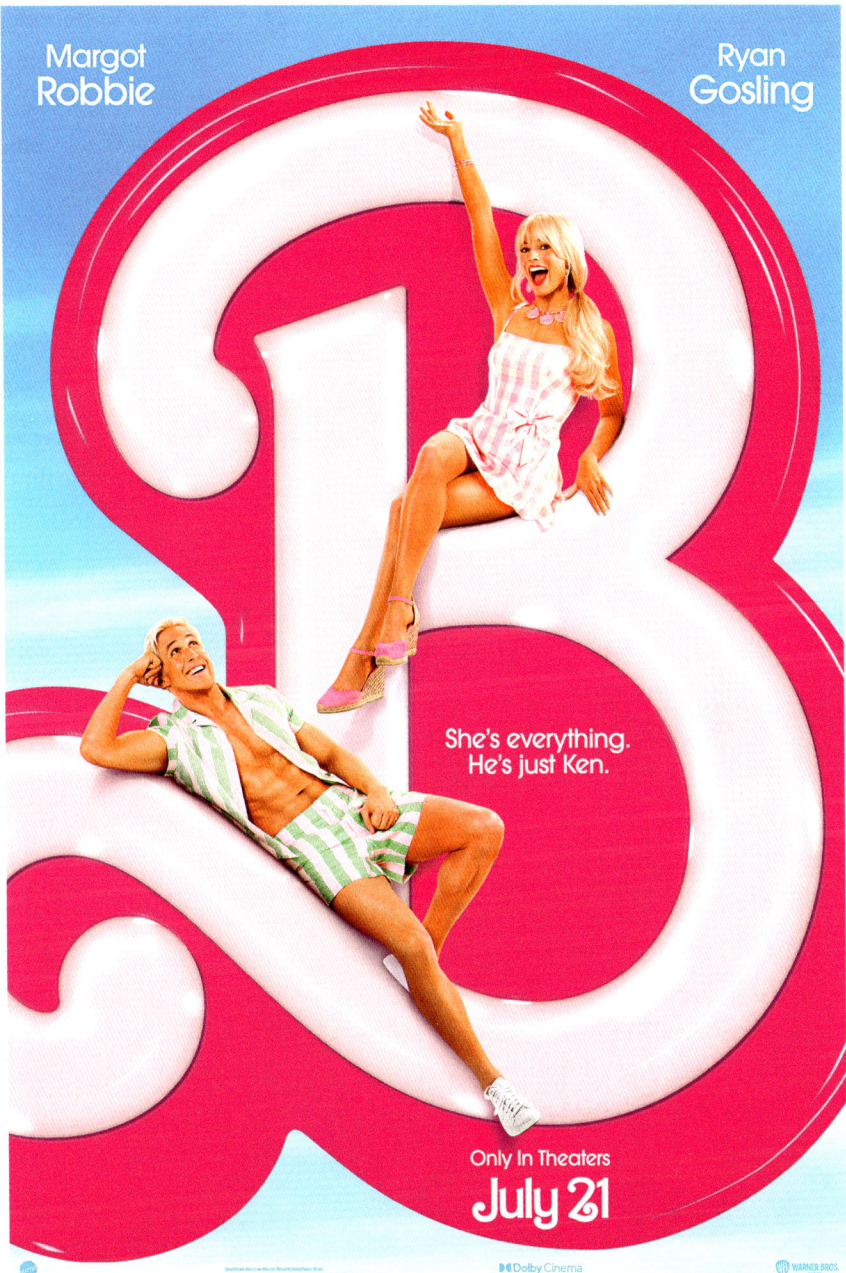

Figure 0.2 *This poster portrays an ebullient, dominant Barbie, highlighting the pathos of her eventual fate at the film's conclusion. Courtesy BFA/Alamy.*

Unexpectedly, and paradoxically, the film makes every effort to underline just how inadequate Margot Barbie actually is, to the point that, at the film's end, she seems to have lost her autonomy. Stripped of her pointedly feminine garments, the despondent and hesitant persona into which she evolves presents a striking contrast to the buoyant and jubilant young woman who opened the film. At the film's conclusion, Barbie, who once drove freely in her own pink convertible, needs to be chauffeured to her doctor's appointment and requires the encouragement of her adopted family to exit their vehicle and proceed unaccompanied to her appointment with her gynecologist.

Barbie manages then, in some ways, by undermining the charisma of its own star, to offer a concept of "woman" that defies the kind of normative standards that Margot Robbie in her role as "Stereotypical Barbie" appears to represent. Sarah Sinwell argues in Chapter 7 that "*Barbie* is both upholding and resisting contemporary notions of femininity, masculinity, and queerness."[38] Certainly, the empty passivity of "Barbie Margot," in contrast with the proactive position taken by those around her, from Weird Barbie to Alan (both "queer" in Sinwell's terms), to Gloria and her daughter Sasha, erodes the credibility of the stereotype that Barbie represents. Sinwell explains that "*Barbie* is rethinking media constructions of American culture by putting queer people and queer women at the center of its storytelling."[39]

Barbie herself as a figure manifests the phenomenon described by the Irish poet W. B. Yeats as "the centre" that "cannot hold" in his famous poem "The Second Coming," with Barbie representing an emblem of twenty-first-century "middle-class despair" according to Pamela Church Gibson and Alexandre Zamboni in Chapter 3. This phenomenon might be described as "the structuring absence" at the heart of the film's narrative, a role that Robbie fills to perfection through her ability to project an almost plastic and depthless perfection.[40] Until well into act three of the film, Robbie's function is to "look good" in a wide array of outfits that often featured what has become known as "Barbie" pink, a role that she continued in her off-screen appearances. This Barbie pink when paired with blue (as it often was) seemed to suggest the "Trans Pride Flag," providing another strand in the queer thread identified by Sinwell.[41]

Amy Skjerseth and Dylan Young opine in Chapter 8, echoing Church Gibson and Zamboni in Chapter 3, that, in contrast with Ken who performed

Figure 0.3 *Ryan Gosling and Margot Robbie with a* Barbie *pink and blue background. Courtesy JEP Celebrity Photos/Alamy.*

or "acted," "Margot Robbie paraded Barbie's outfits in press appearances, with her very photogenic 'looks' stressed inside and outside of the film,"[42] invoking John Berger's famous adage, dating back to the 1970s: "Men *act* and women *appear*."[43] As Church Gibson and Zamboni remark: "Robbie of course has been a Chanel brand ambassador for several years." They conclude: "[R]arely has a movie" sparked so much fashionable activity at viewing theatres.[44]

In her role as the proverbial clothes horse, Robbie's Stereotypical Barbie underlines her function as a structuring absence (she cannot even sing/speak for herself) around which the narrative is created. The goal of her journey is to reveal that she has no center—she has not, as yet, created a self that she could come to "know" in any meaningful way. Ruth Handler, her mentor and creator, a ghost in the film, ends up giving Barbie an imperative: "Now . . . FEEL." The emphasis on feeling on Handler's part dismisses rationality as having a role in determining Barbie's final choice as the film nears its conclusion: should she remain a doll, function as an ideal, a symbol, or become human?

Significantly, her existential crisis, which catalyzes the narrative and her journey, initially takes the form of what she calls "thoughts of death," recalling the Christian tradition of *memento mori* ("Remember you [must] die")—a motif that has its roots in Roman culture. The idea underlying this theme is that a recognition of the inevitability of death should turn the individual away from

Figure 0.4 *Tears: the Real World humanizes Barbie as she learns to feel (Barbie, dir. Greta Gerwig, 2023).*

a preoccupation with the ephemera of this world to ponder the deeper truths of human existence. The *Catholic Reporter* boldly states: "Barbie's memento mori teaches us that reckoning with death shows us how to live."[45] By the end of the film, Barbie comes to realize the emptiness of her life in Barbie Land. Becoming "human" stands in for the "soul" that the Little Mermaid in Hans Christian Andersen's eponymous fairy tale successfully sought to acquire.[46] The beginning of Barbie's self-realization, her loss of innocence, occurs when she first knows tears, early in her visit to the Real World. These tears are a sign of her growing "humanization," culminating in the "Now ... FEEL" sequence during the film's denouement, when, significantly, her tears return.[47]

Greta Gerwig: Coming of age

Unlike popular bonkbuster romances (also known as sex-and-shopping novels) destined for women readers[48] or popular films such as *Fifty Shades of Grey* (dir. Sam Taylor-Johnson, 2015), Gerwig's dramedy of self-discovery avoids the sexual turn that marks so many contemporary screen narratives for adults; instead, she focuses on the eternal questions that underpin the classic portrayal of a coming-of-age chronicle: who am I, what is my destiny? Barbie undertakes a journey, a similar journey to that which figures in Gerwig's earlier films, providing a kind of allegorical *Bildungsroman* (literally a "novel of education") for the contemporary woman, as elaborated by Patricia White and Suzanne Ferriss in Chapters 2 and 6, respectively.[49]

Gerwig's earlier films, in which she participated as actress, screenwriter, and eventually director, revolved around the plight of young women living in the world that inhabitants of the Global North know only too well; as such, they exhibited an almost autobiographical quality. *Lady Bird* (2017), Gerwig's first notable directorial success (though she had previously co-directed a number of mumblecore films), revisits the classic coming-of-age narrative, focusing on the relations between a mother and daughter, with elements that clearly recall her own personal history. In contradistinction, *Barbie* speaks to Gerwig's larger cultural and historical concerns, as White argues in Chapter 2, with *Barbie* revisiting a recognizable icon of what White calls "American girlhood," as does

Figure 0.5 *Greta Gerwig directs Saoirse Ronan in* Lady Bird *(2017). Courtesy Lifestyle Pictures/Alamy.*

Gerwig's second film *Little Women* (2019).[50] This film, the latest adaptation of an iconic novel by Louisa May Alcott, explores the coming of age of a family of sisters, the Marches.[51] With a budget of $40 million, it qualifies as one the rare recent mid-tier films that targets a female audience. The film also might be characterized as a U.S. version of what known as a "heritage" film, a spate of end-of-century British productions.[52]

The characters that inhabit the novel *Little Women*, like Barbie the doll, have become popular figures during the twentieth century, reiterated frequently in literature and cinema directed at young girls and young women. Barbie, like Jo in Gerwig's *Little Women*, undertakes a journey in which "her ending" remains ambiguous. Linking Gerwig's vision to a tradition inaugurated by Alcott, Patricia White remarks that, by "dramatizing a conventional girl-gets-boy happy ending without fully settling the question of its diegetic status," Gerwig leaves us wondering whether Jo, *Little Women*'s organizing sensibility, will marry.[53] The author, Louisa May Alcott, often identified with her character Jo, did not. In a far more obvious manner than in this earlier film, Gerwig underscores that Barbie's ending is not "the end," but a new beginning.

Figure 0.6 *The March sisters in* Little Women *(dir. Greta Gerwig, 2019). Courtesy Entertainment Pictures/Alamy.*

Barbie alone: A "kitsch" paradox

Ultimately, Gerwig does not sentimentalize her heroine's story; she brings a wry, ironic sensibility to her narrative, one that draws back from sentiment while leaning into satire. This darker view of the world suggests the influence of her husband and co-writer Noah Baumbach on the screenplay. A noted auteur director, Baumbach brings an essentially pessimistic view of the human condition to his films. *Barbie* remains ambiguous. It routinely asks women to reconsider the world offered to them by narratives such as *Sex and the City* (HBO, 1998–2004), which share the sex-and-shopping aesthetic of the bonkbuster—a world often represented through the clothing choices made by characters, with self-fashioning an important concern in *Barbie*, as Ferriss elucidates in Chapter 6.[54]

Not coincidentally, Weird Barbie famously presents Barbie's existential choices in terms of shoes when Barbie consults her in response to the series of disfunctions, from "thoughts of death" to flat feet, that afflict her. She illustrates Barbie's dilemma by presenting her with two types of footwear—a cork-soled sandal (a Birkenstock) or a pink stiletto (a Manolo Blahnik). As it turns out, however, Barbie really has one choice, to journey to the Real World, represented by the sandal, a classic brown Birkenstock, which would allow Barbie "to know the truth about the universe." When Margot Barbie hesitates to undertake her journey, Weird Barbie warns her: "Fine, get cellulite, I don't care."

The option of choosing a Birkenstock suggests multiple possible interpretations. For many viewers (but not all) the sense that the film offers *queerness* as a not fully realized, but desirable, possibility is suggested when Barbie as "Barbara" dons pink Birkenstocks for her visit to her gynecologist in the film's final scenes. (Barbie, or Barbara Handler, as the human Barbie calls herself, after her creator, wears pink Birkenstocks at the film's conclusion.) Yet, Birkenstocks have a long history, dating back to 1774, during which both men and women wore the shoe. In recent decades, Birkenstocks have had something of a fashion moment, according to the *Guardian*, "with the luxury e-tailer Yoox reporting that its best-selling shoe of 2022 was the Boston Clog from Birkenstock."[55] Gerwig, a keen observer of human behavior and fashion, is no doubt metaphorically winking at the viewer, while citing the currently popular shoe's fraught history. In 2014, as one of "13 Fashion People on Birkenstocks," she confessed: "I grew up in Northern California, so I was born with Birkenstocks on. So I'm into it."[56]

Paradoxically, the highlighting of the Birkenstock underlines a seeming promotion of a constraining stereotype (whether it be Birkenstocks or Barbie the doll), coexisting with an homage to the history of queer culture, in which the brown Birkenstock has its place, as described by Sinwell in Chapter 7.[57] Consequently, this ambiguity, this ability to contain contradiction, becomes one of the defining features of the film, leading other scholars such as Seán Cubitt in Chapter 14 to link the film's style to a form of postmodernism predicated on paradox, but that, nevertheless, descends into kitsch. In Cubitt's words, "Sharing the unanchored allegories and cognitive dissonance of the postmodern but no longer haunted by the ghosts of the avant garde, kitsch is the available mode of critique after postmodernism," the one that Gerwig mobilizes in *Barbie*.[58] Others, such as Claire Perkins, associate these moments with the irony that characterizes the "smart film" that emerges in the 1990s out of the independent cinema tradition, what Kim Wilkins calls "eccentric cinema."[59] Geneviève Sellier, in Chapter 11, posits this irony as generating a kind of ambiguity that produces an inherently incoherent discourse around consumerism and feminism.[60] Bruce Issacs echoes Sellier, commenting in Chapter 12: "I confess to finding the film a condescending and vacuous fiction portending some form of concern for the individual, with an incoherent message of urgency for various collectives."[61]

The film, thus, offers a lighthearted parable with a dark underbelly, one in which an ostensibly humorously enunciated irony, parody, and, at times, satire mask a more sinister vision of contemporary culture. Authors like Rebecca Stringer and Seán Cubitt underline this double valence. In Chapters 13 and 14, respectively, they draw attention to the fact that the film's appeal is grounded in an industrial system reliant on plastic and the pursuit of self-fulfillment.[62] Greta Gerwig's *Barbie* reminds viewers that fairy tales never promised us a world without difficult decisions in the face of the darker sides of human existence.

Part One

A Fragmented World: The Cultural Moment

The Barbenheimer Phenomenon and the Post-Pandemic Streaming-Era Movie Industry

THOMAS SCHATZ

It goes without saying that *Barbie* was a truly historic hit, and that it undoubtedly would have been at any point in recent decades. But coming when it did— on July 21, 2023, the date of its domestic release—and joined at the hip, so to speak, with *Oppenheimer*, another monumental hit released the same day, renders *Barbie* all the more remarkable. Indeed, its ascent to the very top of the box-office heap in 2023 was positively stunning, considering what it faced as a one-off "woman's picture" from emerging indie auteur Greta Gerwig. *Barbie* swam upstream against multiple industry currents, most notably Hollywood's obsessive commitment to blockbuster franchises geared to global audiences; the onslaught of streaming, both as a delivery system and as a source of original programming from a new breed of studios; and the lingering effects of the Covid-19 pandemic, which crippled the movie business and accelerated the worldwide pivot to streaming. There were other challenges as well, including the writers' and actors' strikes just prior to *Barbie*'s release, as well as the ongoing impact of the #MeToo movement, both of which spoke volumes about the plight of top talent, and particularly women, in the movie industry.

Oddly enough, *Barbie* wasn't up against *Oppenheimer*. The two films initially were seen in competitive terms, particularly by the trade press which gauged Warner Bros.' decision to release *Barbie* on the same day that Universal opened *Oppenheimer* as an act of aggressive counterprogramming and a swipe at former Warner ally Christopher Nolan. But fans of both films (and both filmmakers) saw the pairing differently, coining the "Barbenheimer" portmanteau shortly after the *Oppenheimer* release date was announced and celebrating the two seemingly antithetical productions in symbiotic terms, as the veritable yin and yang of contemporary Hollywood. That notion steadily caught on and dramatically impacted the films' release campaigns, fueling one of the biggest and most unusual opening weekends in Hollywood annals. And the success of both films, in turn, not only bolstered the recovery of the struggling post-pandemic theatrical market but threatened to disrupt the surging streaming industry.

Critical conditions: The state of the movie industry in 2023

To fully appreciate the Barbenheimer phenomenon, we need to situate the two singular productions in the larger industrial context. We might begin by noting that the Hollywood film industry in 2023 was in serious disarray. The most obvious and immediate reasons for this were the combined impact and complex interplay of streaming and the Covid-19 pandemic. But the deeper reasons involve the studios behind *Barbie* and *Oppenheimer*, Warner Bros. and Universal Pictures, along with their parent companies Time Warner and Comcast (owner of NBC Universal) and the rest of the so-called Big Six media conglomerates—Disney, Sony (owner of Columbia), News Corp (Fox), and Viacom (Paramount). That cadre of media powers consolidated control of the U.S. film and television industries in the early 2000s after more than a decade of furious media mergers and acquisition (M&A). That M&A action culminated in 2004 with the launch of NBC Universal (by GE, which later sold the media combine to Comcast), and at that point the Big Six owned all the major film studios, all the broadcast TV networks, and most of the top cable networks. They dominated other media industries as well, but their key assets were their film and television holdings.[1]

Warner and Universal also were involved in a decisive reset in the old guard's response to new media. In 2000, at the height of the dot-com boom, Time Warner merged with the internet giant AOL (in a staggering $165 billion deal) and Universal was acquired by the French conglomerate Vivendi (for $38 billion). The architects of both record-setting deals were betting on high-speed internet—then known as broadband—which was just ramping up. But the rollout of broadband proved to be disastrously slow, which was a key factor in the dot-com bust of the early aughts and the collapse of both the AOL and Vivendi deals in 2002. In the wake of that bust and the consolidation of the Big Six, the major film studios retrenched, doubling down on the traditional theater-driven business and their blockbuster franchises—which went into another register in the new millennium with the *Lord of the Rings*, *Harry Potter*, *Spider-Man*, and *Shrek* series, and Nolan's *Dark Knight* trilogy. The studios fixated, too, on the exploding overseas markets, which couldn't get enough of their franchise fare. After running neck-and-neck with the domestic market for years, Hollywood's overseas markets took off in 2004 and began climbing at a stunning rate, doubling domestic by 2009 and nearly tripling it by 2019. At that point eighty-three of the top one hundred all-time worldwide hits had been released since 2004, and every one of them was a franchise film.[2]

The conservative turn paid off, as the studios reaped record profits and relied more and more heavily on high-cost, low-risk series spectacles. That put the squeeze on mid-range and prestige pictures and sounded the death knell for the indie movement, as the conglomerate-owned Indiewood outfits were decimated, the independent market imploded, and independent hits like *The Passion of the Christ* and *Fahrenheit 9/11* (both 2004), simply stopped happening. The roiling M&A waters also calmed down in 2004. The only major transaction over the next decade involved NBC Universal, interestingly enough, which GE sold to Comcast in a deal that closed in 2013. The first inklings of another M&A wave came in 2018 with AT&T's buyout of Time Warner and Disney's acquisition of 21st Century Fox. More than simply a realignment of the old-media giants, both deals signaled the conglomerates' first serious response to streaming—the delivery technology itself and the growing threat of Netflix and Amazon, as the prospect of broadband finally caught up with the film and television industries.

Both Netflix and Amazon were launched in the late 1990s and parlayed the new DVD technology into early success in the booming home-video market. Both also shrewdly exploited the internet, initially to market their inventory and engage their subscribers, and by the mid-2000s to deliver films and television series. Both moved into original programming in the 2010s, which took off with a run of hit Netflix series in 2013 including *House of Cards* (Netflix, 2013–18) and *Orange Is the New Black* (Netflix, 2013–19). That sparked a stunning five-year surge as Netflix's stockpile of original programming grew from 73 hours in 2013 to over 1,500 in 2018, while its subscriber count grew from 40 million to 140 million and its market value spiked from $22 billion to $130 billion. Netflix also nabbed 112 Emmy nominations in 2018, the first year since 2001 that any network outpaced HBO. Amazon followed at a more modest pace, scoring its first series hit with *Transparent* in 2014 (Amazon Prime, 2014–19). It also was the first of the streamers to score a feature film hit (and two Oscar wins) with *Manchester by the Sea* (dir. Kenneth Lonergan), in 2016. But Netflix was more aggressive in that arena as well, acquiring and streaming more than fifty feature films in 2017, far more releases than Amazon or any of the Hollywood studios. Netflix also began edging into the theatrical realm in 2018 with the Oscar-qualifying limited release of Alfonso Cuarón's *Roma*.

Netflix's arrival as a Hollywood player was signaled in January 2019 when *Roma* was showered with ten Oscar nominations including best picture (resulting in three wins) on the same day that the Motion Picture Association designated Netflix a major Hollywood studio. Those were watershed events for the streaming and movie industries, although Netflix was overshadowed on both fronts that year by Disney. The studio topped the domestic market for the fourth straight year in 2019, grabbing a staggering 33-percent share on just ten theatrical releases, nine of which were franchise blockbusters. Disney's buyout of Fox also closed in March 2019, increasing its heft in the media realm while giving it controlling interest in Hulu, the number two streaming service behind

Netflix. At that point Disney began gearing up for the November launch of its own service, Disney+, the first foray by a legacy Hollywood power into streaming. Disney+ faced stiff competition from Apple, which rolled out its much-hyped Apple TV+ service on November 1. But its meager lineup of original programs and lack of a library attracted few subscribers, and the launch was a bust. Disney+, on the other hand, was an immediate hit, enrolling 10 million subs on day one and surpassing 25 million by late December. Its success was fueled by multiple factors: an ad-free, low-cost service; the momentum of its theatrical hits; its small but incomparable library; and a slate of ten new features and twenty-five original series, including the *Mandalorian*, a Star Wars spinoff hit that established a prototype for its subsequent series offshoots of its LucasFilm and Marvel franchises.

The success of Disney+ spurred the ramp-up of Warner's HBO Max, NBC Universal's Peacock, and ViacomCBS's Paramount+. But it also launched just before the outbreak of Covid-19 and the ensuing pandemic, which hastened the global move to streaming. That rendered Netflix, Amazon, and Apple stronger than ever, while pressuring the legacy media companies that bet on streaming to persevere, despite the crippling startup and content costs. Netflix was the only profitable streaming service during and after the pandemic, netting over $5 billion in 2021 and again in 2022, while the legacy companies lost billions. But the movie business did begin to recover as the pandemic eased, and by 2022 it had climbed to roughly two-thirds of its pre-pandemic level. Franchise fever ran higher than ever, with the top ten hits alone that year—all of them big-budget sequels or franchise films—accounting for over half the ticket sales. The M&A action resumed as well, highlighted by two landmark deals announced in March 2021. One was Amazon's $8.45 billion acquisition of MGM, which gave the tech giant a legendary movie brand and added some 4,000 titles to its massive library. The other saw AT&T, which was struggling with the move to streaming and with mounting debt, unload Warner in a deal with Discovery, a second-tier cable company that paid $43 billion for a minority stake and complete control of the stumbling media giant, which was renamed Warner Bros. Discovery when the deal closed in 2022, with Discovery boss David Zaslav installed as CEO.

Greta Gerwig and Christopher Nolan: Different paths to an unlikely convergence

Thus, *Barbie* and *Oppenheimer* were conceived and executed during a period of enormous churn and uncertainty in Hollywood and in the media ecosystem at large. And as auteur-driven prestige pictures that were financed and distributed by major Hollywood studios which went on to become enormous commercial hits, both were exceedingly rare commodities in an industry overrun by high-stakes sequels, reboots, and superhero spectacles. That said, the backstories and career trajectories of the writer-directors behind the two films were altogether different, with Gerwig emerging from the independent sector as it cratered in the late 2000s, while Nolan with his *Dark Knight* trilogy was among the prime perpetrators of the blockbuster franchise mentality that hastened the indie movement's decline. But, paradoxically, *Oppenheimer* would bring Nolan more critical praise and award-season kudos than Gerwig enjoyed with *Barbie*, which was the linchpin in CEO Ynon Kreiz's objective to "transition [Mattel] from being a toy-manufacturing company, making items, to an I.P. company managing franchises."[3] *Barbie* obviously advanced that effort, which helps explain why the Academy overruled the Writers Guild and categorized the script by Gerwig and her husband (and first-rank indie auteur) Noah Baumbach as an adaptation rather than an original screenplay in its eventual Oscar nomination, due to its basis on preexisting material.[4]

That remarkably wrong-headed decision by the Academy belies the fact that *Barbie* was an original and innovative film that recast its iconic source material, although it did underscore that fact that Gerwig had moved to the Hollywood mainstream after starting her career on the industry margins. Her early work was primarily as an actress in low-budget independent films, before venturing into screenwriting on *Hannah Takes the Stairs* (dir. Joe Swanberg, 2007), and she wrote, co-directed, and co-starred in *Nights and Weekends* (dir. Joe Swanberg and Greta Gerwig, 2008), a no-budget mumblecore outing. Her acting career began taking off after her first film with writer-director Noah Baumbach, *Greenberg* (2012), in which she co-starred with Ben Stiller, and led to roles with top directors like Woody Allen and Whit Stillman. An early breakthrough came in another Baumbach-directed film, *Frances Ha* (2012), a screwball comedy-drama that Gerwig co-wrote with Baumbach, and that she carried to critical and (modest) commercial success in the title role. That put Gerwig on the map as an actress, mainly in mid-range indie pictures, and by then she and Baumbach were living together and starting a family. (They wed in 2023.)

Gerwig's first solo directing effort was *Lady Bird* (2017), a wry and very personal character study that she spent several years writing and developing. The film was a solid hit for indie powerhouse A24 (partnered with Focus, which handled overseas distribution) and a major career boost for Saoirse Ronan in the title role. *Lady Bird* also was a critical and award-season hit, garnering five Oscar nominations including best picture, best director, and best original screenplay. The film's success gave Gerwig the confidence and leverage to convince producer Amy Pascal to hire her to direct *Little Women*, which she began scripting for Sony/Columbia prior to *Lady Bird*. She won the assignment and gave the seventh adaptation of Louisa May Alcott's 1868 novel a very contemporary spin. Gerwig restructured the story as flashbacks, with a stellar cast that included Ronan, Laura Dern, Emma Watson, Timothée Chalamet, and Meryl Streep playing both their older and younger selves. She also foregrounded the story's feminist themes and gave the ending—which Alcott's editor famously insisted include the heroine's betrothal—an ambiguous self-reflexive twist.[5]

Pascal ran interference with the studio, which required some effort. "This is not a movie that studios are making these days," said Pascal shortly before the film's release. "It's not your typical period piece, it's pretty meta, pretty subversive."[6] It was also pretty successful. Released on Christmas Day, 2019, just before Covid struck, *Little Women* finished among the year's top ten box-office hits with a $219 million worldwide gross. It was a critical and award-season hit as well, culminating in six Oscar nods including best picture and best adapted screenplay—but not best director, interestingly enough, which *Variety* deemed "the single biggest snub of this year's nominations," auguring an even more infamous snub a few years later.[7]

By then Gerwig was working on *Barbie*, which she and Baumbach co-scripted during the pandemic. Her champion on that project—and another sympatico woman producer—was Margot Robbie, who of course was starring in the $140 million Warner Bros. production. Robbie's emergence as a star and a Hollywood player paralleled Gerwig's, sparked by a breakout role in Martin Scorsese's *The Wolf of Wall Street* in 2013. She and husband Tom Ackerley founded their production company LuckyChap Entertainment a year later, which had a hit with its first release, *I, Tonya* (dir. Craig Gillespie, 2017), securing Robbie's stardom. She had a strong record with indie-inclined auteurs like Scorsese and Quentin Tarantino (in *Once Upon a Time in Hollywood*, 2019), and her three films prior to *Barbie* were with writer-directors David O. Russell (*Amsterdam*, 2022), Damien Chazelle (*Babylon*, 2022), and Wes Anderson (*Asteroid City*, 2023).

Robbie persuaded Mattel to let LuckyChap produce *Barbie* on the strength of her star appeal and aptness for the title role but little else—i.e., no story, no script, no director. She and Mattel film boss Robbie Brenner took pitches from multiple writers, but nothing clicked until they met with Gerwig, whose ideas for the film bowled them over. Margot Robbie was sold on Gerwig as writer-director early on, but Gerwig wasn't ready to commit until she and Baumbach finished the script.[8] By then she was eager to helm the film and was comfortable working with Robbie as well as Mattel, and her attachment as director was announced in July 2021.[9] Brenner later asserted that the finished film was very much in line with the initial Gerwig-Baumbach draft, which went into production without input or obstruction—or even notes—from Mattel or from Warner Bros. Much of that was due to Robbie and Ackerman insisting on her autonomy and creative control, although Gerwig also thought that "it was *all* so idiosyncratic and so wild, it was almost like no one really knew where to start taking it apart."[10]

In stark contrast to Greta Gerwig's recent ascent was the estimable career of Christopher Nolan, whose stature as a mainstream Hollywood auteur had been steadily rising for decades. His ascent began with his second film, *Memento* (2000), a low-budget independent neo-noir that landed him a directing assignment at Warner Bros. for a mid-range thriller (and modest hit), *Insomnia* (2002). That led directly to Nolan's *Dark Knight* trilogy—*Batman Begins* (2005), *The Dark Knight* (2008), and *The Dark Knight Rises* (2012)—also for Warner Bros., which reaped global revenues of over $1 billion on the second and third installments. *The Dark Knight* also caused a stir when its eight nominations did not include best picture (or best director), compelling the Academy to increase the number of best picture nominees from five to ten.[11]

Nolan began veering away from franchise filmmaking in the 2010s while becoming a franchise unto himself writing, directing, and co-producing (with his wife and partner Emma Thomas) mind-bending, cutting-edge sci-fi thrillers like *Inception* (2010), *Interstellar* (2014), and *Tenet* (2020), as well as a fact-based (but characteristically nonlinear) Second World War drama, *Dunkirk* (2017). The latter did excellent business ($530 million worldwide) and was Nolan's most critically successful film to date. It also anticipated *Oppenheimer*, another Second World War drama that he began developing during the pandemic and was in the same relatively modest (for Nolan) $100 million budget range as *Dunkirk*, roughly half the cost of his CG-heavy spectacles. But *Oppenheimer* was far more ambitious and complex, despite its factual basis, due to its fast pace and frequent temporal leaps, its multistrand plot structure and play of viewpoints, its mixture of color and monochromatic film formats, and its political and scientific complexities—all in a film with an anticipated three-hour runtime.

These challenging factors might have raised a red flag or two with other filmmakers, but not Chris Nolan, who by now enjoyed complete autonomy and was calling the shots on all aspects of his productions. But he would not be calling them at Warner Bros. The studio had handled all of Nolan's films since *Insomnia*, but his (noncontractual) alliance with Warner was irrevocably broken during the pandemic. Tensions began building with the release of *Tenet* in September 2020, which did not fare well critically and failed to break even with a global gross of $365 million. Nolan was unhappy with Warner's handling of the film, but what prompted the split was the announcement in early December that, due to the pandemic and the surge in streaming, Warner Bros. was doing away with the "theatrical window" for its entire slate of 2021 films, which would open simultaneously in theaters and on Warner's streaming platform HBO Max. *Oppenheimer* was at least two years out and there was no telling where Warner's release policy would stand by then, but Nolan wasn't waiting to find out. He began shopping *Oppenheimer* with a straightforward list of demands: complete creative control, 20 percent of the first-dollar gross revenues, full financing of the projected $100 million budget with an equal spend on marketing, a theatrical window of at least a hundred days, and a three-week blackout period on any of the studio's other pictures both before and after *Oppenheimer*'s release. Multiple studios were interested, and in September 2021 Nolan disclosed that Universal would finance and distribute his next opus. Weeks later, Nolan began pre-production and cast Cillian Murphy (in his sixth film with the director) in the title role. Universal also announced the release date: July 21, 2023—the third weekend in July, which had been Nolan's good-luck opening slot since *The Dark Knight*.[12]

By then Gerwig was actively prepping Barbie, and in fact Ryan Gosling was cast as Ken just days after Murphy signed on with Nolan. Both films went into production in early 2022, and both were shot "under wraps" and based far from Hollywood—*Barbie* at Warner's Leavesden studios outside London, and *Oppenheimer* on location in Los Alamos and elsewhere in New Mexico. But there was little to connect the two until April that year, when Warner Bros. revised its summer 2023 schedule and announced *Barbie*'s release date: July 21.[13]

Barbenheimer

Warner's schedule change was widely regarded as both a counterprogramming ploy and a shot at Nolan, although the stakes for both films and for both studios would change significantly while *Barbie* and *Oppenheimer* were in the works. The AT&T-Discovery deal closed in April 2022, and the newly configured Warner Bros. Discovery struggled mightily under David Zaslav. He brought in two new studio heads, Mike De Luca and Pam Abdy, to get the movie division back on track, but the struggles continued into early 2023, punctuated by the disastrous release of two DC superhero films, *Shazam! Fury of the Gods* (dir. David F. Sandberg) in April and *The Flash* (dir. Andy Muschietti) in June. Those flops put increasing pressure on the Robbie-Gerwig venture, as Zaslav declared "Operation Barbie Summer" and focused all the conglomerate's marketing resources on the July release.[14]

Universal, meanwhile, was on a roll, grabbing the top market share in 2022 and again in 2023 with an output of franchise films, family fare, and occasional one-offs—and not a comic-book superhero film in the bunch. Universal had two huge hits in May 2023—*The Super Mario Bros. Movie* and *Fast X*, the tenth *Fast & Furious* installment—which paved the way for *Oppenheimer*, Universal's only release between mid-May and mid-August. Universal pitched it as a Christopher Nolan "event film" par excellence, and as another of his awesome technical achievements—especially the Imax angle, after Kodak created a new 65mm black-and-white film stock that Nolan used for the scenes shot with Imax cameras centering on Oppenheimer's nemesis Lewis Strauss (Robert Downey, Jr.). And while Warner Bros. deployed Robbie and Gosling to promote *Barbie* at every conceivable opportunity, Universal exploited Nolan's all-star lineup of Murphy, Downey, Emily Blunt, Matt Damon et al. to pitch *Oppenheimer*. Moreover, the SAG-AFTRA walkouts began on July 14, which meant, as *Deadline* aptly noted, that *Barbie* "together with *Oppenheimer*, was the last big film before the actors strike to get a fire-breathing global promotion from its cast."[15]

But the most impactful sales campaign for both films was mounted not by their studios but by the fans and online cinephiles who coined the "Barbenheimer" portmanteau, which went viral as soon as the *Barbie* release date was announced. By the summer of 2023 the meme—and the attendant discourses—was everywhere, with the *New York Times* lauding the "organic marketing" campaign that had transformed the competing releases into an unprecedented double bill. The *Times* also quoted experts who questioned whether the extraordinary level of awareness would "translate into attendance," with the opening weekend estimates pegged in the $60 million range for *Barbie* and $45 million for *Oppenheimer*.[16]

The projections actually were off-target, substantially underestimating the success of what *Variety* termed "a double feature for the ages."[17] *Barbie* and *Oppenheimer* fueled the fourth-biggest opening weekend in industry history, grossing $182 million and $82 million, respectively, en route to global box-office dominion. *Barbie* was the bigger hit, eventually topping both the domestic and worldwide markets in 2023 and giving Warner Bros. its most successful release ever at $1.44 billion. *Oppenheimer* was an enormous hit as well—the year's number three release (after *Mario Bros.*) at $977 million. The two were invariably reviewed together and were embraced by the critics; indeed, they were two of the best-reviewed films of the year. But while *Barbie* steadily

Figure 1.1 *Fans created a Barbie-Oppenheimer symbiosis at the box office. Courtesy Valerie Macon/AFP via Getty Images.*

outpaced *Oppenheimer* in terms of ticket sales, the Nolan film became an award-season juggernaut, culminating in its thirteen Oscar nominations and seven wins, including best picture, best director, best actor (for Murphy), and best supporting actor (for Downey).

Barbie made Oscar news as well, of course, but in terms that signaled the growing rift in the Barbenheimer symbiosis with regard to their critical and cultural stature. Barbie scored a single Oscar win (for best original song), and its seven nominations infamously omitted Robbie for best actress and Gerwig for best director. The screenplay's nomination for best adaptation due to its basis on a preexisting property was another obvious slight, adding to the tremendous blowback against the Academy for its handling of *Barbie* and its key creatives, which became a major award-season story in itself in early 2024. It also coincided with the release of multiple reports on diversity and equity in Hollywood in a year ruled by *Barbie*, which indicated that the industry was making little if any headway in terms of the inclusion of women and minorities onscreen, onset, or in the studio's C-suites. In fact, *Barbie* looks increasingly like an exception that proves the rule in an industry steeped in white male privilege.[18]

The Barbenheimer symbiosis itself was clearly an exception to multiple industry rules, and it remains to be seen whether it remains an isolated phenomenon. There would be efforts to repeat it, of course, as with the pairing of *Gladiator II* and *Wicked*, which were released on the same day, November 22, 2024, and hyped as "Glicked." Justin Chang opened his *New Yorker* review of the two films with this: "One of the movie industry's many recent laments is that 2024 has given us no Barbenheimer—no box-office showdown between two thrillingly brainy blockbusters, cemented together in the cultural imagination and the commercial stratosphere." In Chang's view, Glicked didn't come close. Whereas *Barbie* and *Oppenheimer* "struck blows for risk and originality in Hollywood," he wrote, the two new films "suggest a safe retreat to known quantities"—i.e., familiar presold IP.[19] And both were immediately outpaced by *Moana 2*, a massive hit that compelled *Variety*'s Owen Gleiberman to bemoan the fact that the year's top-ten releases "are *all* sequels. Every goddam one of them."[20] *Barbie* and *Oppenheimer* obviously bucked that trend as one-off worldwide hits, and they were equally distinctive as auteur films by indie-inclined writer-directors—a vanishing breed in mainstream Hollywood. Both were "brainy" on multiple levels, including shared thematic undercurrents of alienation and existential dread, with Barbie's motivating query, "Do you guys ever think about dying?", preoccupying *Oppenheimer*'s eponymous protagonist as well.

Barbie and *Oppenheimer* also struck a blow for theatrical moviegoing in the face of streaming, albeit along very different lines. Nolan's split with Warner Bros. was all about the primacy of theatrical release, and it took on another dimension with his decision to shoot much of the film on Imax and large-format Panavision cameras and to release it in both large (70mm) and standard (35mm) formats. That fed the interests of Nolan fan and film techies, who flocked to *Oppenheimer*'s PLF (premium large format) venues. The film did nearly half its opening weekend business on PLF screens, and its Imax run alone ultimately generated $183 million.[21]

While Nolan remained firmly committed to celluloid and theatrical release, Robbie and Gerwig had a more flexible view of streaming. Robbie's follow-up to *Barbie* as co-producer and star was a heavily publicized adaptation of *Wuthering Heights*, and again she tapped a fast-rising female multihyphenate, in this case Emerald Fennell, to helm the picture. Fennell was just coming off *Saltburn* (2023), an Amazon-MGM film co-produced by Robbie that scored both in theaters and online. *Wuthering Heights* was the subject of a fierce bidding war in late 2024, with Netflix reportedly offering $150 million for the film, including its usual Oscar-qualifying limited theatrical release. Robbie and her producing partners opted to go with Warner Bros., ironically enough, which offered only half the Netflix price but guaranteed the film's wide theatrical release and healthy participation deals for Fennell and Robbie.[22]

Meanwhile Gerwig was busy with a Netflix deal to write, direct, and produce two *Chronicles of Narnia* films, which she began working on prior to *Barbie*'s release. Emboldened by that success and inspired by Nolan's strategy on *Oppenheimer*, Gerwig began pressing Netflix for a global PLF release of the Narnia films, with the first one slated for Thanksgiving 2026. The same week that Netflix lost *Wuthering Heights*, the streaming giant acknowledged that it had entered discussions with Imax about releasing the Narnia films—a radical departure from its firm long-standing policy of giving it high-profile films limited theatrical releases.[23] The Gerwig situation was further complicated by Noah Baumbach's alliance with Netflix, which was producing and distributing the writer-director's fourth consecutive film. His previous Netflix productions included one of the streamer's most successful films, *Marriage Story* (2019), co-starring Adam Driver and Scarlet Johansson, and also one of its biggest (and costliest) disappointments, *White Noise* (2022), which co-starred Driver and Greta Gerwig.

Conclusion

While the Baumbach films with their Oscar-qualifying and buzz-generating limited theatrical rollouts were business as usual for Netflix, the Gerwig situation was a possible game-changer in terms of an all-in commitment to franchising as well as a franchise-worthy theatrical rollout. Netflix's bid for *Wuthering Heights* signaled its inclination to compete with the legacy majors, and the success of *Oppenheimer* in large-format venues, which were rapidly proliferating on a global scale, suggested that the theatrical sector's post-pandemic recovery might be even stronger than expected. Netflix and the other streaming powers could ill afford to ignore that prospect, and Gerwig in the wake of *Barbie*'s singular success had both the talent and the leverage to push them even further into the legacy studios' realm. She also was capable of bringing women (and girls) back into movie theaters in record numbers with female-driven fare—no small feat in the post-pandemic steaming era. Indeed, Gerwig and Margot Robbie both seemed determined to roust Hollywood out of its relentless, risk-averse pursuit of young male action hounds and 'toon-hungry families. And that, finally, may prove to be the most significant aspect of *Barbie*'s runaway success, and one that set it distinctly apart from not only mainstream Hollywood but also the Great Man triumphalism of *Oppenheimer*.

The Americanization of Feminine Culture: Female Authorship and the Culture Industry from Alcott to Barbie

PATRICIA WHITE

With the success of *Barbie* (2023), Greta Gerwig's public persona crossed over from auteur to entrepreneur. Aligning her brand with Mattel's, she bridged the distance between authenticity and plastic, indie credibility and corporate power. With a reported budget of approximately $145 million, the film has earned more than $1.47 billion globally, making it the highest grossing female-directed film in history.[1] Yet celebrating the film's success as a feminist breakthrough is ironic, and not necessarily ironic in the manner of Gerwig and partner Noah Baumbach's self-reflexive script. In much of the championing of *Barbie*, feminism just means girl power. Affinity with a 65-year-old, deeply divisive, gender-normative, and imperially marked consumer product predominantly sold to 3–5-year-old girls is taken as metonymic of women's and girls' empowerment, while the film's target demographic is collapsed with the director's identity: generically female. These slippages, which default to a

U.S. American, able-ist celebration of white aspirational heterosexual femininity and call it feminism, are all too familiar to scholars of women and popular culture. Gerwig's film has more imagination.

Female authorship and audience response

My chapter title riffs on cultural critic Ann Douglas's 1977 classic *The Feminization of American Culture,* in which she holds the success of female-authored domestic novels in the nineteenth century responsible for a renunciation of the "tough" U.S. American ideals of Calvinist theology, a "feminization" that ushered in the consumerist values of mass culture in the twentieth century.[2] Douglas is right that popularity does not guarantee good politics, but as many subsequent feminist critics have argued, it is often an indicator that a deep cultural chord has been struck. Allow me to invoke several key feminized popular forms and their feminist critical commentators: the novel (Nina Baym's *Women's Fiction*), silent-era Hollywood (Shelley Stamp's *Movie-Struck Girls*); paperback romance (Tania Modleski's *Loving with a Vengeance*); the women's picture (Mary Ann Doane's *The Desire to Desire*); chick flicks (Hilary Radner's *Neo-Feminist Cinema*); internet culture (Michele White's *Producing Women*; Elana Levine's *Cupcakes, Pinterest, and Ladyporn*); and popular music fandom from the Beatles to BTS (Susan J. Douglas's *Where the Girls Are*; *Bangtan Remixed*, edited by Patty Ahn, Michelle Cho, Vernadette Vicuña Gonzalez, Rani Neutill, Mimi Thi Nguyen, and Yutian Wong).[3] In *The Female Complaint*, Lauren Berlant looks to the racial politics of women's culture for the affective contours of the "intimate public sphere" in the United States.[4] In all of these modes of cultural production, women are indeed targeted as consumers, but their response to genres, formats, and specific texts, while enthusiastic, is excessive; their need is not fully met by the product (hence the need for more products). Such breadth and depth of critical insight on this history of female response, not to mention audience common sense, makes late Hollywood's serial forgetting of the potential of the female box office all the more frustrating—from *Titanic* (dir. James Cameron, 1997) to *Frozen* (dir. Chris Buck and Jennifer Lee, 2013) to *Wonder Woman* (dir. Patty Jenkins,

2017) to *Wicked* (dir. Jon M. Chu, 2024), women audiences are alternatively underestimated and exploited. The Barbie doll as candidate for a contemporary Hollywood IP tentpole offering is a no-brainer. But the way female authorship has been enlisted and activated in the resulting cultural phenomenon can be illuminated by this feminist scholarly history.

The scale and overdetermination of *Barbie*'s success, not only in the marketplace but also in cultural conversations in the twilight of American world dominance, make it a valuable case study of the influential conjuncture of female authorship and audience response in commercialized leisure culture, of global circuits of production and reception crisscrossed by ambivalent signals and subversive strains. Ideologically positioning white women as the *sold* and the *sold to* is key to the rise of consumer capitalism in the American century, and other audiences are carried along in this project. A privileged few women have also been involved in the *selling*. Their power is paradoxical: authorship makes otherwise unexpressed experiences, desires, and resistances affectively accessible, but the culture industry harnesses these desires to capital and empire. This chapter links *Barbie* to the history of women's commercialized popular culture in the United States, arguing that the contradictions it brings into relief around racialized femininity and post-feminism reach back to the nineteenth-century invention of girlhood as a market sector. Greta Gerwig is both an apt student and an avatar of this history.

As Gerwig takes on Mattel's most valuable IP, she is able both to preserve its value for American global dominance (the film also topped the 2023 international box office) and meaningfully to express enduring contradictions of the U.S. model of consumerist femininity. Mattel's toy Barbie is a product of American Cold War optimism. In order to compete in the twenty-first-century IP film marketplace with the videogame and comic-book nostalgia that universalizes adolescent male taste, Gerwig adds some important elements. She addresses adult feminists and classic Hollywood film lovers and introduces a suite of characters—America Ferrera's working mom of color Gloria and her progressive tween daughter Sasha (Ariana Greenblatt), as well the motley multiples of Barbie and Ken in Barbie Land—that index American multiculturalism while they support heroine Stereotypical Barbie (Margot Robbie) through existential crisis and resistance to rogue white male toxicity.

It's rare that a chick flick critiques patriarchy by name. To invoke Eve Sedgwick, Gerwig addresses global audiences with a message that is "kinda subversive, kinda hegemonic."[5] She goes about it by yoking the resistance often enacted in women's and girls' consumer practices to a rendering of, in Richard Dyer's words, "what utopia *feels* like."[6]

"Making art of girlhood materials"

As this chapter will go on to detail, it is no accident that Greta Gerwig's project before *Barbie* was a screen adaptation of Louisa May Alcott's classic *Little Women* (2020). That film consolidated Gerwig's reputation as writer-director for the post-#MeToo era, after her auspicious debut as solo auteur with the semi-autobiographical *Lady Bird* in 2017.[7] As Meghan O'Rourke writes in the *Atlantic* (where Alcott herself found fame),[8] "[Gerwig's] entire career as a filmmaker has, in a sense, been a campaign to make art of girlhood materials."[9] Alcott's bestselling 1868 novel of New England homosocial female domestic cultural power helped establish a lucrative market for girls' fiction that arguably lay the groundwork for the success of Ruth Handler's Barbie doll in the post-Second World War toy market. Gerwig's film had to "transcend" the commodity's association with not only the demeaned, but also the diminutive, feminine to make a twenty-first-century blockbuster that appealed to multiple market sectors. *Barbie* is not aimed exclusively at girls; however, it makes full use of the prodigious imagination and longing bottled up in "girlhood materials" to at least attempt to rewrite the consumerist script.

As the story goes, Handler came up with the idea of Barbie to give her daughter Barbara a grown-up doll, facilitating postwar girls' shift away from the limited repertoire inherent in baby doll play.[10] After her launch in 1959, fashion-forward and career-minded Barbie became a wildly successful made-for-girls commodity that girls and others could do all manner of things with, to, and for.[11] The American cultural industry, which Adorno and Horkheimer had diagnosed when the Handlers established Mattel in 1945, has since diversified, compartmentalized, and globalized.[12] Yet the doll stayed near the top of toy sales for decades, until partially eclipsed by second- and third-wave feminist shifts in ideas about gender roles, "girliness," and their accompanying market extrusions (Bratz, American Girl Dolls, TikTok).[13]

For in addition to being treated dismissively because of its association with the feminine, Barbie, like women's fiction before it, has long been a target of internal feminist critique. Aimed at stereotypical traits—Barbie's whiteness, thinness, sexualization—such critique also became a stereotypical version of feminist dogma that arguably underestimated girls' agency. By the time Mattel Films was established (seemingly anachronistically, in 2018, preceded by Mattel Playground Division five years earlier, and eclipsed by Mattel Studios in 2025)[14] the discourse on Barbie had nearly drowned out Barbie herself. The dolls continued to be updated (significantly, to accommodate diverse body types, hair textures, and skin colors) and sold, but "Barbie" was perhaps best understood as a simulacrum, a copy without an original, at once a signifier of childhood nostalgia for multiple generations of women and others, an offering on girls' birthday parties' potlach pile, and a namecheck for post-feminist irony.

Forgotten in much of the cultural commentary and even trade press coverage of the 2023 film are the forty-plus already existing feature films in the *Barbie* franchise, evidence of a cultural taste hierarchy newly appointed CEO Ynon Kreiz would have to defy. Clearly the first effort of the new film division wouldn't succeed if it were primarily understood as a two-hour-long product placement for little girls' toys. Launched in an era of uncertain box office returns and a reliance on the power of IP bordering on faith in scripture, the *Barbie* movie needed celebrity power. And it needed celebrity authorship. In the post-#MeToo era, with increased public awareness of the dismally low numbers of women directing films in Hollywood, assigning a film like *Barbie* to a male director would be unthinkable. (Even before such attention, women writers and directors who did find employment were traditionally relegated to "girls'" properties.) But the specific connotations of Greta Gerwig's authorship were key to making the concept of a *Barbie* movie a "high" concept.

Feminist film scholars look to female authorship not because they believe in innate differences between woman- and man-made films, but because the work of female-identified creators so often publicly addresses the private experience and structural determinants of life under patriarchy. As Richard Dyer considers in "Believing in Fairies: the Author and the Homosexual," identity categories inform authorship in ways that deserve attention, even for critics who might be skeptical of notions of pure authorial expression or suspicious of opportunistic branding.[15] Gerwig's oeuvre, which combines the visibility of the actor/celebrity, the connotations of interiority of the serious writer, a set of resonant biographical factors, and the evidence of the director's well-informed choices across a coherent set of texts, makes for a revealing authorial case study.

Little Women and *Barbie* rank near the top of any list of malleable, meaningful properties embodying concepts of U.S. femininity. Hence Gerwig's interest in both. In her film versions, this controlling interest takes the form of the protagonist's narrative of self-realization—a resonant version of spirited, independent, and "good" girlhood that her own auteur image amplifies. Producer and star Margot Robbie pitched Gerwig as director to Mattel. Blonde and wholesome, both women offer "positive" real-life Barbie stand-ins, with Gerwig's gawkiness a foil to Robbie's near-uncanny perfection. (Perfection with comedic potential, however: Robbie's "cool blonde" looks were played for black humor in *I, Tonya*, directed by Craig Gillespie in 2017, and similar tensions shaded Carey Mulligan's character in the scorched-earth feminism of *Promising Young Woman*, directed by Emerald Fennell in 2020, also from Robbie's production company, Lucky Chap.) Robbie's choice of Gerwig can in

Figure 2.1 *Margot Robbie's near-uncanny perfection in her role as "Barbie"* (Barbie, *dir. Greta Gerwig, 2023).*

this light be seen as doubling down on an ironic deployment of girl glamor. Gerwig brings her "smart" connotations—she's a Barnard graduate and a two-time Oscar nominee for writing—to a dumb toy.

The feminist auteur and the culture industry

Certainly, as many commentators have noted, the choice of Gerwig to direct *Barbie* cashed in on the filmmaker's reputation as a *feminist* auteur. While her acceptance of the assignment was the occasion for discussions of "selling out," these were largely resolved as "leaning in," positioning *Barbie* to be a juggernaut of what Hilary Radner calls "neo-feminist cinema."[16] Some of Gerwig's choices include: explicitly thematizing patriarchy; downgrading Ken (at least ostensibly); Sasha's lunchroom takedown, which culminates with calling Barbie a fascist; Gloria's Tik Tok-legendary speech about the impossible contradictions of being a woman; the film's ending. Then there's the casting of lesbian, trans, fat, black, and brown celebrity Barbies and Kens, the soundtrack, the solidarity. Other dimensions of the film effectively pull from traditional women's genres: the expressive use of color and *mise en scène*, the multiples as an ensemble cast, the musical numbers, the emphasis on affect, the emphasis on *stuff*. Much of the film convinces as an enactment of how some feminists might script their Barbie play. (Here it has some affinity with experimental films that use Barbie-like dolls, of which Todd Haynes and Cynthia Schneider's *Superstar*, released in 1987, and promptly banned, is the best known and most poignant.) Gerwig strives to maintain her critical position while collaborating with corporate culture, both Mattel and Hollywood.

Gerwig's previous film, *Little Women*, allegorizes working within the cultural industry by showing the compromises Alcott made with the literary marketplace more than 150 years ago, opening and closing her adaptation of the novel with scenes of her protagonist's negotiations with her publisher. On *Barbie*, the writer-director was frank in interviews about the contradictions of working with the Mattel corporation further to monetize a brand that has been emblematic of second wave feminism's critique of social messaging about impossible beauty standards. As she put it in the *New York Times Magazine*:

"Things can be both/and. I'm doing the thing and subverting the thing."[17] And she's doing the thing in style. Gerwig's formula is strikingly similar to the ideological operation that Roland Barthes in *Mythologies* calls "inoculation," through which myth asks for buy-in by showing it is aware of the sell.[18] In fact, Gerwig makes even more of a plot point of the machinations of the culture industry in *Barbie* than in *Little Women*, with much of act three taken up with madcap chases with Mattel executives bent on putting Barbie back in her box. Indeed, the Gerwig/Baumbach screenplay casts Mattel in the narratological slot of "villain," as the all-male board headed by Will Ferrell's character makes every effort to keep quiet the potential brand damage done by Stereotypical Barbie's trip to the Real World.

Obviously, there is no inherent contradiction between being a feminist/female author and a deft manipulator of the culture industry. That is precisely the history into which I argue Gerwig inserts herself both in her scripts and in the scripting of her career and persona. The cultivation of women as consumers calls for female expertise in the shaping and selling of commodities. Twentieth- and twenty-first-century women with image empires, from Handler to Oprah to Martha Stewart, hearken back to those women novelists—including Alcott and Harriet Beecher Stowe—who so angered Nathaniel Hawthorne as a "damned mob of scribbling women" controlling the literary marketplace.[19] As the argument about the nineteenth-century concept of separate spheres goes, women, excluded from public roles in politics, the world of work, and the marketplace, had to "preach" through the novel form and thereby exert "influence" over the cultural realm.

In the blockbuster film space, Gerwig puts a feminist twist on what Timothy Corrigan calls "the auteur of commerce," incorporating a critical take on the economic constraints of her position.[20] Gerwig maintains an interest in the white American female *Bildungsroman* across her work as actor, writer, and director.[21] It is within this framework that she brings Barbie™ to life. The subject/object tensions embodied in white femininity (articulation of selfhood vs. sexual objectification and symbolic national capital) and in girls' culture (creativity and female sociality vs. consumerism, traditional femininity, and heteronormativity) underlie Gerwig's authorial persona, which is informed by her signature film roles as an awkward, half-grown woman. *Lady Bird, Little*

Women, and *Barbie* arose from this legacy, this entitlement. Moreover, her oeuvre identifies authorship itself with white female narratives of self-realization; while the characters Lady Bird and Barbie are not writers per se, their musings share semantic space with the expressions of interiority that have made Jo March such a powerful figure of girl readers' (and women writers') identification since the 1860s. While nonwhites and nonwomen can be and are powerfully interpellated by these heroines, I argue that all three texts solicit the kind of sororal identification that Alcott's book offered. The question "Are you a Jo or an Amy?" allows for small margins of difference. At a slightly further remove from Barbie's own sister Skipper, you can be her best friend—choose white Midge or black Christie. In these associations it is clear that the whiteness and impossible physical proportions of Barbie remain the symbolic capital of femininity. From such objectification, white female authors have wrested a subject position and invited readers to share it.

The sororal mode and product placement

How does the sororal mode derived from *Little Women*'s female family play out in *Barbie*? Barbie Land is imagined as a utopia, a horizontal social organization (with cul-de-sacs) in which both desire and competition are sublimated. Barbie Land espouses sisterhood—every night is girls' night. Weird Barbie, even as played by the lesbian genius Kate McKinnon, isn't invested with enough witchy power to bring out the erotic/subversive potential of the film's feminist utopian colony (the Amazonians in Patty Jenkins's *Wonder Woman*, 2017, go further). Issa Rae as President Barbie, who lives in a pink version of the White House, similarly defers racial commentary to celebrity intertext. Both Latina and "ordinary," Gloria undermines stereotypical Barbie's perfection with her sketches of Cellulite Barbie and, as a mom, introduces a new dimension to Gerwig's coming-of-age narrative. But as Stereotypical Barbie enters the Real World, Gerwig enters the world of IP-driven filmmaking that dominates twenty-first-century Hollywood. While the filmmaker may delight in subverting the Mattel corporate message, the film's aggressive marketing is set to overwhelm authorial and audience resistance alike.

Textually, the film's strategies to "soften" the embrace of dominant corporate values, including the narrative integration of Ruth Handler and the nondiegetic tribute to discontinued Mattel products in the end credits sequence, draw out some of the contradictions of female consumer power. The film claims an alternative corporate genealogy, with Handler trotted out to midwife the film's resolution. Played by Rhea Pearlman as a benevolent Jewish grandmother, Handler "haunts" Mattel headquarters. Her enclave on the seventeenth floor is set up like a kitchen; her domain melds the spaces of production and consumption that links the Alcott/March sisters to *The Gilmore Girls* and beyond. Handler functions like Glinda the Good Witch in the film's resolution, telling Barbie she already has the power she needs: the film's fantasy/reality dialectic is resolved in a pair of pink Birkenstocks worn by flesh-and-blood Barbie, now claiming the name Barbara Handler.

The film's end credits indulge in literal product placement, starting with the original Barbie and her iconic packaging, and proceeding through adjuncts Ken and Christie to a series of infamous Mattel misfires and questionable designs: Happy Family Midge, whose pregnant belly could be detached and the baby popped out for play; the defecating dog Tyler; and the notorious Magical Earring Ken, who, along with Sugar Daddy Ken and Ken's buddy Allan, appears in the film on the side of the Barbies against patriarchy's encroachment into Barbie Land. The credits sequence pays homage to collective authorship, through toy and package design, to collector culture, and, implicitly, to the many misappropriations of the Mattel canon. *Barbie* is thus situated within a corporate lineage of serial production, but also as a little bit rogue, as if the film wishes it too could become a product Mattel will come to regard as too radical or "niche."

But unlike discontinued merchandise that takes on added value in a minor/mirror economy of collectors, there seems to be no outside to Mattel's profiteering from *Barbie*: now Weird Barbie comes in a box. Weird Barbie was Gerwig's name for the ubiquitous phenomenon of mutilation performed by nameless kids who played with Barbie too hard, an attempt to inject the authenticity of children's communal play (conducted with all the ambivalence due the transitional object) into the branded project. Gerwig's brand is indeed bankable, as the terms of her deal to remake the *Chronicles of Narnia* with

Netflix attest, but her authorship retains the marks of spontaneity and imagination associated with girlhood and independent cinema. She skillfully deploys the condensation of consumption and production, object and subject, associated with (white) American femininity.

Women's culture, women's authorship

Gerwig's engagement with issues of authorship and compromise in *Little Women*, her second film as sole author/director, sets up her later approach to *Barbie*.[22] In her version of Alcott's novel, Gerwig thematizes the trade-offs for the woman author in engaging the sentimental subject (as topic and audience). Gerwig's remake of *Little Women* is a deliberate inscription of her signature vision into the history of women's cinema (which includes three Hollywood adaptations before hers).[23] The term "women's cinema" is both an authorial and a market category, like women's (and girls') fiction before it. In the address to a diverse female audience lies the proto-feminist capacity of women's genres, and often their queer and anti-racist potential. As noted above, in the mid-nineteenth century, the phenomenon of women writing was driven by the white and propertied ideology of male and female separate spheres. Men did politics; women did morality and manners, exerting influence through their words rather than acting directly. As is well known, Harriet Beecher Stowe wrote *Uncle Tom's Cabin* (1852) to forward the cause of abolition, and her vision of Christian maternalism outsold everything but the Bible in her time. Louisa May Alcott, her family's principal breadwinner, emulated Stowe, but she was less religious and more practical: ever conscious of the market, she trained herself to write with her left hand when her right failed her.

The shifting figure-ground of female and feminist, of female independence and female collectivity, is apparent in the layers of *Little Women*'s closing scene as Gerwig stages it. Jo March (Saoirse Ronan) negotiates her book contract for the autobiographical *Little Women* in her publisher's office. It isn't only copyright she negotiates for, however; it is the very question of narrative closure, a primary social task of the novel as literary form (and one *Barbie*'s open-ended text explicitly resists: when Will Ferrell's character offers "Barbie loves Ken," Sasha replies scornfully, "That's not an ending!"). Jo's publisher demands that the manuscript's heroine get married, imposing the marriage plot on a story whose fundamental attraction is its utopian female homosocial world. Gerwig sees the publisher's demand precisely as a plot against women's autonomy, and she honors Alcott's own wishes in her ending.

In a letter to her friend Elizabeth Powell, Alcott wrote about these wishes for *Little Women*:

> A sequel will be out early in April, & like all sequels will probably disappoint or disgust most readers, for publishers wont let authors finish up as they like but insist on having people married off in a wholesale manner which much afflicts me. "Jo" should have remained a literary spinster but so many enthusiastic young ladies wrote to me clamorously demanding that she should marry Laurie, or somebody, that I didnt dare to refuse & out of perversity went & made a funny match for her. I expect vials of wrath to be poured out upon my head, but rather enjoy the prospect.[24]

With the full cinematic resources of space, time, and *mise en scène*, Gerwig approached these contradictions in her film adaptation as Alcott could not, dramatizing a conventional girl-gets-boy happy ending without fully settling the question of the scene's diegetic status. Intercut with Jo's meeting with the publisher is a rom com-style race to unite the hetero-couple. However, after Professor Bhaer (Louis Garrel) is brought together with Jo for the kiss that signifies traditional closure, the scene continues, suggesting that the "funny match" might be merely what Jo concedes to her publisher rather than a heterosexual resolution to the film we are watching. A sweeping overhead long take, in motion like much of the film, depicts Bhaer as one among many teachers, family members, and students who fill the halls and grounds of the (integrated and co-ed) school Jo sets up at the home she inherits from her aunt.

Key to this double ending is the identification of Jo with Alcott and the incorporation of the narrative of writing and publishing the book within the film. As Gerwig explains: "The structure truly came out of wanting to introduce this layer of authorship everywhere."[25] Gerwig gives us Jo and her published book as the final clinch, the pairing framed in the film's closing image. Female authorship coupled with feminist address tasks the utopian female-run

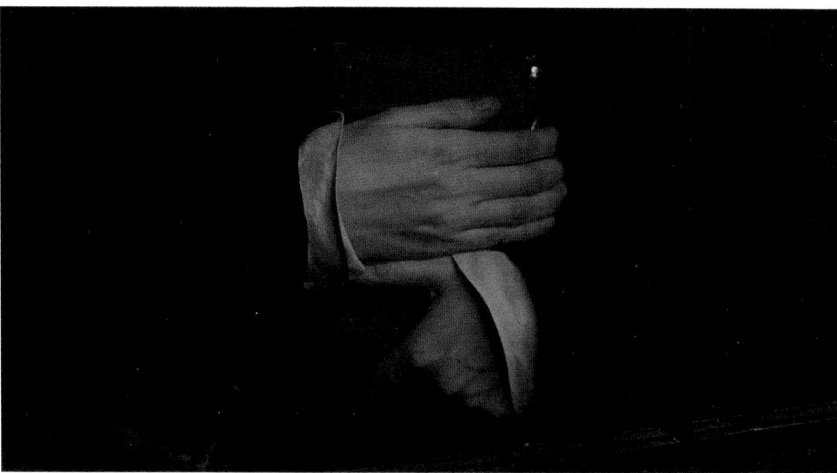

Figure 2.2 *Jo and her published book in the film* Little Women *(dir. Greta Gerwig, 2019).*

collectivity with social transformation. Jo's school is an exemplar of nineteenth-century dreams of an inclusive society modeled on domesticity. In Gerwig's version, Black and white kids painting and playing music side by side signal Alcott's abolitionist politics. Yet *Little Women*'s insular world risks maintaining white femininity as guarantor of female moral authority.

The panoramic hive of activity at the end of *Little Women* might put one in mind of a film studio—we see areas where music, painting, fencing, even the equivalent of craft services are in progress. Coupled with the closing image of Jo with her novel, the scene could be taken as a vision of Hollywood made over in the image of feminist struggle and self-sufficiency that Alcott's novel inspired, a utopian space in which "authors ... finish up as they like." Optimistically, *Barbie* strives to realize this vision. The film's opening tour de force number by Lizzo echoes *Little Women*'s vision of female utopia, now drenched in pink. (A Pantone chip of the film's signature shade is on display at the film's Mattel headquarters, a wink at crafty online consumer/influencers who are another key part of the film's audience.) Recalling the floating camera over Munchkinland that invites the viewer to take in classical Hollywood's Technicolor splendor, *Barbie* reveals a cul-de-sac where each Barbie has a Dreamhouse, all jobs are occupied by women, and the Kens are granted a liminal territory known as "Beach." This multiple address to young girls who could play with Barbie and older ones who used to, to camp audiences, Lizzo fans, and participants in the internet-generated stunt of seeing both *Barbie* and Chris Nolan's overlong, overserious *Oppenheimer* (2023) on the same day bespeaks aggressive blockbuster marketing. And while the scene's vision of racial inclusiveness doesn't extend much beyond *Little Women's* integrated homeschool, the audio relies on Black women's celebrity to create a Barbie Land worth attending to.

Like Gerwig, the multiracial group of marquee-name female pop artists who participate on the film's soundtrack (a number of whom are signed with Warner, the studio that partnered with Mattel to make and release the film) are also grappling with issues of artistic autonomy and commodity compromise. Nicki Minaj and Ice Spice sing, in "Barbie World": "Yellin out, we ain't sellin' out," but their bodies are on the line as author/performers in ways Gerwig's is not. Part of the paradox of being a "little woman" is remaining presexual; when Robbie's Barbie becomes a real girl, her story arc ends offscreen somewhere "between a woman and her doctor." Nicki Minaj and Ice Spice are only visible in the film's ancillary texts; too sexually confident for *Barbie's* PG world, they showcase the film's set and design elements in the "Barbie World" music video, released as a literal teaser for the film. The feminization of American culture still seems to depend on a fiction of white sexual innocence.

Conclusion

Barbie both lays out and enacts a feminist argument about the contradictions of white supremacist patriarchal capitalism; but like *Little Women's* invocation of the self-sufficiency of a female-headed family, it evokes a utopia where contradictions are resolved in individual terms. If only *Barbie's* perfunctory resolution of the Kens' insurrection on election eve could avert what happened in the *real* Real World not long after the film's successful release. The film can't posit a social solution to what it nevertheless acknowledges are social problems.

Barbie needs an ending, Sasha insists, and in the film's memorable last scene, the protagonist is dropped off at a high-rise office building, poised for what looks like C-suite success, only directly to address the receptionist/

camera: "I'm here to see my gynecologist." The film's last line is one of its clear triumphs, a poke at Dobbs-era U.S. rollbacks on reproductive rights and a cheeky insistence on Hollywood's continued alliance with Democratic Party values of accessible family planning, including abortion. Barbie's earlier talk back to the baffling sexism of the Real World, delivered to a group of male construction workers, had been: "I'd like to inform you that I do not have a vagina." Having chosen the Real World, with binary sex as its implicit corollary, she delivers the film's feminist punch line, claiming healthy and sexually autonomous futures for all those encouraged to identify with an overdetermined symbol of conventional femininity turned sharp critical tool. In Gerwig's film, Barbie exercises *choice*: the Ur-trope of post-feminism and its promise of (white) women's economic capacity and neo-liberal self-actualization.[26]

Thus, ventriloquized through a commodity come to life, Gerwig's authorship is more than an expression of personal vision. As a critical construction, I have argued, it carries forward the influential history of American women's roles in mass cultural production and reception. Since the mid-nineteenth century, women authors and audiences have expressed discontent by imagining and endorsing forms of solidarity that are then incorporated into consumerism and traditional roles and hierarchies. *Barbie* contends with the symbolic role of white femininity in that history through both Gerwig's assertion of authorial control and the centering of Stereotypical Barbie's Real Girl narrative. The paradox of Barbie remains the paradox of *Barbie*. Mattel makes the sale but can't control the play.

Fake Feminism and Strident Pink Spectacle: Fashion, Celebrity Culture, and the Marketing of Greta Gerwig's Barbie

PAMELA CHURCH GIBSON AND
ALEXANDRE ZAMBONI

It is vital for cinema, as a medium, that screenings in traditional film theaters continue; this is, after all, the actual format for which films are conceived and created. Films are designed to be viewed in the proper ratio, rather than to be consumed privately on smaller and smaller screens. And the film we are about to discuss certainly sent unprecedented audiences straight to the multiplexes—not, as is usual today, to see the latest superhero film, but to watch a film by a little-known woman director, Greta Gerwig, whose first solo film, *Lady Bird* (2017), was undeniably an "indie" film, and whose second, *Little Women* (2019), a new adaptation of the famed nineteenth-century novel of the same name by Louisa May Alcott, was not exactly mainstream fodder.

Owing to an extraordinarily effective partnership between the fashion industry and our ever-expanding celebrity culture, combined with a global marketing campaign that went way beyond the wildest dreams and the financial reach of the early studio moguls, *Barbie* enjoyed an unanticipated success at the box office. And despite its curious claims to be a feminist film, there is in fact a brief moment of middle-class despair that undermines the film's apparent glorification of contemporary consumerism.

In fact—and worryingly for many—*Barbie* (2023) became the most commercially successful film ever to be made by a woman director. Its cinematic opening was, of course, organized alongside that of *Oppenheimer* (dir. Christopher Nolan, 2023), which became an equally successful film (if not as profitable at the box office), providing an uneasy companion piece; it is, after all, a seemingly uncritical presentation of this real-life womanizing scientist (played by an extremely popular and unusually handsome actor) who created the first effective weapon of mass destruction—and was, therefore, responsible for the death and devastation at Hiroshima and Nagasaki, hardly hinted at in the film.

Barbie, as a milder central protagonist, brought her own—highly fashionable—history to the screen with her. This particular doll has always been of great interest to fashion designers, possibly because of the ludicrous proportions that have angered so many women for so long; it is by now common knowledge that, if Barbie attempted to stand on her tiny feet, she would topple over, while the size of her breasts would also unbalance her, and would mean that she could only move forward by crawling along the ground. The following quotation, from a *Vogue* article of 2009, shows how—long before there was any thought of a cinematic spectacle—the doll was valued and valorized within the world of fashion:

> Despite her diminutive height of 11.5 inches, Barbie has one of the biggest wardrobes ever, designed by over seventy top name fashion designers, and has worn one billion pairs of shoes. Since she burst on to the fashion scene in New York in 1959, she has had the personal touches of Giorgio Armani, Christian Dior, Bill Blass and Oscar de la Renta put on her sizeable wardrobe. She has worn wedding gowns designed by Vera Wang and Carolina Herrera, and Christian Louboutin is designing a special pair of pink shoes for her. And Barbie knows her big brands too. She's been decked out by the likes of Ferrari (naturally, since she drives one) and cult make-up brand MAC.[1]

Barbie, celebrity, and the fashion industry

Somehow, in 2023, this particular fashion icon and 65-year-old celebrity became the heroine of a purportedly feminist film, one vociferously claimed as such by its director and its star. If nothing else, the film is a product of—and surely owes its success to—the now firmly established and extraordinarily effective partnership between the fashion industry and our ever-expanding celebrity culture. "Stereotypical Barbie," the film's heroine, is the epitome of the ever-desirable celebrity look; she is slim, blonde, tanned, carefully made-up, with contoured face and long dark eyelashes, and of course possessed of disproportionately large breasts. She has a global appeal far beyond the reach of most flesh-and-blood celebrities—and it is an enduring appeal, one unhampered by aging.

And in the months prior to its release, the two conjoined behemoths of fashion and celebrity culture managed to hijack what was, as suggested above, intended—according to director Greta Gerwig, and star Margot Robbie—to be a firmly *feminist* film. Gerwig, Robbie et al. were, of course, bankrolled by Mattel, the manufacturers of the doll—toy manufacturers have traditionally been among the main beneficiaries of blockbuster movies (think, for instance, of James Bond's gadget-laden cars and the Harry Potter spin-offs). But in the past, manufacturers have not possessed the level of power over these films that is wielded here by Mattel. We might remember here the words of Nicholas Roeg, maverick English director: "I don't *want* to make commercials for toys."[2] And, like Roeg, the director of this film had her own very different ambitions, as she and her chosen star embarked on their project.

Any examination of the gender politics of this film should, however, begin by noting that the narrative's starting point, Barbie's need to visit the "real world" (in opposition to "Barbie Land," where she initially resides) is in fact motivated not by any intellectual enquiry, but by her need to stop the advance of the cellulite she has detected on her improbably perfect thighs, and to solve the problem of her newly flat feet. And the story line, too, involves the near-deification of Ruth Handler, the original creator of Barbie, and tries to make of her a feminist mother-goddess; this seems a strange endeavor, to exhume and to glorify a millionairess who chose to present so many girl-children with this impossible version of young womanhood.

By the end of the film, Barbie has swapped her stilettos for Birkenstocks, so at least she has the correct—or rather the stereotypical—feminist footwear.[3] More significantly, she also now possesses a flesh-and-blood womb, cervix, vagina et al.—necessitating her first visit to a gynecologist. This could, of course, be seen as feeding into the current furor over "real women" and the resulting fissures within feminism—the so-called "TERF wars."[4]

A "feminist film," of course, is not simply a film intended for a female audience, and it is presumably more than a film *about* women, one simply intended to reflect their interests and concerns; otherwise, the "women's pictures" produced by Hollywood studios in the 1930s and early 40s would be "feminist films." Indeed, one or two academics have tentatively advanced that argument—with reference to certain of these films.[5] The made-in-Hollywood Garbo vehicle *Queen Christina* (dir. Reuben Mamoulian, 1933) is usually singled out here; in its closing moments, its cross-dressing heroine is seen sailing away to an unknown—and solitary, self-sufficient—future.

These films, which were intended for—and very successful with—the female audiences of the time, always had at least one strong woman at the center of the narrative, but their plot resolutions were not necessarily intended to have a wider cultural significance. Of course, these films were directed by men, with one exception—*Dance Girl Dance*, Dorothy Arzner's film of 1940. And they are in fact directly relevant to this discussion of a fashion-conscious film, for their own female stars, the fashion icons of their day, were at the center of extremely successful sales campaigns, structured around these same films, with their synchronized opening nights and themed window displays; these were invariably for clothes, accessories, and cosmetics. However, Charles Eckert, the first scholar to examine this particular phenomenon and who christened "tie-ins" as such, described how *Queen Christina* was also used as a successful way of publicizing Swedish cutlery, which was itself displayed in department-store windows across America to coincide with the opening nights of that film.[6] Eckert's essay of 1978 was arguably the first academic analysis of the links between film and fashion. Originally published in the *Quarterly Review of Film Studies* in 1978, it was reprinted in the first collection of academic essays ever to explore that topic, *Fabrications: Costume and the Female Body* (Gaines and

Herzog, 1990). The "tie- ins" and themed windows of the 1930s are still with us, of course, while the incongruity of the "Swedish flatware" displays of 1933 is surely trumped by the "Barbie-Burger," with its neon-pink filling, which went on sale in the Brazilian branches of Burger King in 2023.[7]

But *Barbie* was at the center of a global—rather than a national—marketing campaign, and of a massive worldwide promotional tour which, in this age of Global Hollywood, exceeded even the most grandiose fantasies of those early studio moguls. The many marketing projects created before, during, and after the release of this film included—alongside clothes, accessories, cosmetics, toys, and soft furnishings— some products not immediately connected with a fashionable doll—a Barbie-pink Xbox, for example, a Barbie boat cruise, and the above-mentioned Barbie Burger. The film itself is, perhaps, a twenty-first-century version of those Hollywood "women's pictures," rather than a "feminist" film, as the director claims. Of Gerwig's own earlier ventures, her first film is a thoughtful exploration of female adolescence and its tribulations, and shows the support and friendship women provide for one another—but there's no particular feminist revelation here. And in her second film, the adaptation of *Little Women*, any feminist work had already been done, over a hundred and fifty years earlier, by the novel's author Louisa May Alcott, herself a committed and openly avowed feminist.

Barbie-core and consumerism

In the film *Barbie*, America Ferrara in her role as Gloria delivers a long and much-quoted speech—penned for her by Gerwig—about the impossibility of being able to meet all the various demands that society in general, and men in particular, make of a woman in contemporary America. Surely this soliloquy is actually a paean of the "middle-class despair" mentioned earlier; the speaker, Gloria—who has a well-paid job, a home, and a family—is largely lamenting the fact that women are still expected to look and behave in a certain way if they are to please men and to "fit in" socially. However, her particular litany of the problems that face the salaried women of the Global North is seen by the director as the most "feminist" thing in the film. Gerwig claimed that both the cast and the crew on set when Ferrara delivered this speech were moved to tears—men as well as women. Reading the speech once more—easy to do online after a swift Google search—it is tempting to think that this same "cast and crew" could benefit from some old-fashioned "consciousness-raising" sessions, focusing on the much more serious situations confronting far too many women.

Here, we must also note the worrying transformation of Gloria's adolescent daughter Sasha. At the start of the film, she is a black-clad and politically aware teenager, the leader of a clique of seemingly strong-minded girls, and she forcefully explains to Barbie exactly how difficult she has made the lives of young women, not only by setting such impossible standards of physical perfection, but by working hand-in-glove with rampant consumerism, In a telling confrontation, Sasha declaims: "You represent everything wrong with our culture. Sexualized capitalism, unrealistic physical ideals . . . You set the feminist movement back fifty years. You destroy girls' innate sense of worth and you are killing the planet with your glorification of rampant consumerism."

Barbie replies: "No, I'm supposed to help you and make you happy and powerful." The "power," however, that Barbie and her fellow dolls exert as they later reclaim their homeland, after the *coup d'état* carried out by Ken and his allies, is surely rather questionable in both essence and operation. The Barbie dolls simply wield what a latter-day Puritan preacher might call their "sexist wiles," using their physical charms first to distract the Kens and then to disempower them. And it's important to note that Ken's own idiosyncratic interpretation of "the patriarchy," which he discovered to be so dominant a factor in the real world, is in fact a relatively harmless variant thereof, given the more unpleasant and violent aspects of contemporary masculine power and behavior. To impose his rule, Ken first puts on extravagant clothes—including a cowboy hat and a vast fur jacket reminiscent of a 1980s rock star. Then, he occupies, rechristens, and repurposes Barbie's Dreamhouse, so that it becomes the "Mojo Dojo Casa House" and provides stabling for his beloved horse. Once installed there, he drinks a lot of beer and strums a guitar, while hanging out day and night with the other Kens. The only really disturbing element here might be the Kens' newfound liking for war games—but these are so stylized and self-conscious that they hardly seem threatening; the Kens don't display any real desire for seeking out *Lebensraum*, let alone world domination.

Of course, the complaints of daughter Sasha, before her worrying change of heart and her surrender to Barbie's values, might have sounded very "second-wave" to those viewers happy with the concepts of post-feminism and neo-feminism.[8] To other women in the audience, however, who might be concerned by the status quo of the new century and who hanker after true equality for all, this declamation might be an echo of their own thoughts. And sadly, strong-minded Sasha is transformed as the narrative progresses into a Barbie-core devotee, abandoning her black outfits for pastel-pink dresses, accessorized with neatly tamed hair and overly "feminine" jewelry. She moves from her earlier hard-line stance to those modes of "feminism" that sit more happily within our neo-liberal climate, celebrated by many feminist scholars but challenged by others—including Angela McRobbie, Diane Negra, and Rosalind Gill.[9]

So, *Barbie* isn't exactly a progressive text, nor a "feminist" film. It is surely, however, a twenty-first-century "woman's picture"—and one which has ensured Gerwig's future and secured her reputation as a director; its extraordinary financial success means that from now on all her new projects will be welcomed—and funded—possibly as opposed to those of other and rather more progressive women directors. If her film has any real precedent, it is perhaps worryingly reminiscent of *Legally Blonde* (dir. Robert Luketic, 2001). That particular movie—which opened with a loving close-up of a well-known brand of shampoo—showed how a young woman overly fond of lurid pink clothes, accessories, and decor could, nevertheless, triumph in the largely male-dominated world of the Harvard law faculty and, later, the criminal courts system. It did not claim to have any feminist credentials, though at all times the heroine is seen to be notably supportive of her female friends and colleagues.

Seemingly as a result of her film's global reach, Greta Gerwig was elected Head of the Jury at the 2024 Cannes Film Festival, a sought-after and very prestigious post. That year, however, Cannes seemed to have become, more than ever, a fashion-and-celebrity circus. Press coverage of the event did not publicize the films nor the actors involved, but focused instead on "celebrities," and in particular on high-fashion models and their constant changes of outfit. Supermodel Bella Hadid was the most photographed attendee, particularly

Figure 3.1 *Greta Gerwig wearing John Galliano for Maison Margiela at the 2024 Cannes Film Festival, where she served as President of the Feature Film Jury. Courtesy Cindy Ord/Getty Images.*

when she appeared for a photocall in a vintage designer dress resembling the Palestinian *keffiyeh.* Interestingly, Gerwig herself wore Parisian couture for all her photocalls, presumably to underline her own newfound celebrity status.

One of Gerwig's designer dresses, created by John Galliano for Maison Margiela, was a rather unfortunate choice—when it was taken out of its extraordinary and highly theatrical catwalk context, without the extravagant styling and the porcelain-complexioned period makeup of the model on the runway. For in the context of a daytime event, this full-skirted candy-striped dress resembled nothing so much as a 1950s housedress, as worn by middle-class self-styled "homemakers" of that period. Only the white Margiela "hoof shoes" sported by the director gave any indication of the outfit's couture origins.[10] Arguably, it was the linked fashion and merchandising, rather than the onscreen content, which created the extraordinary success of her film. The extensive global press tour exemplified the unusual ambition of the project. The multigenerational appeal of *Barbie*, combined with the supposedly "feminist" take on the doll, and an advantageous antagonism, in the period around the film's release, with the opening of *Oppenheimer*—all this created a wave of "Barbie mania," fueled by relentless social media activity.

Fashion is, as suggested, at the film's very core, and Barbie-inspired trends trickled down from the red carpet to the general public, with the birth of the TikTok aesthetic "Barbie-core," and a series of collaborations with fast-fashion companies.[11] The movie arguably functioned as the catalyst of a massive marketing operation, merging fashion, cinema, and celebrity culture, profiting through a worrying symbol of female submission now rebranded as a contemporary icon of emancipation. The hyped-up opening of the film was not only designed to coincide with the opening of *Oppenheimer* over that same weekend—but the public were also encouraged to attend both screenings, ideally on the same day. It seems that many Barbie fans, dutifully dressed in fuchsia pink to honor their plastic heroine, may have obediently sat through a biopic celebrating the man who created the atom bomb. Some of the more adventurous fans were photographed in pink cowboy ensembles and full-skirted gingham dresses, based on two of Robbie's most notable costumes in the film; these were created by leading designer and previous Oscar winner Jaqueline Durran, but accessorized onscreen by Chanel handbags and jewelry,

Figure 3.2 *Margot Robbie as "Stereotypical Barbie" displays the Chanel logo on her bag* (Barbie, *dir. Greta Gerwig, 2023*).

all kept carefully in shot. Robbie of course has been a Chanel brand ambassador for several years; rarely has a movie sparked so much fashionable activity at viewing theaters.

Now—a look back. For the doll's appearance throughout the decades has been shaped by the gaze of leading fashion designers, who have given her more attention than any film star—Oscar de la Renta was the first fashion designer to create a custom-made line for her in 1985. As *Time Magazine* writer Cady Lang explains, one of the first careers that Mattel marketed for Barbie was that of "fashion model," arguing that her impossible proportions were surely made to showcase fashion.[12] They are, of course, the proportions of contemporary *celebrity*, rather than the more boyish models traditionally seen on couturiers' catwalks.

In some ways, Barbie is the single most enduring fashion icon of the last half-century. Since the first Barbie doll was released in 1959, wearing a striped black-and-white bodysuit designed by its creator, Ruth Handler, the doll arguably became the symbol of the modern female consumer, "devoted to waste and self-fashioning."[13] Her willingness to adopt every style made her the ideal canvas on which to project multiple identities, thanks to her plastic nature that allowed a multitude of transformations undreamt of by even the most chameleon-like popstars and actresses. As costume and fashion designer

Bob Mackie, who dressed Barbie in 1990, declared, "She could be anything we wanted her to be"—a description that is worryingly reminiscent of many of the most successful, and most malleable, fashion models. Their profession, of course, is in many ways a paradigm of "women's general compulsion to regulate and discipline their bodies in pursuit of a prescribed yet elusive feminine image."[14] Despite Barbie's seeming versatility, her appearance in popular imagination corresponds to a very specific and immediately recognizable "look."

Barbie the doll favors kitsch outfits invariably adorned with eye-catching accessories featuring bows, hearts, and stars. In Gerwig's movie, the character as played by Margot Robbie is indeed "Stereotypical Barbie," the very embodiment of this fashionable and aesthetic ideal—deeply rooted in an enduring European notion of modern beauty and femininity associated with the Global North.[15] The early 2000s had seen the return of hyper-feminine celebrities, whose maximalist and colorful style replaced that of the heroin-chic fashion icons of the late 1990s and the grunge era.[16] Barbie, with her very different interpretation of dress and self-presentation, was arguably central to this new era, In recent years we have seen, on catwalks and across social media, a growing interest in Y2K fashion,[17] and very soon after the release, in July 2022, of the first pictures of Margot Robbie as the Mattel doll, the aesthetic inspired by Barbie's universe became particularly popular on TikTok. It was baptized "Barbie-core" on social media and became one of the most-used hashtags on the platform across the following year.[18]

The release and marketing of *Barbie*

The theatrical release of the *Barbie* movie cemented the centrality of the trend—mainly thanks to the highly publicized press tour and the presence of several celebrities in the cast, as characters or cameos. Among them we find, for instance, pop superstar Dua Lipa, who also sang on the official soundtrack and collaborated with the house of Versace for its Resort 2024 collection, which was itself inspired by a Barbie-core aesthetic.

The hype around both doll and film manifested itself into millions of social media reels and posts dedicated to the stereotypically feminine and stridently pink aesthetic of Barbie's universe; it was also highly instrumental in fostering Barbie's reappearance as a brand. Warner Bros., the company who distributed the movie, exploited its increasing popularity through a series of collaborations with numerous different brands, over a hundred in all, including several fast-fashion companies like Zara, H&M, Forever21, Shein, and Boohoo.[19]

There were, of course, a few upmarket offers—the Malibu townhouse to rent, for example, decorated throughout to create an adult version of Barbie's Dreamhouse. But it was the multitude of pink-fueled Barbie-inspired fast-fashion collections that sparked criticism from, among others, sustainability activist Livia Firth, founder of Eco Age (a consultancy firm providing bespoke sustainability solutions for brands looking to improve their supply chain), and executive producer of the documentary *The True Cost*, a film denouncing the human and ecological ravages of fast fashion in the Global South.[20]

Firth wrote an enraged post on her Instagram account, pointing out the stark contrast between the empowering message supposedly conveyed by Gerwig's post-feminist manifesto and the living and working conditions of women producing the fast-fashion garments branded as "Barbie":

> Just some of your favorite fast fashion exclusive @barbie collaborations— from @boohoo, @hm, @primark, @sheinofficial, @forever21, and MANY many more—I can guarantee you ONE thing: they ain't produced by any Barbie or liberated woman who gets paid a living wage or works in safe environments with no abuses. AND you ain't going to keep this forever, are you? How long will it last in your wardrobes before it gets thrown away / donated / recycled—aka dumped to a Global South country like Ghana or Kenya where there are no Barbies or liberated women. P.S.: I forgot: they are made of cheap synthetic or polyester fabrics—so you are also wearing Oil. But that's all right . . .[21]

Firth's statement points out a significant contradiction inherent within the current post-feminist cultural landscape and raises questions regarding the true significance of the movie for the feminist cause.

Finally, the red-carpet appearances of Robbie-as-Barbie demand attention.

As Elisabeth Castaldo Lundén has argued in her seminal work on the Oscar ceremonies:

> The relevance of stars and celebrities on the red carpet rests on their function as vessels for disseminating fashion discourses through their attained fame. In this sense, their underlying importance depends on the cultural implications of their transformation into a leading social elite, making some regard them as worthy of emulation.[22]

Thus, Barbie-core and its commercial implications should be understood as a phenomenon directly influenced by the powerful marketing and PR strategies behind Hollywood's continued hegemony—a phenomenon that we could compare to Georg Simmel's conception of fashion characterized by imitation, as a trickle-down rather than a bubble-up system, in anthropologist Ted Polhemus's terms.[23] The dissemination of *Barbie* as a cultural and commercial phenomenon reached its peak at the moment Margot Robbie's cinematic and sartorial performance crossed the set and moved onto the red carpets, becoming the main attraction of the movie's press tour. The actress continued to embody Mattel's doll far beyond the fictional realm, wearing Barbie-inspired looks throughout the promotion of the movie. The overall fashion operation was orchestrated by stylist Andrew Mukamal, who commissioned several Barbie-inspired outfits from leading fashion houses across the world, including Versace, Bottega Veneta, Chanel, Vivienne Westwood, and Miumiu—all of which were collected in a book, *Barbie: The World Tour* (2024).[24]

The impressive collection of "looks" involved several moments that referenced Barbie's fashion past—most frequently referenced were the early 1990s, when sales of the Barbie doll reached their peak, and it became a recognized fashion reference point for designers and stylists. Barbie arguably influenced a new mode of dressing, embodied by real life "Barbies," such as the 1990s supermodels—those true glamorous celebrities of that decade.[25] It is not a coincidence that Robbie wore so many outfits inspired by, or directly copied from, vintage pictures of the leading German model Claudia Schiffer, who was considered at the time to be the new Brigitte Bardot; some say, in fact, that Bardot herself might have been the original inspiration for the first Barbie doll.[26]

There is a fine line, though, between harmless irony and stereotypes perpetuating harmful prejudices. Barbie-core could be interpreted both as a naif and ironic reappropriation of feminine tropes previously denigrated as frivolous, or as a return to a highly standardized idea of what girls and women should wear. And some might see the presence in the Barbie movie of a diversified cast as possibly encouraging; however, as a counter to this, many were angered by the fact that the "out" lesbian actress Kate McKinnon was cast as "Weird Barbie." And, despite her character's growing self-awareness throughout the movie, Robbie rather than Barbie remains the main star of the whole marketing operation. "Stardom" invariably overshadows good intentions and Robbie's recent hegemony inevitably sparks questions as to what might be worthy of attention and adulation in our current celebrity-dominated landscape.

The detailed and well-thought-out collection of the red-carpet looks Robbie wore both on tour and at opening nights is illustrative of a new phenomenon which merges cinematic and fashion narratives. In recent years, the photocalls of a press tour's red-carpet events have become instrumental in the marketing of blockbuster releases. Fashion, in this context, works to create the unique and ephemeral spectacle of this particular red carpet, backdrop for the communion between fashion and cinema ever since the "golden age" of Hollywood.[27] But in recent years this very same press tour red carpet has become increasingly elaborate and more heavily publicized, becoming the most privileged of runways for both emerging fashion designers and established brands in search of further exposure. In the article "The Enchanted Spectacle," Caroline Evans argues that the fashion shows of the late 1990s have to be understood, not only as a commercial spectacle in an increasingly visualized global arena, but at the same time as a form of "theatricalization of social reality and of the self."[28] If we look back at Robbie's theatrical performances during these press tours, we might argue that the cinematic red carpet has become in recent years the very apotheosis of what Evans was describing. The cult of personality and the star power of the actress is merged with the transformative visual appeal of fashion and its ability to create narratives. Arguably, this is a primary example of how celebrity culture and fashion now imitate and influence each other's rituals.

The significant difference between the current situation and the fashion shows of the late 1990s lies in the communication and spread of the events. In the 1990s, television started to broadcast fashion shows; in today's society, internet activity has speeded up the process, transmitting live these pseudo-events, defined by sociologist Daniel Boorstin as activities whose sole purpose is to garner publicity—a definition that seems correct, but diminishes the artistic potential of the performance, considered here only as a commercial operation.[29]

The body of the movie star is obviously at the epicenter of the operation where cinema, celebrity, and fashion collide— what in social media terms is called a "viral moment."[30] Virality is a key concept in any understanding of recent developments in the current social media landscape, where the massive amount of visual content being produced and distributed has profoundly modified the established tactics of the film industry's various PR strategies. The long-established theatricality of the fashion show becomes the perfect medium in which to craft a spectacular moment to gather attention in the midst of the endless flow of content.

And fashion, of course, now enhances the star power of all celebrities who walk those red carpets, arguably fueling the resurgence of glamor as one way of attracting attention to the cinematic experience in the post-pandemic world depicted at the start of this chapter—a world where film theaters stood empty, new streaming platforms flourished, and celebrities—including screen stars and plastic heroines—became the main drivers of global fashion marketing and unbridled consumption.

Conclusion

Earlier in this chapter, America Ferrara's impassioned speech about the demands placed on a woman in contemporary America was described as a "paean of middle-class despair," the lament of a woman gainfully employed and enjoying a comfortable lifestyle, as opposed to the many women who are poor, unemployed, disenfranchised, sometimes threatened and abused. Perhaps "despair"—cutting across age, economic status, and ethnicity—should inform our response to the extraordinary way in which a highly lucrative fashion spectacle was allowed to masquerade as a "feminist film."

Part Two

The Greta Gerwig Touch: A Contemporary Auteur

Greta Gerwig: From Indiewood to Conglomerate Hollywood—New Iterations of the Contemporary Auteur

ALEX DICKIE

In a field that remains male-dominated, Greta Gerwig's visibility as the creative visionary behind a celebrated feminist-coded blockbuster is anomalous and invites consideration of the shifting function of auteurism within contemporary conglomerate Hollywood. Gerwig's billion-dollar-grossing, women-targeted feature *Barbie* (2023) is indicative of a twenty-first-century Hollywood that has reconfigured how film authorship is leveraged within the commercial or event cinema space. As a cinematic project, *Barbie*'s success can be understood as both product-driven and auteur-driven—a seemingly contradictory synthesis that combines the director's authentic indie credibility with the costly demands of the large-scale filmmaking of Hollywood's blockbuster apparatus. Given that Hollywood tentpole films are understood to marry conventional continuity filmmaking principles with expansive cutting-edge spectacle in order to appeal across the four audience quadrants, Gerwig's film is the rare blockbuster created by, and primarily targeting, women.

Gerwig's negotiation, or reconciliation, of this dynamic saw her imbuing Mattel's iconic toy property with idiosyncratic cinephilic panache in her adaptation of the license. Her success in navigating the constraints and the potential threats of studio intervention place her in rare American studio filmmaker company; those operating within the highest budget echelon who are nevertheless perceived as having the clout to retain control and continuity of vision despite the commercial imperatives of conglomerate Hollywood. Such capitalist priorities are frequently interrogated as inhibiting personal expression. The discourse surrounding Disney's *Marvel Cinematic Universe* (2008–) series, for instance, has glommed onto the disclosure that the productions use external support studios like The Third Floor that previsualize elements of the *mise en scène* and choreography. This practice is cited as evidence of how studios interfere, wresting control away from directors to execute visionless committee filmmaking.[1]

Gerwig's case also illustrates how the descriptor "auteur" (borrowed from the French) has been exploited as a brand signifier exploited for marketing and commercial purposes, while remaining closely connected to a longer romantic aesthetic tradition regarding the identifiable presence of an author in a film text. This latter conception of auteurism, valorized by *Cahiers du Cinéma* and Andrew Sarris in the 1950s and 60s, initially celebrated recovering art from Hollywood movies as articulated across a filmmaker's oeuvre. It has since become closely entangled with art, independent, and national cinemas. In particular, auteurism is associated with stylistic features and formal techniques that modify the constructed narrative spaces of film through camera, editorial, and temporal motivations that operate outside the diegesis of the film frame. Auteurist practices, however, present some messy limitations, particularly as it is extending into other screen disciplines to describe visionary control for both the showrunner of the streamed series and the creative directors of AAA videogames. Most pertinently for this discussion, however, auteurism in commercial cinema must grapple with its legacy of exclusion.

The marginalization of women in Hollywood

When auteurism came to prominence in the 1970s during the era of New Hollywood, women, with few exceptions like Elaine May and Claudia Weill, were overwhelmingly excluded from directing studio films. Accordingly, women did not benefit from the subsequent romanization of the golden era that their male counterparts enjoyed. Statistics gathered by a Directors Guild of America committee revealed that of the over 7,300 feature films released by major distributors in Hollywood between 1950 and 1980 a paltry fourteen were directed by women.[2]

While these figures do not include independent productions or films that did not receive major distribution, which have a better record of employing women, they nevertheless paint a bleak legacy of women directors working in Hollywood. The reality of women directors working in mainstream commercial cinema was such a significantly different experience to that of men it is unsurprising that the classic conception of auteurism theory fails to take this into account. It was in this context, after all, where Andrew Sarris devised his seminal work *The American Cinema: Directors and Directions 1929–1968*, ranking the efforts of 113, mostly American, directors by assessing their visual style in relation to their body of work. Those who failed to elaborate cinema syntax by developing aesthetically challenging or thematically transgressive styles were critiqued as journeymen. Sarris's form of classification completely omitted the formal innovations and pioneering work of women directors, such as Alice Guy-Blaché, Maya Deren, and Lois Weber. That Dorothy Arzner was ignored—despite being one of the top studio directors of Hollywood's classic studio era and reputedly the first to use a boom mic in her feature *The Wild Party* (1929)—suggests traditional auteur theory's mission to recognize art within the commercial cinema wholly neglected the role that women played behind the camera.

Given the widespread adoption of auteurism within popular culture, the historic precarity of women directors in an overwhelmingly patriarchal industry has led to critical rebukes of auteurism's limitations and the proposition of alternative historiographies to recover overlooked and marginalized forms of authorship. Scholar Judith Mayne has made the case that because critics lack a significant "body of evidence to suggest how and in what ways female-authored cinema would be substantially different" from works by men, the "classical equation of authorship" can "repress or negate the significant ways in which female signatures do appear on film."[3] Film writer Karina Longworth launched a season of her *You Must Remember This* podcast series dedicated to uncovering the work of Polly Platt, a New Hollywood production designer whose many other contributions to films, such as effectively serving as co-producer on *The Last Picture Show* (dir. Peter Bogdanovich, 1971) and *Paper Moon* (dir. Peter Bogdanovich, 1973) among others, have gone uncredited due to systematic sexism throughout Hollywood. Yvonne Tasker outlined how the rigidity and entrenchment of classical auteurism remains resistant to contemporary women directors who are singled out as "an inappropriate presence" within conventional "romantic, masculine" auteurism discourses.[4] This conceives women auteurs as both outside the hegemonic ideal of a director but also tethers any discussion of their films as a counterpoint to, or departure from, the norm of male directors. Consequently, this risks further fortifying an asymmetrical reception dynamic that perceives the qualities of films by women as inherently peripheral. How does Gerwig, who generates her own material while working at the highest scale of the commercial industry, figure into this framework? Certainly, numerous publications have celebrated her unique navigation of production not typically known for accommodating women-centered narratives. But how does this connect to her identity as a Hollywood auteur or, potentially, a marketable brand?

The new auteur

Theorist Timothy Corrigan developed a framework that decentered the film to instead consider how Hollywood's commodification of a director's surname became a mediating strategy that can enshrine directors as authors through marketing. Corrigan investigated how the auteur film began to "aspire more and more to a critical tautology, capable of being understood and consumed without being seen."[5] This implies that the public profiles of Hollywood filmmakers can be diminished or anonymized when such a system withholds, or constructs for the audience, an identifiable authorial signifier outside of the boundaries, and aesthetics, of the film text. Scholar Thomas James Wardak elaborated upon Corrigan's concept of the director as brand icon through a systematic examination of how such auteur constructions are leveraged by twenty-first-century conglomerate Hollywood's promotional channels to generate specific authorial meanings. He conceives this trend as "the author-industrial complex," which recognizes the symbiotic relationship between authorship and industry as being maintained through peripheral influences that lay outside the hermetic filmic text, such as paratextual materials, promotional strategies, and online fandoms which collectively influence, construct, and imply the values associated with the director.[6] This form of auteurism sees any understanding of a director necessarily tethered to the corresponding historical period in which they are situated while working in the industry. Similarly, film scholar Deb Verhoeven makes the case that contemporary auteurism has decentered the film to instead regard the overall industrial process's impact on a filmmaker's career. Verhoeven summarizes that twenty-first-century auteurism is "less about the consistent performance of personal expressivity than it is about creating the optimum conditions for consistent commercial performance."[7]

Extending this to Gerwig, the discrete circumstances and specific configuration of institutional discourses connected to the release of *Barbie* have together produced a less prescriptive auteurism dynamic that positions a woman as the chief arbiter of the top-grossing film of 2023.[8] Her anomalous commercial success represents a departure from the career trajectories of Generation X women filmmakers like Nicole Holofcener, Rebecca Miller, and Kelly Reichardt, directors born in the 1960s and 70s, who have remained closely associated with indie and independent films throughout their careers. These forms have been debated as providing a space where women fare better than the majors. The editors of *Indie Reframed* identified a common refrain regarding the works of women directors working in Indiewood: their in-betweenness, producing neither comfortably mainstream nor outwardly oppositional cinema, frequently precludes their work from being "readily absorbed into any pre-existing categories" which inhibits their marketplace visibility and careers.[9]

Domestic independent festivals like Sundance, where filmmakers like Ava DuVernay and Chloe Zhao launched their careers, has been identified as a talent pipeline for large-scale Hollywood productions.[10] While both DuVernay and Zhao went on to direct blockbusters for Disney, either preference for smaller-scale features or the lack of opportunities suggests that for contemporary women filmmakers following such a trajectory toward high-budget features largely remains an atypical pathway compared to their male counterparts. A 2023 report from the University of Southern California detailed that only 12.1 percent of directors of the top-grossing domestic films in 2023 were women, which demonstrates that women remain woefully underrepresented behind the camera in this space.[11] The unprecedented success of *Barbie* offers an opportunity to consider how the position of Gerwig within the contemporary Hollywood industry as an auteur is leveraged at both a personal level and strategically amplified and deployed by the studio.

The transformation of Hollywood

The period in which Gerwig shifted to directing was a paradoxical era of both consolidation and expansion for Hollywood. Beginning in 2012, the streaming giants Netflix and Amazon expanded beyond digital delivery services into series production and subsequently supported prestige features like *Manchester by the Sea* (dir. Kenneth Lonergan, 2016) and *Roma* (dir. Alfonso Cuarón, 2018) disrupting the firmament of Hollywood. By late 2019, the proliferation and user adoption of streaming services, which included the launch of both Disney+ and Apple TV+ in early November, was soon fortified by the COVID-19 pandemic as global audiences began embracing the platforms en masse.[12] Predictions that the pandemic would mark the juncture where streaming services would supplant, if not outright end, the theatrical model were proven premature as the market began slowly bouncing back in 2021. The recovery among studios, however, did not occur in a linear fashion. Following AT&T buying out Time Warner for $85 billion in 2018, WarnerMedia, which encompassed various media subsidiaries including Warner Bros. and the streaming service HBO Max, was unceremoniously unloaded to cable company

Discovery in 2021 for $43 billion. Currently operating as Warner Bros. Discovery, the regime change experimented with simultaneous streaming and theatrical releases for their tentpole features. This frustrated auteurs like Denis Villeneuve and has seemingly led to the dissolution of their near-twenty-year working relationship with Christopher Nolan, before announcing their intention to return to traditional exhibition in 2023.[13] This has raised concerns about whether the majors have marginalized certain forms or categories of films.

Thomas Schatz's research delineated that conglomerate Hollywood essentially produces three classes of film that are differentiated by budgets and audience demographics: blockbusters by the major studios priced above $100 million; the output by specialty divisions which produce "modestly budgeted films in the $30 million to $50 million range for more specialized and discriminating audiences"; and the "bottom tier" genuine independents that range anywhere below $10 million.[14] While the latter two sectors used to be home to the contemporary Hollywood auteur film, increasingly the erosion of the mid-tier picture prompts reassessment as some blockbusters now share certain sensibilities associated with auteurism. In the span of three years, the combination of rising production costs and the fallout of the 2008 financial crisis impelled media conglomerates to disband the specialty film divisions Miramax, Paramount Vantage, and Warner Independent and Picturehouse, leaving only Fox Searchlight, Focus Features, and Sony Pictures Classics. This process radically reshaped the industrial structure of the indie scene.

Yannis Tzioumakis's quantitative analysis of specialty film distribution in Hollywood between 2009 and 2019 reveals that in the aftermath of three of the major studios retreating from dedicated indie divisions, a set of companies emerged, including A24, Bleecker Street, STX Entertainment, and Annapurna among others, effectively replacing the studio's shuttered divisions. Across this period, these new entities, in conjunction with the studios, have roughly maintained the same market share for specialty features as Indiewood in its heyday.[15] Tzioumakis characterizes the specialty features produced in this era as "late indie," the prefix signaling their reduced cultural cachet stemming from diminishing trade and popular press coverage and the increasingly commercial orientation of the films compared to the output of the 2000s.[16]

With its estimated combined production and marketing budget of $295 million, a soundtrack featuring artists signed to Warner Bros. Atlantic Records label, its simultaneous release into thousands of theaters around the globe, and being headlined by Hollywood actors Margot Robbie and Ryan Gosling, *Barbie*, in many respects, bears the hallmarks of a standard blockbuster.[17] *Barbie*, however, is also strategically positioned as an auteur event film by Warner Bros., with some posters displaying "a film by Greta Gerwig" alongside the names of *Barbie*'s stars, conjuring traditional associations of glamorous comedy. Other posters withhold this possessory credit altogether, and these variations could be understood as a form of studio risk mitigation for increasingly expensive films, where tailoring specific audience addresses becomes a way to differentiate the product. But outside the economic concerns it speaks to an ambivalence within the blockbuster form. Gerwig's previous features *Lady Bird* (2017) and *Little Women* (2019), with budgets of nearly $10 million and $40 million, respectively, were more modestly scaled third- and mid-tier films.[18] Since Warner Independent Pictures closed in 2008, the studio's excursions into mid-budget indies or specialty features have been largely limited to Clint Eastwood films and few others.[19]

Correspondingly, since this narrowing occurred, the studio's blockbusters are increasingly being furnished with Indiewood qualities. Warner Bros. releases like *Gravity* (dir. Alfonso Cuarón, 2013), *Mad Max: Fury Road* (dir. George Miller, 2015), and *Dune* (dir. Denis Villeneuve, 2021), among others, premiered at festivals and rigorously promoted the visionary authorship of their respective directors at the center of their marketing campaigns. This strand of the blockbuster appeals to niche audiences and is enshrined with the imprimatur of auteur. Often these paradoxical features contain handcrafted, analogue techniques that in the digital age are characterized as conceived outside the dominant norms of commercial cinema despite their inextricable entanglement with the studio machinery. Gerwig, who recognized that blockbusters like *Barbie* "can have a quality of hegemonic capitalism," described the assembled montage of home videos sourced from the cast and crew as "sneaking in humanity to something that everybody thinks is a hunk of plastic."[20] Gerwig implies not only that she has overcome, through personal ingenuity, the impersonal limitations of commercial film, but also that her previous directorial efforts, despite being closely associated with Hollywood, were also not participating in hegemonic capitalism. This perception of hegemony being something that auteurist discourses can counter through narratives surrounding the film's packaging, production style, and promotion proposes that the director's authenticity and creativity are a means to reframe large-scale industrial efforts as personal works.

Barbie: A production history

Barbie was initiated by its star Margot Robbie who through her production company LuckyChap Entertainment approached Mattel in 2018 and successfully negotiated a deal where she would produce and star in a feature film based on the license.[21] Such short-term arrangements, dubbed the package-unit system by scholar Janet Staiger, have been typical in Hollywood since the 1950s, where finance, labor, and the means of production are organized by the producer rather than the studio.[22] A partnership with Warner Bros. Pictures was announced in early 2019, with Greta Gerwig and her co-writer Noah Baumbach personally selected by Robbie as screenwriters in July of that year.[23] With its focus on identity and death, Gerwig joked that she figured their script would likely remain unproduced and join the infamous ranks of the black list.[24] When the New York-based couple finished the script Gerwig became protective of the project, the filmmaker stating: "It felt so clear to me: If they didn't want to make that [version], I didn't need to make it."[25] Still officially employed as a screenwriter, Gerwig began extensive preparations via Zoom calls in winter 2020, assembling the creative team of cinematographer Rodrigo Prieto, production designer Sarah Greenwood, and costume designer Jacqueline Durran before the project received the green light.[26] This unorthodox approach continued with Gerwig forgoing a traditional pitch and instead presenting the executives at Mattel with a "strange and surreal" poem about the struggles of the project that, in her words, communicated "some vibe of the movie."[27] As with *Little Women*, Gerwig ultimately signed on as director years after joining the project in a writing capacity, publicly stating her desire to protect the script.[28] This unconventional approach was carried through into the film's production.

Barbie, an enormous undertaking that saw principal photography split across location shoots in Los Angeles and interiors at Warner Bros. Studios Leavesden between March and July 2022, was a significant departure from the location-based realism of *Lady Bird* and *Little Women*. Working to Gerwig's paradoxical mandate for "authentic artificiality," *Barbie*'s production team devised a highly stylized aesthetic strategy that recalls the year of the doll's invention in 1959.[29] Gerwig's mandate saw her expand the fuchsia-hued production across eight soundstages and a studio backlot. Teaming up with cinematographer Rodrigo Prieto, known for his collaborations with Alejandro González Iñárritu and Martin Scorsese, Gerwig used in-camera photography to emphasize the tangible stages' unfinished qualities. She retained visible strings, painted skies, and cut-out moons, highlighting and underlining the constraints associated with classical Hollywood as part of her filmmaking process. Utilizing a combination of front- and rear-projection, dioramas, matte paintings, and the scaling down of large sets to miniatures to deliberately distort scale and expose the edges of the stage, Gerwig leaned into the constructedness of Barbie's aesthetic.[30] In combination with the lavish, widescreen staging of numbers like "I'm Just Ken" where the imperfectly choreographed performers move against expressive washes of color and gestural outlines serve as referents for the highway expanse, *Barbie* reflexively recalls the abstracted aesthetics of technicolor soundstage musicals.

This visual strategy also serves the purpose of delineating between the constructed spaces of Barbie Land and the ostensible real world. The former uses large-format cameras and wide-angle lenses placed in close proximity to the actors, who are consistently framed either in profile or head-on, to create an effect that resembles playing with miniatures in a tox box; the latter expands the visual vocabulary to include telephoto lenses, distorted framing, and jarring camera moves.[31] As Gerwig's first digital shoot as director and her first extensive engagement with numerous high-end visual effects and technologies,[32] *Barbie* bridged classical Hollywood practical filmmaking while largely adhering to continuity filmmaking norms. The theatrical departures, informed by Gerwig's cinephilia, contains and justifies the stylization narratively. A measure of difference and distinctiveness is felt more profoundly in the grand scale of the blockbuster focused on exploring the relationship dynamics between women

Figure 4.1 *Director Greta Gerwig, in collaboration with cinematographer Rodrigo Prieto, used in-camera photography to emphasize the unfinished qualities of the environment in which actors performed their roles as means of underlining the artifices of the filmmaking process (Barbie, dir. Greta Gerwig, 2023).*

and their surrounding environments, which, due to its rarity, is potentially more alienating for studios than any excessive stylization could be.

A blockbuster with a difference

Gerwig's flippancy during the press cycle, including joking to *60 Minutes* that "literally, the worst thing that can happen is that it's terrible, nobody likes it, and it bankrupts a studio,"[33] and disclosing that she attached a self-deprecating note to America Ferrera's script, pleading, "I wrote a *Barbie* movie, hear me out,"[34] assists in ironizing the blockbuster discourse. While her self-aware irreverence playfully invokes tales of Hollywood hubris, Gerwig simultaneously offers an alternative, more earnest profile that differs from many of her male contemporaries. Describing her role as director as "creating an atmosphere of acceptance, no wrong answers, no judgment" on set, this collaborative approach stands in contrast to auteurs celebrated for their tyrannical, controlling tendencies.[35] Gerwig wholly credits second-unit director George Cottle with designing the film's car chase, a cliché of the blockbuster that, nonetheless, undermines the narrative that camera blocking and *mise en scène* are the privileged right of the auteur.[36]

These challenges to expectations are also maintained discursively through promotional networks that shape the interpretative guidelines for Gerwig's work and persona. Across both Warner's official platforms and indirectly through external channels, these collectively assist in conferring the status of author on certain directors. The paratextual discourse surrounding Gerwig during the award campaigning throughout 2023 and 2024 played a crucial role in maintaining this association and perhaps reshaped normative boundaries of what constitutes an auteur.

For example, during this promotional cycle, Gerwig was featured with the president of the Criterion Collection.[37] During the interview, Gerwig champions the French New Wave filmmakers Jacques Demy and Jean-Luc Godard, both revered auteurs, and acknowledges their personal influence over her style. Accordingly, this recognition invites dedicated viewers to seek out and identify *Barbie*'s overt homages to Nouvelle Vague icons such as Catherine Deneuve and Anna Karina, with Robbie framed to resemble a combination of both. This strategy places both the star and director as part of a tradition that appeals to Criterion's robust network of cinephiles. As an authority dedicated to preserving the best available versions of directors' uncut visions, Criterion typically adheres to conventional notions of Euro-centric auteurism, despite a few notorious departures. Their home releases and their meticulously designed cover art often endow directors with processionary credits that list their names alongside or above the movie stars; their pioneering audio commentaries invite viewers to eavesdrop on conversations with filmmakers and scholars. Accordingly, Criterion has "a legitimizing function that empowers it with an ability to affirm what films should be deemed important,"[38] which indirectly benefits Gerwig's films even though they have yet to receive the Criterion treatment. During this same period, *Barbie* made its home premiere on Max, the streaming service for Warner Bros., where the film is listed alongside a separate entry for Greta Gerwig's commentary. The positioning of the director as its own standalone category on the dashboard ribbon rather than hidden under an extra features option is a unique promotional feature of the platform and not something commonly extended to the other blockbusters on the service.

In doing so, this blockbuster with an indie sensibility, according to a featurette on Warner Bros. social channels, reconciles Gerwig's ambition of "paint[ing] in beautiful broad strokes" with continuing to explore stories about "mothers and daughters."[39] The director insists that despite Barbie being a global brand, it "feels just as intimate as *Lady Bird* or *Little Women*," suggesting that she has imbued what could be an anonymous franchise film with similar values to those expressed in her previous directorial work.[40] In the run-up to the awards season, the WB Awards website hosted Gerwig's interviews alongside celebrated auteurs like Todd Field, Alfonso Cuaron, and Jane Campion, the latter being the only woman director to win both the best director Oscar and the Palme d'Or. When Campion expressed her admiration, she pointedly stresses to Gerwig: "It's so much got your personal flavor, which is the greatest delight, and it's a blockbuster, so I can't imagine how you did this." This in turn provided Gerwig with the opportunity to insist that the canvas that big-budget films offer can be more liberating rather than constraining,[41] while also placing herself in the same category as the famed Antipodean auteur.

Film festivals offer another means of singling out specific mainstream commercial cinema from the mass of industrially produced cultural objects. These not only provide alternative sites for viewing movies deemed culturally significant, but also through the use of museum-style classifications that identify the film's unique features they can privilege and promote the filmmakers as auteurs outside traditional competitions.[42] Hollywood directors such as Joseph Kosinski and James Mangold have premiered their commercially orientated films at Cannes in the hopes of benefiting from the festival as a media event. *Barbie*, however, like Gerwig's other previous debuts at Telluride Film Festival in Colorado and MoMA in New York, premiered stateside at the Shrine Auditorium in Los Angeles. Despite having no direct engagement with the European film circuit, in December 2023, Iris Knobloch, Cannes Festival President, bestowed upon Greta Gerwig the honor of chairing the 2024 Cannes Jury, making her the first American woman director in history to take up that coveted role. Knobloch cites Gerwig's ability to reconcile incompatibilities by "delivering arthouse blockbusters, narrowing the gap between art and industry," a reference to *Barbie*'s more transgressive qualities.[43] Gerwig is both an active agent inside the Hollywood system and an outsider who closely orbits key institutions that fetishize the director as the author. She occupies a liminal space, benefiting from the resources of global media conglomerates, while embracing the artistic institutions that serve to safeguard against, or offer alternatives to, commercial cinema without fully occupying either.

Conclusion

Considering the role auteurism plays in the context of a multiplex global blockbuster such as *Barbie* demonstrates how authorship depends on the industrial structure and priorities of conglomerate Hollywood in which it is located. Studio-sanctioned authorship is commercially exploited as a guarantor of quality to distinguish products. Can the auteur reverse this dynamic to problematize a homogenized sphere of cultural production? Championed for using the massive studio resources of a licensed blockbuster to fit her own idiosyncratic purposes, Gerwig demonstrates the potential for a less prescriptive, more flexible form of auteurism. What remains to be seen is whether this is a viable pathway for others to follow, promising future opportunities for a richer range of voices behind the camera. Or will *Barbie* prove to be a maverick aberration? Streaming services are tempting filmmakers away as talent migrates toward the original series in the absence of feature-length films. Indie darlings like Annapurna Pictures are successfully diversifying their screen portfolios beyond cinema into videogames, refocusing their capacity and remit. It remains unclear how these realities will prepare the next generation of women auteurs to figure in or challenge the blockbuster environment. The inherently paradoxical nature of *Barbie* as a blockbuster, which targets women under and over 25 but nevertheless appeals to young men, incorporates analogue techniques in the digital age, and co-opts Indiewood strategies to promote its director as authentic, suggests once-rigid boundaries are collapsing in this era of consolidation. While directors will undoubtedly continue to mount male-centered auteur films across all budget categories in Hollywood, Gerwig stands out as a director who explored an alternative path.

Barbie, *Irony, and Post-Indie Cinema*

CLAIRE PERKINS

On the positive side of *Barbie*'s critical reception, one of the most recurrent evaluations of Greta Gerwig's much hyped and anticipated blockbuster was that it was "smart." Critics repeatedly expressed both admiration and surprise at the film's efforts to simultaneously celebrate and critique its iconic subject, and to manage an "unexpectedly weighty"[1] range of political and tonal positions: "a balance between kitsch, meta-commentary, and genuine appreciation" in "a movie that wants to have its Dreamhouse and burn it to the ground, too."[2] Implicit in this acknowledgment of how the film is "much weirder than you'd ever expect a *Barbie* motion picture to be"[3] is a nod to what it's not, a 'dumb' film that straightforwardly promotes the toy line it is based on without tackling its considerable gendered baggage. In this way, critics discussing the "intelligence and interrogation"[4] of this 2023 film evoke a more specific and loaded concept of "smart cinema," as a sensibility linked to a group of commercial/independent U.S. films released in the late 1990s and early 2000s that used tonal irony to critique white, middle-class taste and culture in deliberate opposition to Hollywood storytelling.[5] Gerwig's co-writer and husband Noah Baumbach wrote and directed several "smart" films, including *The Squid and the Whale* (2005), *Margot at the Wedding* (2007), and *Greenberg* (2010, starring Gerwig), and Gerwig herself was a central part of the lower-fi "mumblecore" movement that was another key dimension of the American independent scene of the early 2000s. Both types of filmmaking have arguably evolved beyond recognition in the American screen systems and cultures of the 2020s. The prominence of the term "smart" in *Barbie's* reception, then, offers an interesting perspective from which to consider both how irony operates in the film, and on how the film itself—as Gerwig's production—reflects the cultural uses to which an ironic, "indie" sensibility is put in Hollywood today.

This Barbie is being ironic

While Warner Bros. had held the rights for a motion picture based on the Barbie IP since 2009, a project had reportedly not appeared earlier because the studio could not figure out how to make a film that acknowledged Barbie's head-spinning mass of contradictions in a Hollywood newly aware of its "woman problem" while also restoring trust and sales in a declining commodity. As Willa Paskin describes, the film couldn't be a satire because that wouldn't sell product, but it also couldn't be straightforward propaganda because that would be boring.[6] As part of this impossible demand, the project also needed the right person at the helm: a "woman with credibility" who had a sincere interest in and attachment to the property. With this range of knotty contradictions, it's no surprise that the film Gerwig delivered relies on irony as a central mode of expression. When understood as a discursive strategy that operates at the level of language or form, irony is ultimately concerned with destabilizing meaning. It opens a space between what is *said* and what is *meant*, relying on a range of textual and contextual cues to signal the difference. As Linda Hutcheon emphasizes, this process means different things to different players: for the *interpreter* it is the making or inferring of meaning in addition to and different from what is stated, but for the *ironist*, "irony is the intentional transmission of both information and evaluative attitude other than what is explicitly presented."[7] When meaning is made ambiguous, a variety of positions can be true, and a variety of audiences can be addressed, which is precisely what *Barbie* needed to do.

The film uses irony to meet this challenge in a range of ways. The starkest expression is in the film's first ten minutes, where it introduces Barbie and

Barbie Land. The doll's backstory is told against a visual evocation of the opening sequence of *2001: A Space Odyssey* (dir. Stanley Kubrick, 1968), with Helen Mirren's voice-over explaining the revolutionary power of Barbie as a figure who "changed everything": the first adult doll in a world that had only known baby dolls. In an interpretation of Kubrick's famous, slow-motion bone toss, a baby doll is thrown in the air segueing to the film's title and the scene moves to a rapidly expanding range of Barbies, who multiply instantly from Margot Robbie as the original figure to a range of women in different outfits and of different races and abilities: *Thanks to Barbie, all problems of feminism and equal rights have been solved. At least, that's what the Barbies think. They're living in Barbie Land. Who am I to burst their bubble?* This opening, and the walk-through of Barbie Land that follows, gives what is, on the one hand, an entirely accurate account of the toy's narrative. Barbie *did* change everything, and then kept morphing to meet evolving social expectations in a vision of female empowerment. The limitations and the impact of this vision, though, are of course more conflicted; they comprise a raft of "baggage" that the film signals solely through heavy irony in these opening minutes, relying on the viewer's knowledge that all problems of feminism and equal rights have *not* been solved in the real world. This relatively straightforward use of irony, where what is meant is what is not said or explained, underpins the film's tone throughout, breaking through regularly in asides such as the nods to discontinued Mattel products and Barbie creator Ruth Handler's reference to her tax evasion issues. Rehearsing a time-honored strategy of allusion in mainstream filmmaking that offers different layers of meaning for different audiences,[8] this strategy is at the core of *Barbie*'s financial success, insofar as it offered a meticulously formed vision of Barbie for those who "love Barbie," a simultaneously knowing critique of the figure for those who "hate Barbie," and a thoughtful cultural study of an iconic commodity for everyone in between.

But the film's use of an ambiguous and unstable tone works in other ways too. The space opened between expectation and reality in the ironic depiction of Barbie Land also extends to how the contradictions of this world are made literal. As numerous paratexts on the film have revealed, the construction of Barbie Land is unmistakably the work of a cinephile, where Gerwig paid insistent attention to making everything feel "authentically artificial"—fake in a material, not effects-driven, way.[9] What this means in practice is that Barbie Land is a world created with visceral care and thought, not just in the world's physical props but in the way Gerwig brings to life what Barbie's mythology would actually entail. Much of the film's early surreal humor derives from statements or depictions of what is routinely glossed over or unacknowledged when thinking about or playing with Barbie: the way she insistently showers without water and drinks without liquid, her awkward proportions in relation to her highly unroadworthy Dream Car and, most cerebrally, the matter-of-fact description of Barbie as a figure who is, in Gerwig's term, "constrained in multitudes":[10] "all of these women are Barbie, and Barbie is all of these women."

These moments are surprising in the way they open and occupy a space between the said and the unsaid, creating a surreal and frequently existential perspective on what it means to engage in imaginative play. When used in connection with the ironic tone that positions Barbie as the force that has "fixed" the world, the effect is doubly destabilizing, undermining a conception of Barbie Land as straight satire and presenting a vision of her contradictions that is genuinely ambiguous. It is this effect that provoked the endless stream of think-pieces on "whether Barbie is feminist or not"—arguably the most common line of enquiry in all the discourse around the film.[11] Barbie Land is a post-feminist vision—depicting a world where women have won, men are secondary in all things, and feminism is no longer needed. Though in this "utopia," the pressure on women to be *perfect* is relentless, something summed up in the encompassing concept that *Barbie is everything*. The film's ironic perspective thus throws into question not only the plausibility of the world presented, but also how ideal such a scenario could ever be. And it's this latter query that propels the film's plot, where Stereotypical Barbie is driven to explicitly question her existence and purpose in the world.

Gerwig/Barbie

Gerwig's indie background and sensibility as a writer, director, and performer positioned her uniquely for this challenge. The vision of a female protagonist feeling existentially uncertain is entirely in line with her creative oeuvre. Across the films she has directed, co-written, and performed in, she has demonstrated a consistent interest in young women who are struggling to figure out who they are and what they want from life, from *Nights and Weekends* (co-directed with Joe Swanberg, 2008), to *Damsels in Distress* (dir. Whit Stillman, 2011) to *Frances Ha* (2012) and *Mistress America* (2015)—both co-written with Baumbach—to what Caetlin Benson-Allott has described as her "reparative girlhood trilogy:" *Lady Bird* (2017), *Little Women* (2019), and *Barbie*, which "[acknowledge] the trauma of trying to figure out what a woman is and how to become one but also [offer] viewers feminist affirmation and joy."[12] The themes of arrested development, precarity, and the unstable boundary between childhood and adulthood that are centered here are all cornerstones of American indie filmmaking of the 1990s and 2000s. The work that has attracted most attention for these concerns, though, has tended to be that of male "maverick" filmmakers who express them in an overly mannered style—with exaggerated control (Wes Anderson), cynicism (Todd Solondz), or self-conscious referentiality (Noah Baumbach). Across the three stages of her indie career, from mumblecore performer and co-writer to "smart" film collaborator to solo writer-director in increasingly larger productions, Gerwig's affective register is highly distinctive in the way it challenges this dominant brand of indie masculinity. In a sphere that prioritizes *control* at the levels of writing, style, and performance, Gerwig brings qualities of movement and commotion. Her characters deal with familiar problems but behave and express themselves in ways that are disruptive and memorable.

This energy is first made visible in her impact on the tone and style of the work of the male indie directors with whom she collaborated in a range of mumblecore and smart films. As I've previously argued, the mumblecore movement in which Gerwig first found visibility presents a microcosm of this valuing of indie expression, functioning as a form of "men's cinema" that, while adopting much looser stories and styling, notably foregrounds male identity politics in its slight narratives.[13] In *Nights and Weekends*, the character of Mattie (played by Gerwig) is uncharacteristically direct and fluent in expressing her dissatisfaction with her long-distance romantic partner (Swanberg). The effect is to challenge mumblecore's typical vision of millennial men and masculinity in crisis, encouraging instead an identification with the changeable perspective of the female character. The film is squarely centered on the favored mumblecore trope of a relationship juncture but puts this in terms of Mattie's subjectivity: it is her frustration, boredom, and grief that is felt, not only through her articulate dialogue, but through her character's palpably uncomfortable occupation of James's city and apartment. In a similar way, *Frances Ha* and *Mistress America*, both of which Gerwig stars in, tangibly counter the spiky negativity of Baumbach's previous films, including *Kicking and Screaming* (1995), *The Squid and the Whale* (2005), and *Margot at the Wedding* (2007). All these films are centrally concerned with the interpersonal dysfunction of the white middle class, but in Gerwig's collaborations the focus shifts from the nuclear family to the frictions of platonic female relationships, between her character and, respectively, a best friend who is drifting away and a new stepsister. Where Baumbach's earlier films tend toward a cynical outlook where characters appear trapped in their anxieties and neuroses, *Frances Ha* and *Mistress America* are more upbeat and earnest. Neither protagonist has her life remotely figured out, but she faces this precarity with a sense of possibility—finding and expressing buoyancy in small moments and connections.

All these collaborations demonstrate how Gerwig's challenge to a dominant brand of male indie identity occurs primarily at the level of affect. She writes and performs characters and situations where the most prominent cultural markers of indie expression—arrested development and ironic expression—are presented in unfamiliar ways. In her solo work, this culminates most palpably in a sense of qualified optimism on her uncertain protagonists and their lives. Christine "Lady Bird" McPherson and the four March sisters of Gerwig's *Little Women* are classically "indie" figures in that they are consistently focused on the mismatch between their dreams and reality—fixated on their own emotions and aspirations. In both films, this mindset relates specifically to their understanding of the limitations their lives present to becoming the women they want to be. As opposed to reveling in this "stuckness," though, the characters are afforded a measure of emotional growth: Lady Bird, for instance, comes to see the wonder of her childhood environment and how the predicament she feels also impacts her family. These finales resonate with Gerwig's own outlook: she has been said to opine that "if a film doesn't have a happy ending, what are we even doing?"[14] Her affective register blends an upbeat optimism with a palpable and clear-eyed self-awareness that comes across as thoroughly *knowing*. The effect is most evident in *Little Women*, where her outlook is felt in her self-conscious changes to Alcott's original story, and the way this has been dramatized in previous adaptations. These changes situate the film as a "smart" adaptation but are made in a naturalistic style that distinguishes her update from the arch style of modern takes on period texts that foreground a more straightforwardly ironic perspective. Like the type of filmmaking that Hilary Radner terms the "smart-chick film,"[15] this strategy of position-taking carries a different affect and function from the work of smart indie films that use a loaded tone to deliberately bifurcate audiences along the lines of cultural knowledge and taste. Gerwig's tone and choices instead work to signal the complexity and contradictions at work in a well-known text, subtly indicating their ongoing relevance in a modern world. As an original story, the effect in *Lady Bird* is less pronounced but equally evident in her interpretation of highly recognizable tropes of the coming-of-age film, which are expressed in terms of Lady Bird's palpable sense of *expectation*. As Gerwig has revealed on the process of creating the film: "Something Saoirse and I had talked about a lot was this idea of, 'what is the movie playing in her head, which is not the movie that she's in?' She would think that she is in a movie where she is going to find 'the one.'"[16] In my own writing on smart cinema I have argued that a key dimension of the sensibility is the way filmmakers take an informed and knowing stance toward aspects of film history, genre, and culture.[17] While not employing the cynical, deadpan, or densely referenced qualities of many films linked to this sensibility, Gerwig's solo films also demonstrate this quality of knowingness—presenting women who express the paradox of being acutely aware of the predictable nature of their everyday dilemmas, while nonetheless sincerely feeling the emotions that attend these.

Post-indie Barbie

With *Barbie*, Gerwig took on an adaptation of another much-loved cultural product that aims to illuminate its ongoing relevance. As mentioned, though, the reignition of interest in this property carried notably different cultural and commercial stakes from that of *Little Women*, with a substantially inflated set of expectations. In the "Barbenheimer" phenomenon, Gerwig's film was part of a concerted campaign by Hollywood to reignite interest and economic returns in cinema-going itself, in an environment radically disrupted by both the COVID-19 pandemic and increasingly convergent media technologies and cultures. One of the distinctive features of this transformed landscape, specifically in the United States, has been the obscuring of mid-level or "specialty" filmmaking as a category with clear production, distribution, and exhibition operations. This "invisibilizing" is typically understood as an effect of the growing influence of digital technologies and their uptake in large (Hollywood) and small (personal) contexts. As James Fleury, Bryan Hartzheim, and Stephen Mamber have described, while "the tech-media hybrids have embraced a data-driven approach to creative labor that tailors films and television shows to online viewer profiles ... a new generation of talent has built an empire on social media, translating their popularity into film and television deals and lucrative advertising revenue."[18] Sarah Sinwell has examined the specific place of indie cinema in this environment, arguing that audiences and markets for independent cinema are transitioning from movie theaters to televisions and other personal devices, and that "the ability to access independent cinema online not only creates new audiences ... but also redefines independence itself."[19]

In this environment, U.S. films that exhibit the cultural markers of an indie sensibility in symbolic opposition to Hollywood are still being produced but are harder to find and understand as a coherent group than they were in the Indiewood era. Alongside this change, the identity of Hollywood has also transformed. The almost exclusive reliance on existing IP has intensified the situation of what Nicolas Bourriaud called in the early 2000s "postproduction": "the proclivity of filmmakers to interpret, reproduce, remake, and make use of available cultural products—[as] a response to the proliferating chaos of global culture in the information age."[20] As Constantine Verevis has observed, this is a critical-historical moment in which remakes and other serial forms no longer linearly follow and supersede their originals but proliferate and coexist as multiple versions. This is a discursive shift where value is ascribed to an earlier version and filters are identified—technological, cultural, authorial—through which this has been transformed in the new property.[21] It follows that this is a moment where blockbuster films depend primarily for their originality on how they distinguish themselves in relation to these other versions. In this environment, the extent to which a film can take a self-aware or knowing stance toward existing cultural products is its most essential form of innovation. In this move, a critical component of an indie sensibility is folded into Hollywood filmmaking itself.

This phenomenon has occurred alongside other ways in which indie cultural markers have become increasingly mainstreamed, including how the creators, themes, and stylistics historically associated with the sensibility have migrated to cable and streaming television.[22] In understanding this shift, it is frequently the minor, character-driven nature of indie filmmaking that is followed, especially when attending to the productions of female creators in the everyday, nontransformative story lines of series like *Girls*, *Better Things*, *Insecure*, and *One Mississippi*.[23] As I have examined, this space has been an especially rich site for female indie creators, who have contributed to forming the highly visible trope of the imperfect or "messy" millennial.[24] This specific trope fits with a broader raft of texts that have appeared over the last decade or so across multiple popular media formats, where creators and protagonists anchor characters and stories around the revelation and performance of their vulnerabilities and "flaws." At one end is the static specter of what Taylor Nygaard and Jorie Lagerwey have termed "horrible white people," where the emotional suffering of largely privileged white characters is centered in story lines that facilitate minimal growth or transformation.[25] At the other is the therapeutic discourse that grounds bestselling books like Brené Brown's *The Gifts of Imperfection*, in which readers are encouraged to embrace their flaws in an effort to become more authentic and fulfilled.[26] The appeal of these expressions is the *relatability* of an imperfect posture. Audiences "get" the cruelly optimistic[27] point that is often left implicit, which is that the expectations and pressures of a gendered neo-liberal environment are exhausting and overwhelming but, nonetheless, function as a horizon of perfection that is difficult to let go.

With *Barbie*, Gerwig brings her distinctive style to a film that unites these two features of a "post-indie" U.S. environment: a knowing stance toward an existing cultural product and a relatable posture of feminine imperfection. By dramatizing Barbie's discovery of unprecedented flaws—a patch of cellulite, bad breath, flat feet, and irrepressible thoughts of death—the film sets in motion a series of doubled scenarios that dramatize an interplay between perfection and imperfection, producing a surprising and highly allusive perspective on Barbie as commodity and icon. This begins when Weird Barbie offers Stereotypical Barbie the option of staying oblivious and attached to her perfect "pink" world (a pathway symbolized by a pink high heel) or learning the truth by traveling to the imperfect "real" world (a brown Birkenstock). When she and Ken opt for the latter, Barbie finds her counterpart—the real woman Gloria, whose own negative emotions are being transmitted to Barbie through play—and learns about patriarchy as a bluntly inverse world to Barbie Land. These discoveries, which culminate in Ken importing patriarchy back to Barbie Land and brainwashing the Barbies into submission, produce a character who is not just "malfunctioning"—as the Barbies initially diagnose Stereotypical Barbie's flaws—but one who is also psychologically precarious: anxious, disillusioned, and overwhelmed. Faced with the Kens' occupation of the Dreamhouses and alteration of the Constitution, Barbie gives up, collapsing prostrate on the ground before the film cuts to a meticulously constructed ad for "Depression Barbie," a precise expression of "imperfect" feminine attitudes and behavior: *She wears sweatpants all day and night! She spent seven hours today on Instagram*

Figure 5.1 *"Depression Barbie" (*Barbie, *dir. Greta Gerwig, 2023).*

looking at her estranged best friend's engagement photos while eating a family sized pack of Starburst! This moment was evidently one of the best received in the film, with multiple reviewers mentioning that the "painfully, minutely specific" ad drew the biggest laughs from audiences[28] and users all over social media posting about feeling "called out" by the fictitious doll.[29]

Gerwig's choice to tap into this powerful affective current is another ironic choice, relying for its meaning on the viewer's recognition of a whole raft of cues. The response demonstrates how intuitively audiences "got" Barbie's exhaustion with relentless demands to perform femininity with constant optimism and competence, a sentiment put into explicit terms in Gloria's viral monologue, which awakens Barbie shortly after: *You have to never get old, never be rude, never show off, never be selfish, never fall down, never fail, never show fear, never get out of line . . . But always stand out and always be grateful.* Resonating precisely with Angela McRobbie's account of the tyranny of perfection in a gendered neo-liberal environment,[30] this description of what the film calls "the cognitive dissonance of living under patriarchy" becomes the literal key to un-brainwashing the Barbies who, upon hearing Gloria pronounce it, wake with a chime as if from a dream, return to their former selves, and ultimately take back Barbie Land. The action of the speech in driving the plot forward means this world cannot simply return to the status quo of perfection. Having learned that Barbie as a force has not, in fact, rid the real world of inequity and, further, has played her own role in perpetuating patriarchal standards, Barbie must, herself, change. In Barbie Land this change relates most centrally to the Kens, who are encouraged to find their own identities and, as Mirren's voice-over smugly intones, will "one day have as much power and influence in Barbie Land as women have in the real world." While this conclusion works within Barbie Land's initial logic, the disappearing of the violence and misogyny that would realistically follow this evacuation of patriarchal standards makes the ending for the Kens feel like a *deus ex machina*—its own improbably perfect conclusion to the more dire imperfections of the real world that have been discovered.

For Stereotypical Barbie, the reckoning with imperfection is more involved. This is the theme with which the film needed to tie up its thorny contradictions, acknowledging the negative realities of female experience under a system that demands perfection while simultaneously restoring faith in a figure—Barbie—which symbolizes that perfection, and specifically the ways in which its values and boundaries have shifted over time. *Barbie* aims to achieve all of this through the plot twist in which Barbie decides to become human. As the changes in Barbie Land are decided, Barbie admits she is not really sure where she belongs anymore, and does not think she has an ending, at which point Ruth Handler, the creator of Barbie, appears to explain that was always her point: she was created as an idea that would live forever, as a direct counter to how uncomfortable it is to be human. Patriarchy, Ruth pointedly notes, is another idea created for this reason. But Barbie insists that she "[wants] to do the imagining, I don't want to be the idea" and, in what is often referred to as the "Just Feel" scene, Ruth invites her to take her hands, close her eyes, and feel what taking this leap will mean. In these few minutes, the film achieves a startling shift in tone. It literally recedes from the smart humor of Barbie Land as, between worlds, Ruth and Barbie talk under shifting patterns of light and shadow that morph into faded home movies of women captured in celebratory and everyday moments, while Billie Eilish's song "What Was I Made For?" plays on the soundtrack. Leaning on the nostalgic images (collected from the cast and crew) and wistful lyrics—*I don't know how to feel, but I want to try*—to explain how the discomfort and uncertainty of being human is ultimately what makes life worthwhile, the moment conveys the power of being affected through affect itself.[31] While it is enacted very differently than in the moments of recognition that Gerwig's other protagonists experience, it is entirely in keeping with her storytelling practice, where her young female characters reliably come to understand how the aspects of their lives they had regarded as flawed or limited in fact contain multitudes.

With this conclusion, *Barbie* unmistakably mobilizes the theme of imperfection to a populist end. Its protagonist learns to recast her failings as strengths that support an upbeat resilient outlook, finally understanding that she does not need to be perfect or extraordinary to have a meaningful and productive existence. In choosing to become human, Barbie evolves from being "everything" to embodying Gloria's idea of "Ordinary Barbie," who "just has a flattering top and . . . wants to get through the day feeling kind of good about herself"—as is emphasized in her final outfit of jeans, a blazer over a tank top, and, in an exact visual metaphor for a mindset that compromises on "perfect" standards, pink Birkenstocks. This vision of accepting that one is "enough" is not a subversive conclusion. But it is an ultimately ironic one for Barbie, as a brand historically associated with a vision of perfection that has set impossible gendered expectations. Gerwig meets this paradox with a knowing but hopeful perspective that is tonally consistent with her other work, which takes the arch irony common to a mannered style associated with male indie directors and diffuses it into something more natural and personal. In *Barbie*, this approach culminates in a smart, ironic tone that is maximalist not minimalist, encompassing an experience for everyone rather than one for pointedly defined audiences. As the high point to date of Gerwig's own post-indie career, I suggest that this tonal approach also demonstrates a model of post-indie cinema. Ordinary Barbie would make money, a Mattel executive quickly calculates in the film, and so did *Barbie* itself, famously becoming the highest grossing film ever made by a female director. This is a cinema, then, that channels the indie credentials of its creators into a smartly inclusive experience in an IP-driven landscape, openly commodifying transgressive ideas and folding these into a stance on a universe of cultural products that is at once knowing and sincere.

"Authentically Artificial": Embodying the Self in Barbie

SUZANNE FERRISS

Greta Gerwig insisted that the aesthetics of *Barbie* be "authentically artificial."[1] Through elaborate costume, production, and set design, the film creates believably fake cinematic worlds—Barbie Land and Kendom Land—to represent the universe of plastic toys that inspired the narrative. The film's elaborately fabricated dreamworld has a genuine purpose: to expose the constructed nature of gendered existence in contemporary culture. In the real world, as in the film world, we fashion our lives through clothing, decor, and architecture. This chapter will examine the film as representing the complexities of gendered self-fashioning on screen and, by extension, in life.

To fashion

The central conceit of the film *Barbie* is, then, fashioning—on multiple levels. As a verb, "fashion" derives from the Latin *facere* ("to do, make"). To fashion something means "to make or shape," "to fabricate." Applying this sense of the word, Stephen Greenblatt has argued the sixteenth century saw the emergence of an "increased self-consciousness about the fashioning of human identity as a manipulable, artful process." Fashion became self-fashioning, shaping "a distinctive personality, a characteristic address to the world, a consistent mode of perceiving and behaving."[2] Sociologists as well as fashion theorists have argued that fashion—clothing—is a critical component of self-fashioning in the modern era. Connecting our bodies and the world, our inner lives to our outward appearance, clothing is essential to the presentation or performance of the self. Clothing is that "most closely attached to the corporal self": "it frames much of what we see when we see another" and thus serves as a "visual metaphor for identity."[3] In Joanne Entwistle's words: "It is the insignia by which we are read and come to read others."[4] Dress is a means of broadcasting identity. "Through clothes," as Jennifer Craik has argued, "we ... fabricate ourselves."[5]

Heightened attention to fashioning a self through fashion is a thread linking *Barbie* to Gerwig's previous work, from *Frances Ha* (2012), which she co-wrote with director Noah Baumbach and in which she played the title role, to her solo-directed films: *Lady Bird* (2017) and *Little Women* (2019). All meticulously re-create imagined worlds that resonate with viewers in the present for what they have to say about identity and relationships in contemporary culture, particularly for women. The narrative anchor of each film is a young woman at

Figure 6.1 *Greta Gerwig as "Frances" in* Frances Ha *(dir. Greta Gerwig, 2013). Courtesy Moviestore Collection Ltd/Alamy.*

a moment of transition. As Hilary Radner has argued, *Frances Ha* reimagines the hero's journey as a woman's story, introducing a theme that marks the films Gerwig subsequently directed.[6] The film follows 27-year-old aspiring dancer Frances Halladay as she seeks a professional life after graduating from Vassar. As she pivots from New York to Sacramento to Paris, she sets herself apart from her contemporaries and their trending fashions by wearing a vintage leather bomber jacket over sundresses and tights.[7] It is an androgynous choice that alludes to the fluidity of attraction she displays. Oversized, the jacket also broadcasts her lack of fit—in terms of career and home. Finally returning to Manhattan, she rebrands herself as a choreographer, signing her name as "Frances Ha," when her full name, Frances Halladay, fails to fit on her mailbox, and abandoning her off-duty dancer's leggings for a white shirt and black pencil skirt.

In several respects, the titular protagonist of *Lady Bird* is a younger version of Frances, poised to leave high school for college and life as an adult. Her evolution necessitates establishing an identity apart from her mother Marion, trading her given name, Christine McPherson, for an imagined persona of her own: Lady Bird. Self-styled by her thrift-store wardrobe as well as her name, she distances herself from her past to launch herself into the future. Jo Marsh, the focus of *Little Women*, is determined to set herself apart from her sisters and embark on a writing career, signaled by her choice to cast off conventional nineteenth-century feminine dress and gestures. Jo's sisters Meg and Amy act as foils, striving after aristocratic dress and manners as a means of securing a future through marriage, rather than professional accomplishment. Barbie, though older than Lady Bird or Jo, finds herself belatedly at a similar inflection point: should she settle for a life of conventional femininity or abandon plastic perfection for the messy reality of life as a human woman? Her transition is traced in the gradual shift from mannered costume to naturalistic dress. In each of Gerwig's films, the protagonist's self-fashioning as a defiant and independent individual is visible onscreen through her choices in fashion.

The filmed worlds the characters inhabit are equally fashioned: through elaborate design Gerwig re-creates with inventive fidelity the characters' tangible, material circumstances. Fashion, naturally, is not singular but plural, referring in an extended sense to defining patterns in music, decor, architecture, and manners. Through collaboration with production, sound, and music teams, as well as costume designers, the director fabricates illusory worlds onscreen employing materials—tactile and aural, as well as visual—to manifest identifiable worlds of the past and present, from post-Civil War Massachusetts in *Little Women* to suburban Sacramento in *Lady Bird*. These are, of course, cinematic representations, and *Barbie* departs from Gerwig's previous films in its heightened attention to artifice, a deliberate representation of the manufactured world occupied by Mattel toys and the constructed dreamworld of cinema. The paradoxical formulation "authentically artificial" expresses Gerwig's intent to create a believable cinematic universe inhabited by adult humans acting as inanimate dolls, who nonetheless experience genuine emotion as they grapple with existential questions about identity and purpose. The film's deliberate artifice grounds a narrative that resonates with viewers in the real world for its authentic portrayal of gendered existence.

A plastic doll

In the most elementary sense of fashion as fabrication, Barbie, the doll, was crafted out of artificial materials, and the highly stylized spaces and decor of Barbie Land emphasize her construction. A real woman—actress Margot Robbie, who also produced the film—plays Stereotypical Barbie, the idealized blonde derived from the original 1959 model, and her surroundings and actions cast her as a plastic toy. The objects she grasps during the opening scenes of her morning routine—a toothbrush, a hairbrush, a milk carton—are disproportionately large, heightening her doll-like stature. The solidity and rigidity of the material of the toys is conveyed cinematically as Barbie glides across the hard surface of the pool. Her feet do not sink into the sand. Ken (Ryan Gosling) bounces off the stiff faces of the waves.

Yet plastic is equally a material that is pliant, flexible, and changeable, suggesting another level of fashioning: as dolls, Barbie and Ken are fashioned, transformed through clothing. They are fashioned through fashion, fabricated by fabrics, made to appear as their human owners wish through their dress. Barbie dresses herself by opening the clear Lucite doors to her closet, a representation of the plastic casing of the package containing an outfit and accessories girls purchase for their dolls. In a shower of stars the dress appears on her body, and another takes its place in the "closet." Subsequent stop-motion call outs of vintage products with the Mattel trademark—Pajama Jam in Amsterdam Set, Pretty Paisley Palazzo Pants—reinforce that her invisible human owner fashions Barbie as she desires, in the ensembles she has purchased, not as Barbie herself chooses. The film equally stresses that her movements are also controlled by an absent human. Her Dreamhouse has no walls. There are no stairs, because "why would a doll deign to descend a flight of steps when she could take a circular pink slide or, even better, float gracefully down from the roof" into her convertible?—which, naturally, moves without her hands on the wheel.[8] While the audience may infer the source of Barbie's movements, she and the other Barbies (apart from Weird Barbie) do not, accepting what is indistinguishable from magic for the mundane reality of everyday actions in Barbie Land.

Both Barbie and Barbie Land embody the "stereotypical" femininity of the original doll. As Stereotypical Barbie, Robbie initially wears a pink-and-white gingham dress, with the flared skirt and cinched waist typical of the 1950s, her cascading blonde hair tied back by a white bow. Pink, a classic signifier of femininity from the same postwar period, links her dress to her surroundings.[9] Color enforces the manufactured nature of the space: a riot of bright pinks and other colors that have no real-world equivalent, especially the dominant fluorescent magenta known as "Barbie Pink," the color Pantone designed for Mattel in 2011.[10] A complementary palette of bright yellows, turquoises, and greens contrasts with the more natural, neutral tones of the Real World.

Gender politics

Barbie Land's visual artifice reflects its fantastical gender politics. Unlike their human owners in the Real World, the Barbies inhabit a manufactured space of frictionless femininity, untouched by patriarchy. In fact, inspired by John Milton's *Paradise Lost*, Gerwig modeled their world on Eden "before The Fall, which is not immaterial to the world we were trying to create in Barbie Land.

There's no shame, there's no aging, there's no death, there's no pain . . . There is no separation between self and environment."[11] The perfection of what Isabelle McNeill calls "a matriarchal dream world"[12] reveals itself in their physical surroundings and their appearance. Women hold all positions of power, all while beautifully dressed. A montage showcases the Barbies harmoniously at work, their clothing signs of their occupations, from the utilitarian uniforms of the trash collectors and construction workers to the designer suits of the U.S. president, her staff, and the attorneys at the Supreme Court. The variety of Barbies and their individualized costumes reinforces the post-feminist dimensions of their world.

In fact, women hold all the jobs. The men have no occupations. Not lifeguards or even surfers, the Kens simply "do Beach," and their costumes—board shorts and shirt—stress their uniformity. In an explicit sign of Barbie Land's hierarchical inversion of conventional gender roles, they are accessories to the Barbies, relegated to second-class status. Athletic, with chiseled abs, they, rather than the Barbies, are sexualized and objectified, any threat they pose as men in the real world neutralized by their superfluousness and their missing genitals. Every night is girls' night, as the "giant blowout party" scene makes clear: the Kens are the back-up dancers to Barbie, all dressed uniformly in white jumpsuits. They dance in unison, their swinging arms indicating their status as playthings in Barbie Land: a doll's arm can swing but can't bend.[13]

Barbie Land's artifice alludes to the aspirational ideals inculcated in its human owners, as the opening parody of Stanley Kubrick's *2001: A Space Odyssey* (1968) reinforces. Margot Robbie appears as a towering version of original Barbie in place of the monolith, marking the transition from a pre-feminist past to a post-feminist future. "Since the beginning of time," Helen Mirren says in voice-over, girls played with baby dolls. Dressed in muted naturals and browns, the first girls who ever existed play listlessly in a dry, almost colorless landscape, bored because "they can only play at being mother"—until Barbie appears and "changes everything." They can play *with* her but also play at *being* her: "Because Barbie can be anything"—a doctor, astronaut, lawyer, Supreme Court Justice, U.S. president, Nobel-prize winner— "women can be anything," Mirren explains. Changing her clothes alters her: by putting her in scrubs, she becomes a doctor. In a suit, she's an attorney or President of the United States. In a space suit, she's an astronaut. With a fishtail skirt, she's a step away from a mermaid.

Dressing up: An existential crisis

Fashion—it's what Barbie, the toy, was made for. Her creator Ruth Handler crafted her as an adult-bodied doll, a miniature mannequin designed for dress up, who could reflect the professional aspirations of her owner. "Unlike play with a baby doll—in which a little girl is pretty much limited to assuming the role of Mommy—Barbie has always represented the fact that a woman has choices," Handler wrote in her memoir, *Dream Doll: The Ruth Handler Story*. "Even in her early years Barbie did not have to settle for being only Ken's girlfriend or an inveterate shopper. She had the clothes, for example, to launch a career as a nurse, a stewardess, a nightclub singer."[14] Carol Spencer, one of the four original fashion designers for Barbie, recalls that they were given instructions to "think of Barbie as a real person . . . [She] was stylish; she was a career girl and she lived a wonderful fantasy life; little girls should be able to project similar dreams as they played with her."[15] As girls transformed her professional and personal identity through dress, they could themselves imaginatively try on future identities as adult women, as the film makes clear. Following a pan over a row of adult women dressed in various professional guises (astronomer, engineer, pilot, broadcaster, etc.), a parallel sequence begins of girls dressed in imitation of their Barbies, displayed on pedestals, as Mirren explains: "girls can grow into women who can achieve everything and anything they set their minds to." In other words, fashioning Barbie is related to fashioning a self. Her plasticity is linked to malleability of identity.

Barbie, the doll, might have been fashioned to be fashioned by others, but Gerwig's Barbie asks, "What Was I Made For?" Artifice and authenticity, fashioning and self-fashioning are separated by a permeable membrane connecting Barbie Land to the Real World. Barbie interrupts the carefully choreographed dance party to ask, "Have you guys ever thought about dying?"

This is, of course, a profound question about human existence, an inquiry into mortality that is of no import to plastic toys, but has deep significance for humanity as a whole, one that has preoccupied Western European philosophy for the last two hundred years.[16] Barbie's existential crisis opens, in the words of Weird Barbie, "a portal . . . a rift in the continuum, the membrane between Barbie Land and the Real World," propelling her on a classic quest of self-discovery.

But, as Weird Barbie (Kate McKinnon) informs her, Barbie's thoughts are influenced by those of her owner Gloria (America Ferrera): "her thoughts and feelings are interfering with your dollness." However, Barbie's thoughts of mortality and aging equally affect Gloria's consciousness, as she sketches "Irresistible Thoughts of Death" Barbie, "Full Body Cellulite" Barbie, "Crippling Shame" Barbie. They are fashion illustrations of Barbie's thoughts and the clothes we have seen her wearing in Barbie Land and in the Real World. Importantly, they are on paper bearing the Mattel logo and motto, "Empowering the next generation through play," a direct allusion to the reciprocal nature of self-fashioning between the doll and its owner. (A Barbie dressed in pink can be spotted on Gloria's desk.)

Weird Barbie's observation—"We're all being played with"—does not refer, as it initially appears, to the Barbies alone but equally to their owners. The dolls' cloistered existence and rigid gender divisions have their inverse equivalent in the male-dominated Real World, as Barbie and Ken (Ryan Gosling) discover when they voyage there. As in the scenes in Barbie Land, color delineates the Real World. As the dolls enter the Real World on skates, the fluorescent colors of their costumes and highlighter-yellow rollerblades contrast markedly with the clothing of the Los Angelenos, all wearing realistic colors of blue, olive, khaki, and other neutral shades. A pan matching Barbie's drive past the brightly dressed, busy construction workers in Barbie Land reveals a group of their real-world counterparts as idle males, their pale clothing bleached by the glaring sunlight. Objectified by their mocking gaze, she feels self-conscious for the first time, aware of an "undertone of violence." She recognizes simultaneously that she is judged by her physical appearance and through an appraisingly critical male gaze entirely absent from Barbie Land's world of feminine artifice.

Transitions

While she is beginning to acquire human knowledge and feeling, the transition is not complete, as the film's costume designer deftly signals. When Barbie and Ken realize their fluorescent clothes set them apart, they still select costumes as replacements, not ordinary clothing. They emerge in Western wear, complete with cowboy hats and fringe. A wide shot reinforces the point: Barbie's ensemble is mirrored on the mannequin on the right—and it is emphatically pink. Ken's transformation is more complete, as his costume suggests: he's wearing black, a color banished from Barbie Land.[17] He dresses as a cowboy, one of the icons of masculinity he discovers on his solo stroll through Los Angeles' Century City, a business district constructed on land once owned by the real-world actor-cowboy Tom Mix, a silent-film star.[18]

Ken becomes cognizant simultaneously of patriarchy and its manifestations in masculine dress. As Ken ascends the elevator, he sees a bank of four screens showing, in addition to a cowboy on horseback, a baseball player, and U.S. presidents Bill Clinton and Ronald Reagan. But his realization that "patriarchy is where men and horses run everything" culminates in an alternate sartorial choice. He sees three images of Sylvester Stallone, the star of the boxing film *Rocky* (dir. John G. Avildsen, 1976), whose posters were displayed on the wall

Figure 6.2 *Barbie's pink Western wear is identical to the costume on the mannequin on the right (*Barbie, *dir. Greta Gerwig, 2023).*

of a gym. The middle panel is a macho, fur-clad, caveman version of his shirtless beach garb.

When Ken returns to Barbie Land, his takeover visually conveys the messy reality of the Real World as well as his garbled understanding of patriarchal rule as he attempts to refashion the feminine world as masculine. Barbie's Dreamhouse has been converted into "Kendom Saloon" (originally and humorously misspelled Salon), with swinging doors in faux wood and horses playing on multiple television screens, an intrusion of muddy browns into the pink world. A toy horse stands on the pool, next to an inflatable motorcycle. Other parodic tokens of masculinity are haphazardly scattered about: beer (or "brewski beers," as the Kens call them), mini-fridges, barbeques, golf clubs, balls of every variety (baseballs, footballs, soccer balls). Ken combines the Western theme with *Rocky*: he's topped his black-and-white cowboy outfit with a "Fauxjo Mojo Mink" and sports a headband in place of his hat (though an array of cowboy hats decorates one wall). He wears boxing shoes and his fanny pack inscribed "Ken" in heavy-metal script is a nod to Rocky's heavyweight title belt.[19] He is accessorized by multiple watches over sweatbands in a bright red, the same color as his boxing gloves and the trim on his punching bag. His fur coat is lined with red fabric imprinted with horses' heads outlined in white. The fur, along with faux wood and frayed denim, introduces natural

Figure 6.3 *Ken combines Western wear with a Rocky theme (Barbie, dir. Greta Gerwig, 2023).*

texture. The manginess of the pelt and his mussed hair communicate his fuzzy understanding of masculinity, but also the imperfections of the Real World. Visually, Kendom is the inverse of Barbie Land: chaos in place of order, natural colors and textures in place of plastic perfection, stupidity in place of expertise. Every night is now boys' night. "How's that feel?" Ken asks Barbie. She can stay in his Mojo Dojo Casa House only as his "bridewife" or "his long-term, casual, low-commitment, distant girlfriend."

The visual imperfections of Ken's intrusions in Barbie Land reinforce the film's critique of conventional gender divisions. His icons of masculinity—cowboys and Sly Stallone—are remnants of the discarded past, from the frontier days of America's westward expansion to the macho 1970s. The Kens' dream ballet takes its cue from the 1950s: they dance in Gene Kelly-esque black tees, tailored slacks, and loafers, an homage to *Singin' in the Rain* (dir. Stanley Donan and Gene Kelly, 1952). The film also invokes *Grease* (dir. Randal Kleiser, 1978), a musical from the 1970s that revives the rock 'n' roll era of black-leather jackets and pompadour hairstyles, called out as one Ken (Ken Watanabe) slicks his hair back. (Ken's doubled pair of cat's eye sunglasses also invokes the period and is a nod to the director character in *The Red Shoes* [dir. Michael Powell and Emeric Pressburger, 1948] another film that inspired the dream ballet.) The parodic beachside battle of the Kens as they fight against each other for dominance, using toys in place of real weapons, emphasizes the impotence of their assertions of machismo, a point already made visually by their outmoded style.

In Kendom, or Ken Land, or Kendom Land, as he variously proclaims it, the Barbies are now accessories. Their attire proclaims that: a doctor and a physicist, now "helpful decorations," wear sexy maid outfits in black and white, an echo of Ken's colors, and a clichéd throwback to the era of Playboy bunnies. Others wear feminine versions of Western wear. Once the Barbies hatch their plot to regain control, they blend in as decoys, wearing red and denim. Working together to restore their Constitution, they wear pink coveralls, the equivalent of the Kens' white jumpsuits—in their case, though, to disguise their machinations under a false image of innocuous uniformity.

Ultimately, Barbie chooses authenticity over artifice, departing from Barbie Land for the Real World. Her decision is made evident through alterations in dress. She gradually appears less "stereotypical." Initially, in frustration with Ken's subversion of Barbie Land's perfection, she tears off her hat and suit jacket and becomes like a discarded doll: she sits artificially with her legs straight out in front of her, falls sideways, flips onto her back, and rolls face down into the astroturf. After Gloria's monologue about womanhood raises her consciousness, she transforms herself: first when she, like the other Barbies, wears an anonymous pink jumpsuit, then a modest pale yellow dress and white wedge sandals with her hair tied casually behind her, rather than elaborately styled. The naturalness of her physical appearance reflects her embrace of authentic over plastic existence, simultaneously understood as the conventional happy ending of the rom-com *and* the inevitability of heterosexual romance and marriage in real life as well as cinema.

"That is not her ending," we're told. That is what Ken expects—he claims: "It's Barbie and Ken. There is no just Ken." He holds fast to the conventional, gendered norms and their fabricated inscriptions in architecture and clothing. But she tells him: "You're not your girlfriend. You're not your house. You're not your mink." Barbie dismisses "male property ownership, male privilege and heteronormative romance structures in one fell swoop," Stacy Gillis notes.[20] Ken then realizes: "Ken is me." He tosses his mink away as if to prove it, discarding the sartorial signs of identification with his patriarchal icons and their masculinist conceptions of coupledom.

In fact, the film depicts both Ken and Barbie seeking authenticity over artifice, genuine feeling over contrived behavior. Parallel dream sequences enforce the link: Ken's dream ballet and Barbie's encounter with her "creator" Ruth Handler. Both take place against a backdrop of pale blue and pink. In each, the doll character wants more than "a life of blond fragility," as Ken sings. He wants to "feel the real thing." Not content to be "number two," Ken asks that Barbie "see the man behind the tan." He does not get the ending he desires—to be the dominant one in their couple—but instead finds self-definition outside of heterosexual romance.

In a greater sense, Ken and the other Barbies and Kens who remain in Barbie Land have no ending for they are dolls. As their creator Ruth Handler explains: "humans have only one ending. Ideas live forever." Gerwig's Barbie, however, decides: "I want to be part of the people that make meaning, not the thing that's made. I want to do the imagining. I don't want to be the idea." In other words, she does not want to be fabricated, to be fashioned; she wants to fashion herself. In a scene clearly modeled on *The Wizard of Oz* (dir. Victor Fleming, 1939), a film that Gerwig identified as one of thirty-three that inspired her own (proleptically announced to the spectator through a poster, on view as Barbie drives by in her convertible), Barbie discovers she has had the power to choose an authentic existence as a human in the Real World all along.[21] Dorothy has to click her heels together three times and recite "there's no place like home." Barbie is told simply to close her eyes and "now feel."

We see a close-up of her heart pendant and one eye. When she closes her eyes, Barbie sees a montage of mothers and daughters. She recognizes that being human is being a daughter and possibly having one (as her owner Gloria does). The film's closing scene shows Barbie entering an office, not to apply for a job but to visit the gynecologist. She gives her name as "Handler, Barbara," identifying herself as the "child" of the woman who created her. She wears a brown blazer and jeans, colors and fabrics of the Real World, and pink Birkenstock sandals. She'd been given the choice between high heels and Birkenstocks before voyaging to the Real World, between the plastic perfection of arched feet in stilettos or flat feet, cellulite and aging in the Real World. Weird Babie asks her before she leaves: "So what will it be? You can go back to the way your life was—(holding the high heel up) . . . or you can know the truth about the universe (holds up the Birkenstock)."[22] She is in Birkenstocks, yes, but they are pastel pink. As Helen Mirren says in voice-over: "Barbie left behind the pastels and plastics of Barbie Land for the pastels and plastics of Los Angeles." After all, she exists only onscreen,[23] in the dreamworld created by Greta Gerwig and her collaborators—and in our collective imagination.

Conclusion

Barbie remains "authentically artificial." Actress Margot Robbie endows the doll with genuine emotion, granting the illusion of a Pinocchio-like transformation from toy to human. Still, she is fabricated through the imaginations of Gerwig and her co-screenwriter Noah Baumbach and shaped through the cinematic artistry of the director, cinematographer, and costume and production design teams. As Isabelle McNeill puts it: "If Barbie becomes 'real' it is both through flesh and through screen image, both through matter and dream."[24] The Real World Barbie chooses is as much a cinematic illusion as Barbie Land, as the film's self-reflexive references to film and literature continually reminds us. She was fashioned to be self-fashioning.

Ultimately, then, *Barbie* reminds viewers that self-fashioning in the real world is akin to that in the film's Real World: it operates within constraints imposed not by the filmmaker but by contemporary culture and biology, against the realities of aging and ongoing efforts (in the United States, for instance) to curtail the reproductive freedoms Barbie appears to be seeking.[25] Greenblatt argued that "the dream of autonomous agency" propelling self-fashioning was "only a dream." Still, he acknowledged it was "intensely experienced and tenaciously embraced."[26] In other words, the artifice of female autonomy can be felt as authentic possibility. The permeable membrane connecting Gerwig's dreamworld to the real world captures the contradictions of lived experience, the "cognitive dissonance required to be a woman under patriarchy," as Barbie puts it in reaction to Gloria's monologue. Her words resonated with female viewers experiencing the limits placed on their agency stemming from ingrained notions of femininity. In the film, articulating the contradictory pressures robbed the patriarchy of its power and allowed the women to reinstitute their Constitution through collective political action, leaving viewers with the idea that a world that is fashioned can be refashioned.

Acknowledgments: Portions of this chapter were previously published in a different format in Suzanne Ferriss, *Greta Gerwig: Filmmaker* (Edinburgh: Edinburgh University Press, March 2026).

Part Three

Identity

Queer Barbie, Weird Barbie, and Greta Gerwig's Many Queer Kens

SARAH E. S. SINWELL

From the iconic Indigo Girls song "Closer to Fine," Billie Eilish's "What Was I Made For?," and Sam Smith's "Man I Am," to the presence of Weird Barbie, Earring Magic Ken, Sugar Daddy Ken, and Allan, Gerwig's *Barbie* (2023) pushes the boundaries of both feminist and queer understandings of Barbie by reimagining the interrelationships between hegemonic femininity, queerness, and heteronormativity. Delving into ideas of female friendship, queer community, and the construction of family while also confronting the challenges and opportunities of living in Barbie Land and Kendom, *Barbie* enables a rethinking of binary imaginings of both femininity and masculinity.

Using feminist theory, queer theory, and critical cultural studies approaches, this chapter argues that *Barbie* pushes up against gender conformity and heteronormativity within media culture, drawing attention not only to the absence of LGBTQIA+ characters within media and cultural histories more generally but, also, to alternative possibilities for more inclusive representation. In this way, *Barbie* is rethinking media constructions of American culture by putting queer people and queer women at the center of its storytelling. By examining the queer references and queer coding in *Barbie*—including references to *The Wizard of Oz* (dir. Victor Fleming, 1939) and friends of

Dorothy; its queer characters, Weird Barbie, Allan, Sugar Daddy Ken, and Earring Magic Ken; and its queer casting, Kate McKinnon, Hari Nef, Alexandra Shipp, and Scott Evans—this chapter argues that *Barbie* is both upholding and resisting contemporary notions of femininity, masculinity, and queerness.

To this end, first, I will give a brief history of Barbie in relation to feminism and queer theory. Second, I will analyze the many incarnations of Barbie within the film itself. Finally, I will discuss the characters of Ken, Allan, and Gerwig's many other queer Kens as a means of exploring additional aspects of queerness and queer coding that occur within the film, from the musical selections to self-reflexive film references to its casting.

"What Was I Made For?" — Feminism, queer theory, and *Barbie*

Generating a worldwide box office of over $1.47 billion, *Barbie* is the biggest debut ever for a film directed by a woman, the highest grossing film of 2023, and the highest grossing film ever released by Warner Bros.[1] Before Helen Mirren's iconic voice-over even starts, the pinkening of the Warner Bros. logo and the appearance of the Mattel logo serve as a reminder that *Barbie* is part of Mattel's product line, reconfirming its capitalistic origins.[2] As the voice-over narration of Helen Mirren briefly explains Barbie's history, Richard Strauss's *Also sprach Zarathustra* plays in the background (familiar to many as the soundtrack accompanying the opening of *2001: A Space Odyssey* [dir. Stanley Kubrick, 1968]).[3]

From the beginning of the film, Mirren proclaims: "Barbie changed everything. Then she changed it all again. All of these women are Barbie. And, Barbie is all of these women . . . Because Barbie can be anything, women can be anything." And, in fact, Gerwig's Barbies include physicists, doctors, Nobel-prize winners, presidents, journalists, diplomats, astronauts, and mermaids. They include Midge (the pregnant Barbie that was released in 1963 but then discontinued due to concerns that she would promote teen pregnancy), Teen Talk Barbie (introduced in 1992 with such sayings as "Let's plan our dream wedding!" and "Want to go shopping?" and later discontinued for having a voice box that said "Math class is tough!"), Barbie Video Girl (a Barbie with a video camera on her back that was created in 2010 and discontinued due to sparking concerns with the FBI that it would be used to film child pornography), and Growing Up Skipper (a Skipper who was released in 1975 and discontinued because of her controversial growable breasts).[4] There are also Barbies with nonnormative bodies, including a Barbie in a wheelchair, a Barbie played by trans actress Hari Nef, and a Barbie played by LGBTQ+ actress Alexandra Shipp. As Mirren reminds us: "Thanks to Barbie, all problems of feminism and equal rights have been solved . . . at least that's what the Barbies think." From the very beginning of the film, this ironic tone self-reflexively critiques patriarchy at the same time as it upholds it as audiences are reminded of the omnipresence of restrictive gender roles even as the film appears to question them.

But Gerwig's incarnation of Barbie in 2023 is not the first one to invoke understandings of feminism and queerness. In her 1996 book *Barbie's Queer Accessories*, Erica Rand posed that Barbie (and her consumers) enable the subversion of cultural norms through radical play and reimagining ideas of feminism and heteronormativity. As she writes:

> *Barbie's Queer Accessories* concerns the use and circulation of Barbie: what you can, and could formerly, buy from Mattel; what Mattel tells you to do, and not to do, with Barbie; what people have done with Barbie as adults and as kids; what Barbie play suggests about the place of the consumer in cultural studies, about the place of queerness in relation to mainstream and margin, about the effects of cultural products on ideology, and about the limits and possibilities of cultural subversion as a strategy of political activism.[5]

In 2023, following the release of Gerwig's *Barbie*, *Glamour UK* also published an article entitled "The queerest Barbie moments of all time: Bring back Earring Magic Ken, you cowards,"[6] while Samantha Puc in *The Mary Sue* pointed out: "Queer Barbies Go Back Further Than You Might Think,"[7] and more recently Clara Bradbury-Rance has analyzed the possibilities of imagining "Butch Barbie."[8]

As Alexander Doty has noted in both *Making Things Perfectly Queer* and *Flaming Classics*, reading texts is yet another means of queering those texts, particularly in terms of the ways in which they resist easy categorization. Writing in *Making Things Perfectly Queer*, Alexander Doty argues: "Queer readings aren't 'alternative' readings, wistful or willful misreadings, or 'reading too much into things' readings. They result from the recognition and articulation of the complex range of queerness that has been in popular culture texts and their audiences all along."[9] Like Judith Butler's use of the term "undoing" in *Undoing Gender* (2004), I propose that "queering" can also be employed as a means of analyzing *Barbie*. "Queer" is not just a way of being, not just the text itself, but it is also a way of doing and undoing, of framing and seeing. As queer theorists such as Adrienne Rich (1980), Eve Sedgwick (1990; 1997), Judith Butler (1990; 2004), Gayle Rubin (1993), Alexander Doty (1993), Michael Warner (1993), David Halperin (1995), Annamarie Jagose (1996), Lee Edelman (2004), Sara Ahmed (2006), Jack Halberstam (2005; 2011), José Esteban Muñoz (2009), Kara Keeling (2019), and Eliza Steinbock (2019) have argued, seeing through a queer lens allows us to undo the work of heteronormative ideology and create a space for alternative means of understanding sexualities, identities, and subjectivities.[10] Thus, I would argue that *Barbie*'s queerness intervenes into traditional understandings of both gender and sexuality by resisting both patriarchy and heteronormativity. As Alexander Doty attests: "[S]ome of the most exciting deployments of 'queer/ queerness' are related to the word's ability to describe those complex circumstances in texts, spectators, and production that resist easy categorization, but that definitely escape or defy the heteronormative."[11]

"Closer to Fine": Stereotypical Barbie, Weird Barbie, and Crippling Shame Barbie

Though Amy Schumer, Anne Hathaway, and Gal Gadot were also possibilities for casting Barbie, when it was announced that Margot Robbie would be cast as Stereotypical Barbie, "Even with so many other potential women who could've played Barbie over the years, Margot Robbie's work anchoring Barbie is so iconic that it's incomprehensible that moviegoers were ever going to say 'hi, Barbie!' to anyone else."[12] Very soon after we are introduced to Barbie and

Barbie Land, Margot Robbie's performance as Stereotypical Barbie breaks down the effervescence and seemingly perfect cotton candy world of Barbie Land as she is suddenly plagued with bad breath, burnt waffles, and flat feet. Along with her cellulite, she is inundated with complicated emotions, including sadness, anxiety, and thoughts of death. These aspects of real life incorporate not only Barbie's interiority and emotions, but they also impact her body and her desirability, threatening her everyday existence in Barbie Land. Thus, it is Barbie's ever-changing body, feelings, and emotions that necessitate her introduction to Weird Barbie and the Real World. As Erica Rand argued in *Barbie's Queer Accessories*:

> One potential limit to Lesbian Barbie obsessed me: Barbie's closet may be diversely stocked, assuming one can make what one can't buy, but her body, with its permanently pointed breasts and feet, seemed unalterably fem. Could Barbie, firmly premolded by Mattel, really be liberated from it? Barbie seemed like a great tool for discussing the difficulties as well as the subversive potential of cultural subversion.[13]

Played by out actress Kate McKinnon, Weird Barbie is deformed "because she was played with too much." Though she is "always in the splits," she is the only Barbie who understands the Real World. So, when there is a rift in the continuum between Barbie Land and the Real World (one that manifests itself

Figure 7.1 *Barbie must choose between pink high heels and Birkenstocks (Barbie, dir. Greta Gerwig, 2023).*

in Barbie's flat feet, cellulite, and bad breath), Weird Barbie is the only Barbie who Stereotypical Barbie can ask for advice. Weird Barbie guides Stereotypical Barbie to choose between the pink high heels of Barbie Land and the stereotypical flat (iconically lesbian) footwear of the Birkenstocks of the Real World, much like the choice between the red and blue pill in the Wachowskis' 1999 film *The Matrix*. At first resisting this choice, Margot Robbie responds: "I'm not adventure Barbie, I'm stereotypical Barbie." Following this moment, the film attempts to answer the question: What would happen if Barbie entered the real world? In the Real World, Barbie is objectified while Ken is admired and discovers the patriarchy (horses and Hummers, Ronald Reagan and Bill Clinton, baseball and golf, and Sylvester Stallone's iconic Rocky).

Through the characters of Gloria (played by America Ferrera) and her daughter Sasha (played by Ariana Greenblatt), Barbie is introduced to the challenges of participating in beauty culture and the limitations of understanding the aging female body in the Real World. Gloria, a Mattel employee, invents new Barbies with titles such as "Irresponsible Thoughts of Death Barbie," "Full Body Cellulite Barbie," and "Crippling Shame Barbie," while Sasha tells Barbie: "You've been making women feel bad about themselves since you were invented. You represent everything wrong with our culture, like sexualized capitalism and unrealistic physical ideals. You destroyed girls' innate sense of worth." Like the lyrics to the Indigo Girls "Closer to Fine" and Billie Eilish's "What Was I Made For?" Barbie not only wonders what she is made for, but is inundated with thoughts of fear, uncertainty, and sadness.

Once Barbie leaves Barbie Land for the Real World, she is constantly confronted with the challenges of living under patriarchy. After Barbie is kidnapped and returned to Mattel headquarters in the Real World, not only does CEO of Mattel Will Ferrell demand of Barbie, "Get into the box you Jezebel," but Mattel headquarters are run by men (and only white middle-aged men of a certain age, class, and status). Though the CEO insists: "Women are at the foundation of this company! There was a female CEO in the 90s and then another one . . . at some point. So that's two right there!," it is clear that Mattel is run by (remarkably inept) men.

Though Barbie eventually meets co-founder of Mattel and creator of Barbie, Ruth Handler (played by Rhea Perlman), Barbie is still bodily and emotionally subject to the confines of the patriarchy, as she realizes: "Either you are brainwashed or you're weird and ugly. There is no in-between." In fact, the repetition of "Hey Barbie" and the song "I'm Just Ken" reiterate the binaries between the Barbies and Kens even as they invite a multiplicity of meanings.

"I'm (Not) Just Ken": Queering Ken, Allan, and Greta Gerwig's many other queer Kens

In 1961, two years after Barbie's debut, Ken Carson was introduced as Barbie's male counterpart and boyfriend. Named after Barbie creator Ruth Handler's son Kenneth, Ken was created to be both a companion to accompany Barbie on her adventures and a "boy next door" who might enable Barbie to fulfill her heteronormative expectations. As Erica Rand writes in her history of Barbie and Ken: "So Ken the artifact came into the world lumpless and intentionally unsexy, with an origin heralded alternately for expanding and foreclosing Barbie's options."[14] This history is complicated not only by the creation of Ken's desexualized "lump,"[15] but also by Mattel's simultaneous reinforcement and denial of Ken as Barbie's dream date.

In Gerwig's *Barbie*, the introduction of Ken and his role in the film asserts that Ken only exists through Barbie's gaze. As Helen Mirren narrates: "Barbie has a great day everyday, but Ken only has a great day if Barbie looks at him." As Ken is introduced onscreen, everyone says "Hi Barbie," ignoring Ken. Ken's job is just "beach," not lifeguard. Thus, Ken is only defined through his relationship (or lack thereof) with Barbie. Countering the intentions of creating a heterosexual and romantic relationship between Barbie and Ken, instead Gerwig's *Barbie* continues to see Ken as superfluous, distracting, and even in opposition to the ideals and understandings of female (and feminist) community in Barbie Land.

Significantly, when Ken leans in for a kiss (a kiss that Barbie fans may or not have looked forward to or assumed would happen), Barbie refuses to kiss him and chooses the other Barbies, rejecting Ken, saying "you can go now" and "I don't want you here." Barbie's incantations of "This is Barbie's dreamhouse, it's not Ken's dreamhouse" and "It's girls' night every night, forever" resist both the patriarchal and heteronormative understandings of Barbie and Ken and the traditional gendered expectations of Barbie Land. In fact, throughout the film, Barbie Land is defined by the Barbies themselves, and *not* by the heteronormative patriarchy.

When Barbie looks at Ken, it is not with desire but with friendliness, but it is a friendliness that is not sexualized and limited to Ken, but rather it is inclusive of all the Kens and Barbies in Barbie Land. In *Barbie*, this kinship takes the form of the creation of female and feminist community in Barbie Land.[16] Defying Hollywood conventions of the gaze as described in Laura Mulvey's seminal 1975 essay "Visual Pleasure and Narrative Cinema," the film incorporates alternatives to the gaze that resists the binary understandings of active and passive, male and female, narrative and spectacle to reconstruct a queer gaze that resists sexualization and instead incorporates queer kinship and friendship, family and familiarity.[17] Though these gazes are still limited by their tendencies to be both white and defined by body privilege and class difference (as noted in Lisa Henderson's work on the class character of the gaze in her 2013 book *Love and Money*), they offer up the possibilities of breaking from classical understandings of heteronormative desire in order to reimagine familial and friendly forms of looking.[18] Unlike Mulvey's passive and active binary understanding of looking, Nicholas de Villiers argues that this form of queer looking can be instead understood in relation to the stare or the glance.[19]

Gerwig's other queer Kens also speak to how the film challenges and resists patriarchal and heteronormative norms. For example, Allan (played by Michael Cera) was introduced as "Ken's buddy" in 1964, just three years after Ken himself debuted. Named after Mattel co-founder Ruth Handler's son-in-law, Allan was designed to fit into Ken's clothes and eventually became Midge's husband in the early 1990s. In Gerwig's *Barbie*, he's the only non-Ken man in Barbie Land. As the narrator states: "There are no multiples of Allan, he's just Allan." Though all of Allan's clothes fit Ken, it is understood that Allan's fashion and aesthetic is queer (he wears a rainbow knit shirt), and his inability to fit in among the Kens and ability to fit in among the Barbies also speaks to the possibility that he could be the Barbie's "gay male best friend."

In addition to Allan, Gerwig's other queer Kens include Mermaid Ken (played by John Cena), Sugar Daddy Ken (played by Rob Brydon), and Earring

Figure 7.2 *Allan greets the crowd at Beach (Barbie, dir. Greta Gerwig, 2023).*

Figure 7.3 *Sugar Daddy Ken and Earring Magic Ken are among fellow discontinued toys at Weird Barbie's abode (Barbie, dir. Greta Gerwig, 2023).*

Magic Ken (played by Tom Stourton). All of these Kens are constructed through camp and queerness, from the billowing blond hair of the male mermaid to the flamboyant rave wear of Earring Magic Ken. Created in 1992, Earring Magic Ken—colloquially known as "Cock Ring Ken—is possibly the most overtly queer Ken. In fact, it was very quickly discontinued six months later after *Chicago Reader* columnist Dan Savage remarked that one of the doll's accessories looked suspiciously like the "cock ring" sex toys favored by gay men of the era.[20] Gerwig's Kens also include additional nonnormatively bodied versions of Ken such as Simu Liu, Ncuti Gatwa, Kingsley Ben-Adir, and out gay actor Scott Evans. These Kens' covert and overt queerness speaks to Gerwig's attempt to combat the patriarchal and heteronormative aspects of Barbie Land and Kendom by including not only queer fashion and queer iconography, but also by resisting the idea that there is only one "stereotypical" version of Barbie and Ken.

The lyrics and performance of "I'm Just Ken" at the Beach Off also contribute to this reimagining of Ken outside the patriarchy. This sequence overtly references the extended musical sequences from Gene Kelly and Stanley Donen's *Singin' in the Rain* (1952) and Victor Fleming's *The Wizard of Oz* (1939) as the Kens perform a choreographed dance on the steps. In her analysis of the use of camp in these scenes, Clara Bradbury-Rance points out:

> It is through its excessive stylisation that camp, according to Katrin Horn, is "capable of intervening in naturalized and naturalizing discourses of gender and sexuality, while granting access to otherwise oppressive systems of meaning- and pleasure-making" . . . By stylising the neon and pastel Barbie Land as a camp utopia—modelled on *The Wizard of Oz* (Victor Fleming, 1939) no less—the film de-naturalises the association of femininity and femaleness, making femininity for everyone.[21]

In Beach Ken's song, sung by Ryan Gosling, "I'm Just Ken," he laments how Barbie looks on him simply as a shallow blond stereotype. He asks: "Is it my destiny to live and die a life of blonde fragility?" Instead, he longs for her to see the man behind the superficial image—someone with real feelings, someone who is vulnerable. He reveals that, most of all, he yearns to know what it is like to love and be loved. He croons: "I wanna know what's like to love, to be the real thing."[22]

This imagining of Ken not only is self-reflexive about his blondeness and fragility, but it also resists the idea that Ken is Barbie's romantic ideal. In fact, it is Ken that wants romance not Barbie. And, it is Ken who is put in what is known as "the friend zone," as noted in "I'm Just Ken." Not only is Ken unable to define his feelings, not only does he understand that he may not be as romantically or sexually attractive to Barbie *because* of his feelings, but all he wants is to be seen by Barbie and to be seen as her ideal. At the same time, the line, "My name's Ken (and so am I) . . . Put that manly hand in mine" is simultaneously a reminder that there are many different versions of Ken but that stereotypical Beach Ken is the only Ken that fits that patriarchal and heteronormative romantic ideal. The insistence that Ken "put that manly hand in mine" also undercuts and reinforces Ken's heteronormativity. His need to understand his hands (and the other Ken's hands) as manly and his desire to create male friendship and community also resists patriarchy as he shows his desire for physical and emotional intimacy between men. Thus, this now iconic song opens up the possibilities for many different versions of Ken (and many different varieties of understanding both masculinity and heteronormativity).

As Ken asks: "Why didn't Barbie tell me about patriarchy?", he also realizes: "There is no just Ken, I was only created within the warmth of your gaze." Though Barbie ends the film by returning to the Real World, Ken still does not quite understand his place in the world. Rather, he is left in Barbie Land and faced with the challenges of both resisting and upholding both patriarchy and heteronormativity in a world that continues to be ruled by women.

Conclusion

As noted in their work on queer female fandom, Mel Stanfill discusses the concept of "structurally lesbian media" and its "interrelated characteristics: primary homosocial intensity, transient heterosexuality, and homosocial-homosexual slippage."[23] Stanfill opines:

> [D]rawing on Alexander Doty's (1993) argument that *Laverne and Shirley* (1976–1983), *The Mary Tyler Moore Show* (1970–1977), *Designing Women*

(1986–1993), and *The Golden Girls* (1985–1992) should be understood as "lesbian sitcoms" because the primary relationships in them are between women, and men as love interests are generally transient and not central to the ongoing development of the story or characters, I argue that all media (not just sitcoms) that center on or are driven by a relationship between women are structurally lesbian media.[24]

This is also true of *Barbie*. Throughout the film, not only does Barbie reject Ken in favor of socializing with the other Barbies, but she continually counters the patriarchy by giving voice to so many versions of Barbie. Even as the film subverts patriarchy, it also participates in it. With Barbie's proclamation that she is not in love with Ken and her return to the Real World where she is "here to see (her) gynecologist," the film reminds us of how it resists heteronormativity. The film, however, also participates in the same heteronormativity by equating Barbie with her genitalia and body parts.

In an interview with *Gay Times* following the release of *Barbie*, Erica Rand reclaims Barbie's queerness through not only her appearance, but also her pronouns, partners, and narratives, saying: "It doesn't take much to chop Barbie's hair off, switch Barbie's clothes, pronouns, partners, voice, or story. I think that's partly why some people fondly remember what they did with Barbie as an early hint of their own queerness, and why adults gravitate to Barbie as a vehicle for play, protest, and parody."[25] One could argue that Gerwig's version of *Barbie* enables even more invitations for "play, protest, and parody" through its many incarnations of Barbie and Ken, as well as through Weird Barbie, Allan, and her many other queer Kens. However, as Clara Bradbury-Rance has also argued, Gerwig's version of *Barbie* also omits the intersectional potential of this inclusion by insisting upon Barbie and Ken's whiteness and gender normativity, writing: "But *Barbie*'s narrative trajectory sidelines decades of political and legal theory and activism by feminists of colour who have highlighted how dominant conceptions of discrimination condition us to think about subordination as disadvantage occurring along a single categorical axis."[26] Thus, though *Barbie* may be a reminder of Barbie's queer *potential*, perhaps only a sequel featuring Weird Barbie and Greta Gerwig's many queer Kens at the center of its storytelling may fully achieve it. When Barbie "went to the doctor," she was given answers "pointing in a crooked line," and all we can hope is that she will be "closer to fine."[27]

"What Was I Made For?" and "I'm Just Ken": The Musical Binary of Barbie

AMY SKJERSETH AND DYLAN YOUNG

The *Barbie* soundtrack notoriously features two songs about its dueling main characters: the epic anthem "I'm Just Ken" and the title character's introspective ballad "What Was I Made For?" Both songs had large streaming numbers and were nominated for the Critics' Choice Awards, Grammy Awards, and Academy Awards. Especially during awards season, it was an open question whether "I'm Just Ken" would be eclipsed by Barbie's song in popularity and acclaim. Ken's success was ironic, given the movie's emphasis on neo-feminist empowerment via consumerism and neo-liberalism. The Barbie-versus-Ken debate was further complicated by the ways that the film's promotion and reception leaned into a gender binary. While Margot Robbie paraded Barbie's outfits in press appearances, with her very photogenic "looks" stressed inside and outside of the film, Ryan Gosling was both a face *and* a *voice* thanks to the success of "I'm Just Ken." The song arguably threatened to dominate discussions about the soundtrack and the movie during the awards season. "What Was I Made For?" (though presented as Barbie's internal monologue within the film) was often interpreted by fans and critics through the star persona of singer Billie Eilish and her signature whispery vocals, rather than in terms of the film's lead character, undermining the importance of the star who played her, Margot Robbie. Ryan Gosling, in contrast, sang his own songs, becoming irrevocably associated with his role as "Ken."[1] Notwithstanding, "What Was I Made For?" (Eilish's song) walked away with all the awards, though it was Gosling who charmed the audience at the Oscars with "his" song's "internet breaking live performance."[2] The songs' reception reflected that of the film, which unexpectedly drew a significant and vocal male audience despite a majority female audience.[3] These award season duels, in turn, contributed to circulating a message of gendered competition beyond the film.

Barbie operates on the terms of, and reproduces, a gender binary in several ways, not only in its plot and characters, but also—and especially—in its music. How does the music—and its life outside of the film—heighten awareness of gendered tropes and narratives? What do the songs' structures and semiotics—their placement within and across scenes, their relation to tropes associated with the musical, and their ancillary PR, media, and awards outside the film (paratexts)—tell us about Hollywood's constructions of gendered binaries, and the ways spectators can take or make meaning from them?

The film's musical structure—or, Is *Barbie* a musical?

Barbie featured several original pop songs by mainstream artists, as well as an original score by Mark Ronson and Andrew Wyatt. The score is typical of Conglomerate Hollywood movies, which often have mixed styles of music, including preexisting and original material, creating compilation soundtracks that double as promotional tools.[4] The film blends original scoring and preexisting and original songs, as well as diegetic/extra-diegetic/metadiegetic (or subjective) sound, to create a balance of make-believe and reality—to offer a commentary on the film's binary divisions, in particular by suggesting the interplay of "real" and imagined worlds.[5] The story world in which the characters live, and in which their actions take place, operates in terms of what one character describes as a "membrane" with a "rip" in it,[6] such that the barrier between the story world (the diegesis, or diegetic space) and the viewer's world (extra-diegetic space) is unstable, with music having a significant role in demarcating—but also blurring—divisions in narrative space.

Barbie's song structure serves the plot's division of Barbie Land and Kendom Land, with music to go with each. The music of Barbie Land includes the celebratory "Pink" (Lizzo) and "Dance the Night Away" (Dua Lipa). But when the Kens take over, so does the music of Ken, from the original songs "Man I Am" and "I'm Just Ken" to infinite covers of Matchbox Twenty's "I Wanna Push You Around." Only when the Barbies recuperate ownership of Barbie Land, in act three of the film, does "What Was I Made For?" arrive, in a sequence referred to as the "Now . . . FEEL" scene. With this structure, *Barbie* sets up two clear and distinctive sound worlds for Barbie and Ken, which reinforce the gender binary present across the film's narrative and paratexts. This music operates in a long tradition of Hollywood musical codes that pit the sounds of femininity against those of masculinity: John Williams, for example, composed themes attached to specific *Star Wars* characters—delicate flutes and strings for female characters versus triumphant brass for male characters.[7] While *Barbie*'s orchestral score merits further attention, and played a crucial role in the film's success, isolating the two characters' centerpiece songs sheds light on how contemporary Hollywood movies perpetuate gendered divisions through both story and song.

Barbie's combination of story and song is achieved through the soundtrack's employment of conventions and tropes from the Hollywood musical. As Rick Altman explains, typical film scores rarely cross the diegetic/nondiegetic border in an overt way, keeping both the "music track" and the "diegetic track" separate.[8] In the musical film, however, both tracks merge through a technique that Altman defines as "the audio dissolve": they continually pass between nondiegetic and diegetic, which muddles an assumed border between both sound worlds.[9]

While *Barbie* cannot be described as a musical in a traditional sense, with only two instances of onscreen singing ("Push" and "I'm Just Ken"), the film nevertheless takes inspiration from the Hollywood musical. The film's opening establishes that Barbie Land allows for the crossing of the "diegetic track" and "the music track": Lizzo's "Pink" provides a metacommentary by narrating Barbie's actions as if the song were an encapsulation of Barbie's internal monologue (a strategy that is reiterated more forcefully with Billie Eilish's song "What Was I Made For?"). The song sequence at once provides omniscient but also personal narration; this initiating narrative space is further complicated by Helen Mirren's omniscient voice-over, which precedes "Pink," accompanied by an orchestral score that cites the opening of Richard Strauss's *Also sprach Zarathustra* (also used in Stanley's Kubrick's *2001: A Space Odessey* [1968]). The film begins, then, by evoking a complex overlapping of narrative spaces that continues to mark its story as it develops. Such diegetic/nondiegetic boundary crossing pervades *Barbie*'s soundtrack. Sequences such as "Dance the Night" demonstrate that it is not unusual for the denizens of Barbie Land to burst into stylized performances and choreographed dances. Thus, while *Barbie* may not be able to be labeled as a musical, there are certainly instances where conventions of film musicals take over, blurring the status of the film as belonging to a specific, well-defined genre.

"I'm Just Ken"

"I'm Just Ken" follows the diegetically presented "Push," which foreshadows the peacocking and binaristic musical masculinity to come. In "I'm Just Ken," a 1980s power ballad, the Kens' hypermasculine peacocking stems from their overt flaunting of heterosexuality and masculinity, perpetuated by patriarchal rhetoric that eventually turns them against each other. Yet, the song begins as a soft, heartfelt ballad from Ken. Gosling sings this in a high register of his voice, expressing vulnerability, and underneath his voice are gentle piano chords, both of which are understood as signifiers of the "anti-masculine."[10] These anti-masculine musical "signs" convey Ken's prelapsarian state, providing a musical reminder of Ken's innocence, emphasizing that he has no knowledge of harmful masculinity before venturing to the Real World. Thus, before leaving Barbie Land, Ken is visually marked as androgynous. His hairlessness, "prettiness," and submissiveness disrupt the binarism of a male/female dichotomy that attempts to keep threats of masculinity at bay.[11] His unthreatening behavior leads to a perception of masculinity that reverses the viewer's expectations about hegemonic masculinity—a perception that is ultimately shattered when Ken enters the Real World and is introduced to systemic patriarchy.

This soft ballad shortly gives way to a change in the music's style. This new section overflows with masculine musical codes, featuring distorted guitars, a lower vocal register, heavy drums, and wailing virtuosic guitar solos—all signifiers of the genre known as "cock rock."[12] As Lucia Kramer notes, rock is predominantly male-dominated and deifies lifestyles of sexual excess, perpetuating a version of masculinity that emphasizes virility and sexual prowess.[13] Within the context of glam rock and hair metal, masculinity is largely equated with sexual proclivity, hence the genre's moniker, "cock rock." Here the use of makeup, long hair, and bright, ostentatious, and tight clothing that could be seen as feminizing are counteracted by an "extreme flaunting of heterosexuality."[14] This heterosexual, macho behavior is exhibited by Ken and the Kens after Ryan Gosling's Ken returns to Barbie Land. On Ken's return, Barbie Land is transformed into Kendom Land, where the Kens develop homosocial behaviors, creating and maintaining male societal dominance and power. As a result, the Barbies become objects of desire for the Kens, who seek to "own" the Barbies, making them their "slaves." The Kens heavily flaunt heterosexuality (equated with domination and violence) to compensate for their potential feminization through their bright clothing and lack of genitalia.

Figure 8.1 *Ken flaunts his masculinity "cock rock" style as he launches into battle* (Barbie, *dir. Greta Gerwig, 2023).*

This ultimately comes to a head in a violent confrontation during the "I'm Just Ken" sequence.

The fight sequence of "I'm Just Ken" features the most masculine-coded music, which, combined with comedic and ludicrous action choreography that Gerwig describes as being somewhere between dancing and vaudevillian physical comedy, serves to parody "macho" masculinity.[15] Instances such as Ken's removal of his fur coat, accompanied by what songwriter Mark Ronson describes as "crazy shred solos" performed by Wolfgang Van Halen, son of 1980s rock guitarist Eddie Van Halen, highlight the masculine peacocking of the scene.[16] Stylistically in keeping with the guitar performance of "cock rock," this scene takes masculine-coded music, heavily associated with the objectification of women, and combines it with incredibly campy action—for example, the faux slow motion and the use of toys as weapons. The music enhances the comedy of the scene, parodying and perhaps commenting on the patriarchal masculine desire for domination and power. Between cuts in the sequence, signifiers of rock are systematically removed from the score. In the first instance, when the camera cuts to the Barbies watching the battle, triumphant strings play as the Barbies realize that their plot to use masculinity to pit the Kens against each other in order to regain their control of Barbie Land has worked. In the second, when the camera returns to the battle from the perspective of Will Ferrell's Mattel CEO, synthesizers dominate the score. Rock is presented as representing the perspective of the Kens, establishing a musically gendered binary between Barbie and Ken. Barbie's musical signifiers rely on tropes associated with "pop music," as a soft mainstream category appealing to a broad audience, whereas Ken's musical language is "cock rock." The stark contrast between the styles of music not only sets up this binary, but also heavily reinforces the masculine codes of "I'm Just Ken," underlining Ken's parodic interpretation of hegemonic masculinity and patriarchy.

According to Gerwig, the inspiration for "I'm Just Ken" came from musicals, describing the sequence as "[her] own version of Starlight Express," a song from the 1984 Andrew Lloyd Webber musical of the same name.[17] While the soundtrack generally plays with the diegesis, interweaving material that provides metacommentary on the film, "I'm Just Ken" constitutes the most overt example of a musical number within the film. While *Barbie* is by no means a musical, "I'm Just Ken" takes over the diegesis of the film, ensuring that both diegetic and music tracks are focused on him, paralleling Ken's temporary conquest of Barbie Land itself. "I'm Just Ken" acts as a reminder not only of Ken's takeover of Barbie Land but also reinforces his masculine domination and control, which revolves around "macho" behavior, heterosexuality, and a desire to mansplain.

The spontaneity of Ken bursting into song alongside the 1980s power ballad style allows this moment to be heavily comedic. The out-of-place musical style, in the context of *Barbie*'s soundtrack, and the surprise element of a musical number with no forewarning, highlights the humor of the scene and the masculine elements presented within the sequence. The spontaneity and unpredictability of the inclusion of a musical number outside of a musical— alongside a change in musical style—comedically comments on masculinity in a way that is not unique to *Barbie*.

Popular media has long played with the concept of spontaneous musical numbers as comedic. For example, "Nothing Suits Me Like a Suit" from the sitcom *How I Met Your Mother* (CBS, 2005–14), has Barney Stinson, a hypermasculine playboy character whose identity revolves around his sexual prowess, imagine a musical number where he bursts into a stylized performance regarding suits. This song is full of sexual innuendo and is used to display Barney's materialistic mindset as well as his manipulation of women; however, the use of a musical number outside of the contexts of a musical allows the song to work comedically due to the sudden change of genre.

Similarly, *Frozen 2*'s (dir. Chris Buck and Jennifer Lee, 2019) "Lost in the Woods" cannily displays comedy through music. Despite being a Disney musical, the randomness of the 1980s ballad style enhances the comedy of Kristoff (an animated male figure appearing in the *Frozen* franchise) singing with a herd of reindeer. This song also acts to portray masculine desire. Across the song Kristoff demonstrates that he does not understand the emotions and desires of his partner, Anna. Rather than focusing on the potential danger in which the characters have found themselves, Kristoff worries about being misunderstood in his attempts to propose to Anna. Foreshadowing "I'm Just Ken," *Frozen 2* uses cock rock to portray Kristoff's masculine desire and frustration at being unable to express his emotions. Despite the song's serious subject matter, the singing reindeer and juxtaposition of musical style convey comedy. These songs' comedic styles thus offer a parodic version of the "masculine" elements of the scene, a parody that "I'm Just Ken" arguably pushes even further.

The very act of having a musical number with stylized performances subverts the vision of masculinity that Ken is trying to portray, that he himself believes to be "hegemonic," in the sense of signifying and even conferring knowledge and status. Musical numbers, as Lloyd Whitesell points out, are "a sign of weakness, betraying tendencies towards escapism, unbridled sentimentality and decorative form, all of which go against deep-seated codes of masculine behavior."[18] The trait of stylized performance, as Kelly Kessler argues, is more often associated with "sentiment-driven" femininity rather than traditional hegemonic masculinity.[19] Indeed, "I'm Just Ken" remains the moment in the film at which Ken truly expresses his feelings regarding Barbie's attitudes and behavior toward him. Bursting into song gives him a method of expressing emotion. In a kind of musical existentialism, the altered reality of the film musical's self-expression allows Ken to still believe in his masculinity, while parodying hegemonic masculinity through singing accompanied by stylized campy actions and dance.

"What Was I Made For?"

The buzz of "I'm Just Ken"—both musically in the film and in the song's offscreen afterlife—meant that "What Was I Made For?," as the song that defined the film's conclusion and Barbie's interior monologue, had a tough act to follow. While "I'm Just Ken" occurs during a lengthy battle scene, "Made For" occurs during a three-and-a-half-minute introspective interlude, after the Barbies have regained control of Barbie Land. There are, however, a few similarities between these centerpieces: like Ken's performance, Barbie's song also pauses the plot, deferring the final scenes of the film to allow her to reflect on her identity in a white room that is neither part of Barbie Land nor the Real World. Ken's dream ballet-inspired sequence is blue and pink, and Barbie's is white. Both color schemes might suggest attempts to find nonbinary spaces of self-realization for these characters. Their song genres, blocking, and subject matter each express the gender aligned with the central character; and yet, both songs also address other gendered experiences.

"Made For" follows the "Now Feel" scene, which has little dialogue and in which Mattel creator Ruth Handler invites Barbie to "now ... feel" in a blank space, after which Barbie closes her eyes and Eilish's song begins. The sparse scene complements Eilish's choice to sing this pop ballad in a "very soft, held back, upper-range falsetto." To Eilish, this style was "what the song wanted," to sound "heartbroken, almost like you were just crying and now you're singing."[20] Such high, delicate singing is typically associated with femininity. For Jilly Boyce Kay, "the gendering of speech ... and the invisibilized but deeply ingrained assumptions about who is entitled to speak in public—all contribute to broader structures of gender injustice and the continuing subordination of women and other 'others' in public life and culture more broadly."[21] Eilish knows the stereotypes surrounding her breathy vocal style well. As Eilish told Brittany Spanos: "Anytime I see an impression [of me whispering] on the internet, it just reminds me how little the internet knows about me."[22] Critics have long typecast Eilish as an emotional little girl, dismissing the training and talent it takes to sing emotively. And yet, Eilish is exacting about the style each of her songs demand, putting "Made For" among "the top three hardest songs

Figure 8.2 *Ruth Handler instructs Barbie to "Now ... FEEL" (*Barbie, *dir. Greta Gerwig, 2023).*

I've ever had to record." Eilish's introspective interviews about the growth of her voice—both as an "instrument" she "can play with" and as a metaphor for speaking her mind—signals a yearning to have a conversation with critics who boil her down to a stereotype.[23] Importantly, this conversational ethos infuses the *Barbie* scene and also the song's creation.

Eilish and FINNEAS (Finneas O'Connell)—her brother, a well-known music producer and her constant collaborator—wrote the song after Gerwig showed them the film's first half-hour and pivotal moments, including the "Now Feel" scene, which Gerwig said needed Barbie's song.[24] Roughly twenty-four hours after seeing the rough cut, Eilish and FINNEAS had a slow day in the studio (working on the 2024 album *Hit Me Hard and Soft*, which deals in dichotomies of gendered and sexual expression), and they decided to work on Barbie's song. After the first verse and line "What was I made for?" came to Eilish, the siblings wrote the song in one sitting.

Eilish and FINNEAS completed the song while Ronson and Wyatt were beginning to compose the film's underscore. Ronson and Wyatt incorporated the song's melodies in their score in a way that FINNEAS deemed a "full circle": their melodies were transcribed into orchestral instruments by Matt Dunkley (who arranged the theme song for the 2021 James Bond film *No Time to Die* that earned Eilish and FINNEAS their first Grammy and Oscar), and then FINNEAS looped the orchestral recordings into the final edit of the song. The score's basis on "What Was I Made For?" is, in Kate McQuiston's terms, a "hybrid score," a score that uses "existing music plus original music written to strongly relate to it . . . [using] shared musical traits, such as instrumentation, a distinctive style, melodic, harmonic, rhythmic material, etc."[25] The underscore's orchestral "covers" of "Made For"—especially the first four notes Eilish sings—reward careful listening for viewers and superfans who have already seen the movie or listened to the prereleased soundtrack.

For example, a half-hour into the film, when Barbie and Ken are in the Real World and Barbie is searching for who is playing with her, she closes her eyes to envision a montage of Gloria (America Ferrera) and Sasha (Ariana Greenblatt), which triggers the first orchestral instance of "Made For." In a parallel to the "Now Feel" sequence (the penultimate sequence of the film), Barbie ends up crying, anticipating the unarticulated internal struggle that is developed fully in this later sequence. In this initial moment, the score speaks for her, breathing the beginnings of Barbie's song into existence. As McQuiston writes: "The spectrum of existing to newly crafted music in the hybrid score illustrates and celebrates the pleasures of making believe, whether that making is tangible and goal-directed, or whether it idealizes or otherwise remakes the past in variously precise acts of remembering."[26] The hybrid score puts song and score—and characters, filmmakers, and audiences—into a conversation of meaning-making that hinges on making believe through our memories.

"What Was I Made For?" sets up a dialogue between not only Handler and Barbie, but also Barbie and Eilish, Eilish and her critics, and the film and its audiences—especially through the scene's montage sequence. According to Gerwig, the montage sequence, which features found footage of women of all ages during personal moments in their lives, is composed of footage of the cast and crew's family members.[27] *Variety* reported that TikTokers made their own "Barbie montages" that reflect what Eilish calls "this groundbreaking, astounding piece about being a woman and the female experience and the human experience and growing up and all of these real things that we all experience and go through."[28] The song puts Barbie on the threshold of choosing who she wants to be for herself outside the world Mattel has built for her. Given that both Barbie and Ken's centerpiece songs question their identities in a liminal space, viewers might consider how both characters' songs offer a threshold to negotiate between Barbie Land/Kendom Land and the Real

Figure 8.3 *Barbie (Margot Robbie) makes her final decision (Barbie, dir. Greta Gerwig, 2023).*

World. "What Was I Made For?" becomes even more of a meeting space in the film because its melodies permeate the underscore. Thus, the melody incorporated into the underscore accompanies Barbie's introduction to the Real World when she first arrives with Ken. In indeterminate ways, it foretells Barbie's questioning of herself. The song invites a circular conversation about life's crossroads and thresholds, expressing a yearning to move beyond the binary.

Song paratexts: To binary or not to binary

As much as these characters' songs are opposed in the film's structure, they are not so far apart in their subsequent afterlives in online discussions and in awards announcements. The titles alone, "I'm Just Ken" and "What Was I Made For?," speak to both characters' existential crises. The film's focus, despite its mononymous title, was made more ambiguous in the minds of potential viewers by the twinned existence of these two songs and the debates throughout the awards season, both on- and offline.

"I'm Just Ken" received a large amount of attention following the film's release. The marketability of Ryan Gosling/Ken as a popular icon meant that the song featured in trailers and even received its own extended play recording—a transmedia expansion that Robbie's Stereotypical Barbie was not granted. Online, the boyfriends of the *Barbie* audience also tended to focus on Ken. Popular culture reverence for the song resulted in SNL's "I'm Just Pete" which, rather than providing a political critique, exemplified how "I'm Just Ken" had been used to further discussion about Gosling, Ken, and contemporary masculinity.[29] The track's fame led to awards nominations, winning the best song at the 29th annual Critics Choice Award, sparking discussion about the attention that Ryan Gosling's performance received, often to the detriment of Margot Robbie as star and Greta Gerwig as director. Additionally, his nomination for best song at the Oscars led to a performance of "I'm Just Ken," which had over 17 million views on YouTube, considerably more views than any of the other Oscar performances.[30] While the ensuing debates about the hype around Ken raised criticism for missing the movie's message, many will remember *Barbie* through discussion about Ken and his music, rather than Barbie.

Does "I'm Just Ken" ultimately situate Gosling as the star of the film, or do Billie Eilish's and FINNEAS's awards have a competing story to tell? Eilish and FINNEAS won Best Original Song at the Oscars, the Golden Globe Awards, the Grammy Awards, the Guild of Music Supervisors Awards, and many more, far eclipsing the Critics' Choice Awards win of "I'm Just Ken." Clearly, "What Was I Made For?" captured the hearts of many listeners who identified with the song and with Barbie's—and, to perhaps equal extent, Ken's—existential crisis. As Eilish says, she and FINNEAS

> wrote from the perspective of a character and her life and the way she sees the world through her eyes and her experiences, and it wasn't until two days later that I was listening to it and I was like, "this is me, this is my life and how I feel," and it was pretty weird to not realize that my subconscious was doing that and also that I related a lot to this character.[31]

Gerwig describes Eilish's creation as "Barbie's heart song—the song that is deep inside her core that she doesn't even completely know is there but that she starts to hear more clearly throughout the film."[32] The depression that critics and scholars often associate with Eilish and her songs does not neatly square with Barbie's existential crisis, or even with Eilish herself, who has recently expressed that she does not wish to continue speaking publicly about mental health.[33] While a singer's star persona is important to the success of a song, listeners also identify with shared experiences of yearning, for which "What Was I Made For?" offers more of a blank slate than "I'm Just Ken." Eilish's open existential rumination is a mirror that we can hold up to ourselves, much like the song's accompanying montage prompted exponential TikTok recreations.

Ultimately, *Barbie*'s music structures gender binaries while creating thresholds that unsettle these same structures. Its songs and the discussion these generated, particularly with regard to the awards both won, may have led to a more polarized binary between Barbie and Ken in the film's afterlife among fans and critics. For *Barbie* is a road movie: the heroes cross a threshold into a new world of self-discovery before they must return to their world.

In *Barbie*, the song that plays on the stereo during Barbie's road trips is the Indigo Girls' "Closer to Fine" (1989). "Closer to Fine" is a threshold song, a portal to a world that is not governed by binaries, not only because it is used to travel between Barbie Land and the Real World, but also between Barbie and Gloria, make believe and real life, and, given the commentaries surrounding the song and film, straight and queer (the song is a lesbian touchstone, but also a favorite of Gerwig's generation).[34] In a film with largely subtle queer references (the characters Allan and the lesbian Birkenstock, Sam Smith's "Man I Am," etc.), the song stands out and draws attention to itself. Penned by Emily Saliers and sung by the Indigo Girls, who also include Amy Ray, it is considered an LGBTQ+ anthem.[35] In this sense, "Closer to Fine" seems an odd choice among the film's insistent binaries in plot, characters, and music. Yet, Brandi Carlisle, a successful songwriter and LGBTQ+ activist, commended the film for reinstating the song. She opined: "The real injustice of how the Indigo Girls have been treated throughout these last few decades is that they've been used as kind of this dog whistling acceptable way to sort of parody lesbians, and I always felt destabilized by it."[36]

"Closer to Fine" also was a signature song for Gerwig's generation more generally.[37] The *New York Times* reported that "Closer to Fine" was "a song Gerwig has loved since growing up among 'hippie Christians' in a Unitarian church,"[38] suggesting why Gerwig herself selected the song as the way that Barbie (and later, Gloria and Sasha—it appears multiple times in the film) navigates back and forth between a gender binary, between a world founded on relations between women and another generated by patriarchy. It speaks very literally of a journey: "I went to the doctor, I went to the mountains."[39] The lyrics later further specify that the doctor is a "doctor of philosophy," qualifying the character's journey as an existential one: "And I went to see the doctor of philosophy / With a poster of Rasputin and a beard down to his knee / . . . I spent four years prostrate to the higher mind / Got my paper and I was free."[40]

If there is any way to summarize *Barbie*'s music in one line, it would be that it represents the existential crisis of Barbie (and Ken) on a winding road that expresses a yearning for a place beyond binaries.

"*Barbieist vs. Oppenheimerist*": A Gender-Based Reception Study of Barbie *in Turkey*

MELIS BEHLIL AND RUKEN DOĞU ERDEDE

Some of the best memes of 2023 featured images that brought together the unlikely pair of Margot Robbie's *Barbie* and Cillian Murphy's J. Robert Oppenheimer. At a time when box office numbers across the globe were struggling to reach pre-pandemic levels, the much-publicized release of *Barbie* (dir. Greta Gerwig, 2023) alongside another (and vastly different in tone) blockbuster in *Oppenheimer* (dir. Christopher Nolan, 2023) resulted in what has been termed the "Barbenheimer" phenomenon. Both films did phenomenally well at the box office, with the exuberant *Barbie* "beating" the more somber *Oppenheimer*, a biopic about the "father" of the atomic bomb, in the number of domestic and international entries. There have been, however, several countries where the results were reversed.

In this chapter, we examine the case of Turkey, where *Oppenheimer* sold 24 percent more tickets. Against this background, this chapter will rely on discourse analysis and reception study to explore the reasons behind this reversal of fortune. Through an examination of comments from leading popular film critics, as well as online forums, we argue that this preference for

Oppenheimer is a manifestation of the country's dominantly patriarchal culture, also revealing the effect of the ruling Justice and Development Party's (AKP) anti-feminist and heteronormative rhetoric. We start with a brief analysis of the two films' box office performance across the world, then turn to the Turkish case, where we survey the views of mainstream critics as well as online commentary, ultimately focusing on the most polarized cases: a popular online forum with a thread on being "Barbieist vs. Oppenheimerist," and three YouTube videos that have been the most-viewed content in Turkish on the subject. The vulgar discourse evident in these commentaries epitomizes the sexist debates surrounding the two films.

Barbie vs. *Oppenheimer*

The juxtaposition of two films that appear to be worlds apart created a buzz in social media platforms that was quickly exploited by the filmmakers and studios themselves.[1] While the films differed greatly in genre, style, and certainly color palette, one could argue that they also shared similarities, highlighting the existential inner journeys of their main characters, and capitalizing on a particularly American brand of nostalgia.[2] At the end of the day, both involved a significant investment by their studios, *Barbie* having cost an estimated $145 million to produce and another $150 million to market,[3] with *Oppenheimer* having a $100 million production budget and $65–100 million for marketing.[4] Warner Bros. and Universal, the respective production companies, benefited from the hype created by the Barbenheimer phenomenon, as did the rest of the industry, struggling with the writers' and actors' unions strikes that had started just around the time of the release of the films.

Upon their release, industry specialists fomented the competition and ensuing discussion by closely following the box office performance of the two films, terming it a "battle."[5] Overall, *Barbie*'s box office tallied up to nearly $1.5 billion, with 56 percent international, and *Oppenheimer*'s to almost $1 billion, with 66.2 percent from outside the United States and Canada.[6] Domestically as well, *Barbie* was the clear winner with almost double the box office, a point that elicited laughter when *Barbie*'s Ryan Gosling and *Oppenheimer*'s Emily

Figure 9.1 *Barbenheimer poster art by Sean Longmore. Courtesy Blue Robin Collectables/Alamy.*

Blunt presented jointly at the 96th Academy Awards the following March. In the international market, however, *Barbie's* lead was narrower, with *Oppenheimer* being staggeringly more successful in Asian countries like South Korea, Japan, and China, and notably more successful in Middle Eastern countries such as the United Arab Emirates and Turkey (see the table below). Granted, *Barbie* had the advantage in terms of its length and the rating it received (114 min. vs. 180 min. and PG-13 vs. R) within the U.S. market. Within the international market, however, each country has its own dynamics and determining factors.[7]

| Country/Region | Box Office | | O/B |
	Barbie	*Oppenheimer*	Percentage
Total	$1,447,038,421	$975,811,333	67.4%
Domestic	$636,238,421	$330,078,895	51.8%
International	$810,800,000	$645,732,438	79.6%
South Korea	$4,312,632	$25,840,720	599.1%
Japan	$3,883,578	$12,204,045	314.2%
United Arab Emirates	$4,238,121	$7,954,884	187.3%
China (incl. HK)	$40,345,361	$71,468,577	177.1%
Turkey	$4,132,029	$7,100,774	171.8%

Source: *boxofficemojo.com*,https://www.boxofficemojo.com/title/tt1517268/?ref_=bo_se_r_1.

Barbie the doll is not as widely recognized in East Asia, leading to a general lack of interest in the film.[8] In China, however, *Barbie* had a limited release and still performed above expectations when it was adopted by Chinese feminists and its popularity spread through word of mouth.[9] Conversely, in South Korea, where *Barbie* is considered a flop, the strong feminist message of the film is seen as a possible reason why it did not connect with audiences.[10] Japan presents a particular case, as the Barbenheimer phenomenon actually damaged *Barbie's* performance. Upon interacting positively with fan posts featuring an image of Barbie accompanied by mushroom clouds evoking the atomic bomb on social media, the U.S. Twitter account of Warner Bros. was formally criticized by the Japanese branch, eliciting an apology for its "insensitive social media engagement."[11] While *Barbie* was released in August, *Oppenheimer* was withheld from theaters until March 2024, after the film's seven wins at the Academy Awards. Despite the sensitive subject (or perhaps because of it), Japanese audiences showed great interest in the film.[12] *Barbie* also encountered problems in the United Arab Emirates and other Arab nations due to its gender politics.[13] Another case is Turkey; though *Barbie* performed slightly better on its opening weekend, *Oppenheimer* ultimately "won" the battle.

Before we delve into the reception of these films in Turkey, we find it necessary to briefly describe the cinematic ecosystem of the country. Like Japan, South Korea, and India, Turkey has a significant film industry, and for the last twenty years, local productions have been solidly outperforming imported releases.[14] In the top-thirty box office of all time based on number of tickets sold, there is not a single Hollywood production.[15] *Oppenheimer* is the highest performing film directed by Christopher Nolan on this list at number 92; *Barbie* is not in the top 100. We also need to note, however, that movie theaters have been underperforming since the COVID-19 shutdowns and box

Figure 9.2 *Fan-made Barbenheimer memes retweeted by the Warner Bros. social media account, which sparked a backlash in Japan. Courtesy Pictorial Press Limited/ Alamy.*

office numbers are far from their pre-pandemic levels. This is largely due to the financial crisis in the country, where the high rate of inflation caused the average ticket price to rise by over 1,000 percent.[16] Additionally, several potential domestic hits were snatched by online platforms Disney+ and Netflix in 2022 and 2023, without any theatrical release. With this background, it is not surprising that both *Oppenheimer* and *Barbie* found themselves in the top ten for 2023.

Barbie and *Oppenheimer*'s "official" reception in Turkey

The initial reception of both films in Turkey was not all that different from around the world. *Barbie* has a 6.8 rating on IMDb, and 5.6 on its Turkish equivalent, Beyazperde, whereas *Oppenheimer* has 8.3 and 7, respectively (Turkish audiences seem to be more discerning on both counts). While film criticism in traditional media, such as television and newspapers, is increasingly rare in Turkey and there is currently no print film magazine, there are numerous blogs and YouTube accounts dedicated to cinema, and Letterboxd is particularly popular among younger viewers.

Leading critics were mostly lukewarm in response to *Barbie*. Unlike in the United States, where America Ferrera's tirade about being a woman was embraced as the film's proof of its feminist credentials, Turkish critics found the scene (and generally the last half-hour of the movie) to be too "obvious"[17] and "tagged on."[18] Several publications close to the conservative government tried to attack the film's gender-fluid approach by publishing "warnings" just before its release. *Yeni Şafak* declared that the film "makes men look disgusting" and Barbie "is now LGBT,"[19] whereas *Milliyet* claimed that families were worried about their children being "subjected to LGBT imposition."[20] Conversely, the LGBTI+ publication *KaosGL* accused the film of being reductionist, essentialist, and heteronormative: "After the director's insistence on not looking at the sexual orientation aspect from the beginning of the film, Barbie, who is human, goes to the gynecologist first thing, that is, the film's linking of 'real' womanhood to the genitalia makes us finish the film as if we were in an uncomfortable pink corset in the middle of the right, LGBTI+ exclusionist, privileged Hollywood feminism."[21] Critics popular on Letterboxd viewed *Barbie* favorably: Aslı Ildır gave the film 3.5 out of 5, Öykü Sofuoğlu 2.5 stars, and media personality Melikşah Altuntaş 3 stars. Figures particularly popular among Generation Z viewers were even more enthusiastic, as Ali Aktaş furnished the film with 3.5 stars, and Zeynep Sanem gave it the full 5 stars.

In the most popular and most commented video reviews on YouTube, the film received both positive and negative criticism. In a video with approximately 158,000 views on the channel Ezgi'nin Kanalı (Ezgi's Channel), the young female vlogger talks about the movie's story in general and states that watching *Barbie* in the cinema is an event.[22] She discusses the merchandise products given at the prescreening for social media personalities, and how the people who came were fully dressed in pink. While referring to the Barbenheimer frenzy, the commentator notes that it should not be considered a competition between the two films. She argues that *Oppenheimer* is a "film that rolls up its sleeves to use the possibilities of cinematic art," but *Barbie* is like an event to celebrate the Barbie icon. It is intriguing that *Barbie* is not considered to be in the same league as *Oppenheimer* even in this positive review because it is not regarded as an authentic "movie" in conventional terms. Moreover, probably taking into account the polarization between *Barbie*'s and *Oppenheimer*'s fans on social media in Turkey, the reviewer adds that the movie has a humanist approach to gender relations rather than a feminist one, which she believes "shouldn't scare men away." Consequently, the video delineates *Barbie* as an "event" aimed at providing entertainment to a general audience while not overtly giving feminist messages about gender relations.

Another review video published on the YouTube channel Filme Gitmeden Önce (Before Going to the Movie), with approximately 380,000 views, offers a lukewarm commentary on *Barbie*.[23] The young male commentator admits, "under normal circumstances, I would not attend a Barbie film, nor would I assess a Barbie film by the same standards applied to conventional films." He adds, however, that he watched the movie and "even got teary-eyed at times or laughed at jokes." The emphasis on "even" is significant. By emphasizing that a film highlighting the challenges women face in a patriarchal society elicited an emotional response in him as a man, the commentator elevates *Barbie* to the status of a "conventional film." Additionally, by expressing emotion where masculinity prohibits male spectators from showing emotions as an audience, particularly in the form of tears,[24] the commentator differentiates his position from the masculine opposition to *Barbie* in Turkey's social media. The video asserts that although the film occasionally becomes shallow and its attitudes toward male characters are sometimes aggressive, *Barbie* effectively portrays the challenges of living as a woman. The video receives positive comments from users for providing a "balanced" critique.

In another popular YouTube channel, Kutsal Motor (Holy Motor), feminist criticism is directed at *Barbie* by the outspoken feminist commentator and the male film critic.[25] They claim that Gerwig's *Barbie* sets out with an intent akin to "feminism for dummies," adopting a taboo-breaking vision. They see it, however, as a shallow and mediocre film that fails to achieve these goals. Commentators suggest that *Barbie* should be understood as aligning itself with the agenda of Hollywood studios to alter their image in the post-#MeToo context, which is reflected in the production of a spate of feminist films. They also claim that the film has been favorably received by male critics especially for these reasons. Unlike other videos, the commentators do not engage in any comparison with *Oppenheimer* and focus exclusively on *Barbie*'s place within Gerwig's cinematic oeuvre. The critiques in the video are consistent with feminist criticism raised against *Barbie* globally. The difference from other videos discussed here is that most of the comments responding to the video find the criticisms too harsh, the commenters unabashedly stating that they enjoyed the film.

Barbieist vs. Oppenheimerist

A discussion thread titled "Barbieist vs. Oppenheimerist" was initiated on Ekşi Sözlük, the oldest and still very popular social media platform in Turkey, during the release of *Barbie* and *Oppenheimer*, where fans of both films confronted one another.[26] It has been observed that many entries across various subjects on Ekşi Sözlük tend to propagate hate speech,[27] a fact also evident in the current example. The heading, which refers to overtly polarized social, cultural, and political attitudes in Turkey,[28] is noteworthy for the prominence of anti-feminist and homophobic views. In these entries, choosing to watch *Barbie* is linked to "femininity" and a "low level of intelligence," and men who prefer *Barbie* over *Oppenheimer* are marked as "f*****" and "being not men enough."[29]

There are also some review videos on YouTube that adopt similar discourses. The need to analyze these videos arises from not only the overt misogynistic narratives they propagate, but also their status as the most-viewed content on the platform on this subject. What's striking about these videos is that, despite being labeled as *Barbie* film reviews, the creators' primary focus is on expressing their opinions about gender dynamics in society rather than the film itself. Among these, in the most-viewed video titled, "Pembesi Gitti Tozu Kaldı," with 2.9 million views, the commentator Murat Soner, a radio personality-turned-YouTuber who does not espouse overtly political views, differentiates himself from the pronouncement that "men do not go to *Barbie*" by stating that he watched the film with his daughter.[30] Nevertheless, in the video, he criticizes women who have cosmetic surgery and share their images on social media instead of focusing on the film. To illustrate his points, he adds images and clips of women from different social media accounts. The tone of the criticism goes beyond insulting to accusing the women in question of being "the real misogynists" because they promote certain looks affecting other women's choices. Consequently, Soner instrumentalizes *Barbie* to communicate his conservative beliefs that belittle and antagonize the decisions women make about their own bodies and social media.

In another video, the commentator focuses on what he calls *Barbie*'s "political correctness bullshit," by invoking the term "SJW," in its English formulation.[31] As a catchphrase emanating from alt-right online presences, the term "social justice warrior," commonly shorthanded as SJW, is "used as a pejorative within these communities to describe individuals who they claim are overly invested in identity politics and political correctness."[32] In the video, the term "SJW" refers to feminists and feminist politics. At times, the term "Feminazis"[33] is also employed interchangeably. Asserting that the claims of feminist politics regarding gender inequality are "absurd," he argues that feminists have taken positive discrimination to an "excessive level," leading to the oppression of men. He condemns *Barbie* as a film that exemplifies these attitudes. He makes only positive comments about the film from a distinctly sexist perspective; as he "found parts of the film humorous," he suggests that "a man must be in the team," referring to Greta Gerwig's co-writer Noah Baumbach.

Another video generates anti-feminist and misogynistic discourse in an even more vulgar manner and has accumulated almost half a million views.[34] As a video about the Barbenheimer frenzy, it begins the discussion by asserting that Nolan and Gerwig cannot be compared, stating that Nolan is a well-known, successful director while Gerwig is a no-name. He separates *Barbie,* "where they work their asses off to sell toys," from *Oppenheimer*, "a masterpiece." Similar to the comments on Ekşi Sözlük, he discusses, in a disparaging tone, his decision not to attend the special screening of *Barbie* in Turkey because that could be taken to mean he is gay. At the same time, he uses vulgar profanities about the influencers promoting *Barbie* on social media and who criticize Nolan's cinema. In the end, the video attacks *Barbie* as representing "feminist screeching." The images accompanying these statements utilize photographs taken during the Feminist Night March, previously held annually on the 8th of March, thereby targeting the feminist movement within the country as well.

Figure 9.3 *A putdown of Gerwig on Filmler ve Filimler YouTube channel, "BARBENHEIMER- ELESTIREL PARODI,"* youtube.com, *August 5, 2023, 11:56, https://www.youtube.com/watch?v=2HApjzJ2_0k.*

Backlash against feminism

These misogynistic and anti-feminist sentiments that emerged in the reception of *Barbie* in Turkey can be explained by the global phenomenon of male backlash in the twenty-first century, a period in which the gains of the feminist movement increased.[35] However, as is evident in the previous video, there are also indications of a dynamics of gender politics that is specific to Turkey. Turkey is a country with a strong women's movement that spans many years and has seen the emergence of different feminisms.[36] Over the years, this powerful feminist movement has achieved various gains in the political, social, and judicial spheres such as improvements in "regulations in the penal law regarding violence against women."[37]

The ruling Justice and Development Party (AKP), however, has been reversing gender equality reforms.[38] These actions, starting with the banning of the Pride March and Feminist Night March, and the brutalization by the police force of those who took to the streets, reached their peak with the country's withdrawal from the Istanbul Convention, a Council of Europe Action against violence against women and domestic violence.[39] Politicians in AKP have claimed that the Istanbul Convention is "a threat to Turkish values and identity and promotes same-sex relations." Pro-government media outlets have published articles on this issue referring to the provisions in the Convention that aim to prevent gender discrimination.[40] The smear articles published by the same outlets about *Barbie* as being "LGBT" and as making "men look disgusting" demonstrate how the government's prevailing anti-feminist and heteronormative rhetoric is registered in the reception of *Barbie*. Although neither the writers in Ekşi Sözlük nor YouTubers mentioned in this article are affiliated with the AKP, we observe that they produce a similar discourse, particularly defining men who watch *Barbie* as "gay" and as participating in a homosexual milieu, using derogatory terms.

In addition to LGBT rights, Turkey's feminist movement has also been targeted, particularly by the AKP party leader, President Erdoğan. In a now infamous speech following outrage in the society after the murder of a young woman, he argued that "the nature[s] of men and women are different" and feminists "who advocate for the concept of equality are distanced from justice."[41] While they do not necessarily use the same words, we have observed similar sentiments in the aforementioned critiques. In particular, videos that label feminists as "Feminazis" and assert that feminist politics are nonsense, by *Filmograf* and *Filmler and Filimler*, point to differences between "the natures" of women and men, and claim that the pursuit of equality have reached an "absurd level." In doing so, they reference the fact that women in Barbie Land are in positions of authority in all jobs as a sign of "injustice to men."

This attitude is also prominent in the soft anti-gender actions of the AKP government, such as the codification of women into domestic labor and motherhood, defending and implementing the discourse of "the most sacred duty of a woman is motherhood."[42] Whether the government's approach is related to its core patriarchal and Islamist values, or about compensating for the neo-liberal crisis of unemployment in the country as suggested by some scholars,[43] the result is depriving women of participating in the labor force and confining them to motherhood and domesticity. The discourse of undermining Gerwig's directorial position and glorifying Nolan as "the director" in some critiques can be considered as the reflection of a rhetoric that codifies women as restricted to certain social spaces.

Conclusion

While the obsession of men with the Second World War is an often-observed situation that underlies the relation between masculinity and war,[44] understanding why a Second World War biopic––*Oppenheimer*––was chosen over *Barbie* in Turkey illuminates the country's dominantly patriarchal culture. In social media platforms and online forums, while *Barbie* is linked to femininity and a low level of intellectuality, men who prefer *Barbie* over *Oppenheimer* are marked as "gay," which connotates "being not men enough" in this particular context. This situation reveals the effect of the ruling AKP's anti-feminist and heteronormative rhetoric in society. The actions of the government, starting with the bans and violent interventions on marches, followed by legal action in the form of the country's withdrawal from the Istanbul Convention, have resulted in a hostile environment for women and

LGBTQI+ groups.[45] In addition to these harsh policies, there are also soft anti-gender actions, such as the codification of women as domestic labor and mothers. In parallel, a rhetoric that extolls masculinity, positing men as under threat, is gaining momentum both in the political and public sphere. Not to end on a pessimistic note, all these developments have also resulted in a new feminist mobilization,[46] as manifested by the feminist critiques of *Barbie*. It appears that *Barbie* served to crystallize displays of gender trouble. We hope that this analysis of the Turkish case will be relevant wherever similar discussions are held around the globe––namely, everywhere.

Deeper into Ken: The Accessibility of Ryan Gosling

MICHAEL DEANGELIS

If Barbie's experiences in the Real World prompt her decision to leave Barbie Land forever, Greta Gerwig's *Barbie* offers Ken his own existential journey, traversing the rocky terrain of patriarchal ideology and toxic masculinity before culminating in the single, bittersweet self-affirmation, "I am Ken." The well-defined chest, abs, and biceps that he displays underneath open vests and flash furs are certainly integral to Ken's characterization, but this version of Ken is much more than a ripped body. Through Ryan Gosling's portrayal, Ken emerges as a prototype for a post-millennial masculinity that pairs body aesthetics with an affective resonance that invites audience identification by sustaining an image as unthreatening and wholly nontoxic. The accessibility of Gosling's persona provides a template for viewers to construct *versions* of the star that are responsive to their perceptions of gender and sexuality. At once, this star persona both addresses and has been shaped by a "Literally Me" masculinity of the consummate, directionless loner hell-bent on redemption; a fan base of women, many of whom have come to perceive Gosling as the quintessential male feminist advocate; and a gay male contingent welcoming the arrival of a discontinued Earring Magic Ken come to life. In the context of a long-standing masculinity crisis, this chapter examines how the portrayal of

Ken is informed by Ryan Gosling's accessible star persona, integrating aspects of Ken's characterization with the actor who plays him, and encompassing publicity, interviews, fan articulations, film criticism, and reports of the celebrity's "offscreen" life.

"Toxic masculinity"

Through star discourse that draws upon both the actor's film roles and the extratextual aspects of his persona, Gosling has been identified as an actor who is attentive to the political developments that have framed post-millennial gender relations, in which "toxic masculinity," in the words of a blogger on a popular website writing under the name of "Valvour," has emerged as a term that encompasses "the negative behaviors and beliefs society has traditionally tied to masculinity."[1] The American Psychological Association, which issued its first guidelines ever for clinical practice with men and boys in 2019, includes stoicism, dominance, aggression, and emotional suppression among these traits.[2] The APA's guidelines also address male behavioral toxicity, encompassing the debilitating psychological symptoms that men harbor in response to the unhealthy behaviors they are expected to emulate—responses that include substance abuse, depression, anxiety, and suicide, the instances of which have been dramatically increasing in recent years among American men.[3] If that weren't enough to bear, many of the performative attributes once considered to be integrally masculine have outworn their gender-exclusivity: masculinity is no longer exclusively associated with the role of provider; fewer jobs require intensive male strength; and men are more vulnerable to having their jobs replaced by automation.[4]

As a strategy of intervention, masculinity theorist Michael Kimmel stresses the importance of dissociating the concept of masculinity from the practice of the unhealthy behavioral patterns that have come to define it. The need for such an effort was indicated when Kimmel asked West Point male cadets to differentiate the traits of "good men" and "real men." The "good men" traits included honor, integrity, sacrifice, and generosity—none of which is inherently affiliated with gender. The "real man" traits, however, were all linked to hegemonically normative expectations of male performance, including strength, a competitive "win at all costs" mindset, and an ability to "play through pain."[5] As Kimmel defines it, the purpose of this intervention would be to "upgrade" masculinity and to de-gender positive feminine traits so that they might be recognized as "human" traits.

Considered as a work in progress, *Barbie*'s Ken provides an affirmative response to this contemporary masculinity crisis. He reveals his narrow conception of male gender identity through stress-induced demonstrations of invulnerability, determined to conquer the beach's plastic waves to impress Barbie (he's hospitalized for his efforts), challenging another Ken (Simu Liu) to a "beach-off," and bemoaning his inability to do a back flip. By the end of the film, however, Ken has begun to accept the infringement of vulnerability as a source of human, rather than feminized, behavior. He reveals the "real man" traits as performative, and demonstrating "empathy, kindness, and emotional intelligence"—traits that have been associated with femininity.[6]

"Ken" and Ryan Gosling: Authenticity and celebrity

Variety suggests that the role of Ken is "not a break from his past work—it's a continuation of it," and Gosling has stated: "In some ways, everything I've done led to it."[7] A relevant precursor of his Ken role that had already demonstrated how one can project an entire life upon a seemingly lifeless doll is Lars Lindstrom in *Lars and the Real Girl* (dir. Craig Gillespie, 2007), in which the eponymous, socially withdrawn protagonist falls in love with a sex doll whom he names Bianca. Lars, whose mother died in childbirth, lives alone in a garage adjacent to his childhood home. After animating Bianca, Lars develops a social life and devotes himself to his companion's needs. Family and townsfolk initially consider Lars's behavior as pathological, yet as they witness the authenticity of his devotion to Bianca, they soon find themselves integrating her presence into the rhythm of their own lives, taking her to doctors' visits, praising her volunteer work at the church, and ultimately bemoaning the loss of their treasured friend at her funeral. Claire Sisco King and Isaac West's assertion that "The fact that Bianca is defined by her 'surface' does not differentiate her from humans but manifests a shared condition" points to another parallel in these two protagonists' identity crises, whereby identification with the star persona prompts a profound transformation of character.[8] The sense of "completion" initially missing in Ken's and Lars's lives is ultimately attained by projecting aspects of personality onto an inanimate being. As he makes Bianca "real," Lars also realizes that he must relinquish control over his own creation, while Barbie's proclamation that she was not designed to be Ken's "one and only" prompts a similar realization. Curiously, Lars's animation of Bianca parallels the viewer's own animation of the Ken doll in *Barbie*, with both films enabling a dynamic in which an agent tailors a lifeless creature to the conditions of one's own reality. Gosling's persona serves as both agent and object in this dynamic.

Unlike Gosling's portrayal of the socially awkward Lars, however, the audience's connection to Ken also plays out in the contours of the actor's *own* body, the surface of which is frequently on display—under an unbuttoned pink and blue striped shirt, a sleeveless jeans jacket, a white knee-length fur coat, and occasionally, entirely uncovered. As a physical being, Gosling-as-Ken correlates with a contemporary version of idealized male form that differs significantly

Figure 10.1 *Lars (Ryan Gosling) with Bianca in* Lars and the Real Girl *(dir. Craig Gillespie, 2007). Courtesy Metro-Goldwyn-Mayer/Photofest.*

from muscled icons like Sylvester Stallone and Arnold Schwarzenegger in the 1980s and 90s.[9] As a 2014 issue of *Men's Journal* reports: "Actors rarely bulk up anymore; they're all trying to be Tyler Durden";[10] and according to personal trainer Tim Walker: "Muscular excess no longer serves as a cultural ideal. He looks great but he's not massive. He's just got really good abs, good arms, and an alright chest. And that's what people want: to be lean, to have a six pack."[11] As I have argued in "Soft and Hard: Accessible Masculinity, Celebrity, and Post-Millennial Cuteness," the accessible contemporary male celebrity body is defined less by excess than by subtraction, requiring the elimination of softer, more pliable tissues to accentuate the sculpted frame that lies underneath. The resulting appearance has gained popularity largely because it constitutes a "look" that is faster and easier for actors to attain, and that is also less threatening and more accessible to those men who might identify with it.[12]

Ryan Gosling started baring his chest long before his portrayal of Ken. Immediately after Jacob (Gosling) takes off his shirt in *Crazy, Stupid, Love* (dir. Glen Ficarra and John Requa, 2011), his love interest Hannah (Emma Stone) exclaims: "Dude, it looks like you're Photoshopped!" In another scene, the crotch of Jacob's front-facing naked body is obscured only by the back of Cal's (Steve Carell) head, while Jacob dispenses relationship advice to Cal in a steam room.[13] In the context of this film, however, such body revelations position

Figure 10.2 *Despite the actor having turned 42 by the time of shooting* Barbie *in 2023, Ken's appearance is also more youthful, and his body is a* harder *body (*Barbie, *dir. Greta Gerwig, 2023).*

Gosling's character as a dominant male with none of the puppy-dog cuteness that characterizes Ken. The version of Gosling in *Barbie* is also leaner than the muscled body of *Crazy, Stupid, Love.* Despite the actor having turned 42 by the time of shooting *Barbie* in 2023, Ken's appearance is also more youthful, and his body is a *harder* body.

The actor's physical body strength contrasts with the vulnerability that Ken exhibits through his failed attempts to claim Barbie as his own, especially when she ignores him, rejects him, or announces to the "real world" that Ken "does not have a penis." ("I have all the genitals," he retorts.) With respect to star discourse, however, Gosling's comments about his physical preparation for the role strategically undercut the character's self-obsession. Gosling's commentary on his own image attests to his modesty. After the host of *The Tonight Show with Jimmy Fallon* solicits Gosling's feelings about the overwhelming online fan response upon the release of the first Ken photos ("It officially broke the internet," Fallon exclaims), the actor expresses surprise and makes light of the attention to the point of self-effacement.[14] An article entitled "Ryan Gosling's Ken Workout & Diet Plan" ends with the author's admission that "the actor is a private individual who doesn't share a lot of personal information. Hence, to scavenge the internet in search of a faithful Ryan Gosling workout plan is to touch down on a lot of secondhand accounts and anecdotes."[15] After relegating any suggestions of rigor in Gosling's workout process to the status of unverifiable hearsay, the author playfully comments upon a lapse in the actor's dietary restrictions by noting his "weakness for Twizzlers."[16] On those occasions when Gosling *does* discuss his preparation for the role, he refrains entirely from aggrandizing the physical process of "becoming" Ken. After an *Access Hollywood* reporter comments that Simu Liu's Ken, whom Gosling's Ken initially sees as a rival, waxed his entire body to render it authentic as a doll, the reporter asks Gosling if he followed suit. Ryan obliquely responds: "You know, that's the Ken life, man. That's just the Ken life."[17] And in the rare cases when the actor does discuss body preparation, he dispels any sense of narcissism with refinement:

> I like to exercise, but I don't like working out at the gym. I like to do ballet and gymnastics … Making muscles is boring and they don't do anything—

they are just like pets eventually. You have to feed them, take care of them, and they are useless. Gym muscles are useless. And they look stupid: you can't do anything with them … They have no practical use.[18]

Rather than characterizing him as a slacker, however, Gosling's disinterest in gym-based workouts reinforces the actor's identity as an authentic, self-made man even while it maintains a lack of obsession about his looks. Known to question social norms and to reject them outright, Gosling has been appropriated as a "loner" figure who plays by his own rules, largely because of what his characters do not express verbally, and this independent loner image had become integral to his star persona long before *Barbie* was conceived. The composite image of Gosling is a man who attends to others while diverting attention from himself. As noted in an article in the *Guardian, People* magazine "tried to name Gosling their sexiest man of the year on four separate occasions, and he reportedly refused each time."[19] While verbal communication is essential to *Barbie*, in other films Gosling's loner image manifests in emotional expression registered only by the face, and more specifically, the eyes. In his analysis of *Drive* (dir. Nicholas Winding Refn, 2011), David Greven notes Gosling's "blank stare [which] starts to suggest alternative possibilities, becoming not so much a mutable canvas as a canvas that mutates."[20] This scarcity of verbal expression also prompted Nancy Epton's fascinating study of the affective properties of silence in these Gosling films, which she treats as the consequent emotional repression of male figures who register intense emotion both because and despite of what they do not express in words.[21]

"Literally Me" and the loner image

Correlating with this silence is the actor's place in "Literally Me," a viral internet trend initiated by a male teenager posting to the popular *4chan* imageboard community. One of the first "Literally Me" memes comprised a set of six images of male stars in outsider roles, three of which feature Gosling—as K in *Blade Runner 2049* (dir. Denis Villeneuve, 2017), as Luke in *The Place Beyond the Pines* (dir. Derek Cianfrance, 2012), and as the driver in *Drive*. Directly beneath these images is a photo of a teenage male (allegedly, the content creator) staring at his notebook computer screen, below the caption, "Wow, this is literally me."[22] The trend has been taken up largely by disaffected teenagers (mostly but not exclusively male) who relate to "male characters who play traditional masculine roles in their respective societies but are eventually alienated from the mundaneness of modern life," and Faris Firoozye cites antecedents in Travis Bickle from *Taxi Driver* (dir. Martin Scorsese, 1976) and Jim Stark from *Rebel Without a Cause* (dir. Nicholas Ray, 1955).[23] Integral to the common identity of these characters is a movement from social alienation to redemption initiated by a radical act of self-sacrifice. The actor's affiliation with "Literally Me" marks a fan focus upon the image (or more literally, the cluster of such images) of the loner star persona as a product of stasis (still, instead of moving, images) and a silence that accommodates the fan's close contemplation of the object of vision, thereby facilitating identification with the star persona.

"Doesn't everyone feel like an outsider?" Gosling asks in a 2008 interview. "I mean, we all do."[24] Although Ken himself may not qualify as a loner, as an already established attribute of an always evolving star persona Ryan Gosling's affiliation with "Literally Me" still informs his role in *Barbie*. In an *El Pais* article entitled "'Literally me': Why do so many straight guys love Ryan Gosling?", the author suggests that "the sad and solitary characters the actor has played" have established an identificatory connection with "a kind of lone wolf archetype that has become popular in recent years."[25] Gosling has played "misunderstood, reclusive protagonists who hide under a shell of hostility—but who, deep inside, are actually empathetic and supportive."[26]

Gosling's loner/outsider "Literally Me" association provides a gateway to his performance in the Real World of *Barbie*, where men have established a level of dominance unimaginable to him and his fellow Kens. Sporting a white cowboy hat and Western fringe shirt with a pink tie around his neck (to match the color of Barbie's outfit), however, Ken's articulated swagger in these scenes registers more as a self-conscious, parodic *performance* of hegemonic masculinity than a celebration of a newfound patriarchy. Despite his drastic transformation of Barbie Land into Kendom, the toxic male fantasy resort where he luxuriates in his "mojo dojo casa house," the abrupt shift from insecure, lovesick puppy-dog to insensitive macho man never registers as ingenuous. As he later reveals to Barbie: "It was hard running stuff. I didn't love it," and he admits to her that he engaged with patriarchy only because he thought it involved horses. As such, Ken reveals his brief embrace of toxic masculinity as an ill-chosen, vengeful response to his frustration at Barbie's insistence on setting the rules of the game. ("You failed me!" he exclaims.)

Feminism and the "Hey Girl" phenomenon

Further evidence of a rejection of toxic masculinity in Gosling's star persona in *Barbie* can be found in popular press reports on the actor's advocacy for gender equality. As with the "Literally Me" meme, Ken's appeal remains a phenomenon of close identification; here, however, the evidence supporting this affiliation with feminism is also extratextual, originating from outside of his film characterizations, and connected to the conditions of his upbringing. Biographer Nick Johnstone notes that Gosling was raised primarily by women, and he quotes from an unidentified article in the *Sunday Times* in which the actor allegedly revealed: "I feel that I think like a girl, just through osmosis, really, living with my mom and sister."[27] An article in *Pink News* quotes the actor as saying: "I think women are better than men . . . They are stronger. More evolved. You can tell especially when you have daughters and you see their early stages, they are just leaps and bounds beyond boys immediately."[28] "I think like a girl," Gosling states in a 2011 interview. "And I just feel like I wouldn't know how to think any other way."[29]

Affiliations with cultural traits more often read as feminine than masculine populate Joanna Benecke's 2013 book *100 Reasons to Love Ryan Gosling*. Some of these "reasons" involve acquired skills that have been coded as feminine (#72: "He likes knitting"), while others document his sex appeal and suitability as husband material, but the bulk of the reasons highlight his generosity, empathy, loyalty, respect, and trustworthiness—qualities not regularly tied to male gender identity. Cuteness plays a role in reason #27, "He loves animals," with text opposite a photo of Gosling walking his dog George, whom he has identified as his "soulmate," and the explanation that he takes George everywhere he goes and carries him through airports: "Ryan and George's bond is one of perfect love and trust, apparently designed to melt the average woman's heart into a warm puddle of pheromones and corn syrup."[30]

Gosling's appeal to women also stems from his hyper-awarenesss of their objectification and the violence that men have inflicted upon them. Reason #28 of Benecke's book, "He doesn't buy into The Game," emphasizes the male toxicity evident in certain of his past onscreen characterizations.[31] Reason #28 pertains to his role as the womanizing Jacob in *Crazy, Stupid, Love*, who teaches his less experienced friend Cal (Steve Carell) that the best way to attract women is first to disorient them with an insult and then to feign total disinterest. "Obviously his Ryness was not a fan of this icky method," Benecke explains. Quoting Gosling, she continues: "I read the book *The Game*. I like to call it 'The Lame.'"[32] Another testament to Gosling's empathy and compassion surfaces in the thirty-minute YouTube video "Ken—How Ryan Gosling Lives and How Much He Earns," which references an incident on the set of *All Good Things* (dir. Andrew Jarecki, 2010) where the script called for Gosling to pull the hair of his co-star Kirsten Dunst. During one take, he ended up pulling harder than he meant to and unintentionally inflicted pain. Acknowledging this action as a mistake in performance, the narrator comments that "it was so unpleasant to him that the next day, he sent flowers to his filming partner as a sign of apology."[33]

Such unsolicited acts of empathy and kindness demonstrate that the actor does much more than pay lip service to feminism and gender equality. He speaks out. As documented in a 2017 *People* magazine article, Gosling voiced his concern about the Motion Picture Association of America's (MPAA) decision to issue *Blue Valentine* (dir. Derek Cianfrance, 2010) an NC-17 rating on the basis of a scene in which Cindy (Michelle Williams) receives oral sex from her husband Dean (Gosling). The actor described the decision as "clearly a product of a patriarchy-dominant society, which tries to control how women are depicted on-screen," noting a double standard at work, whereby it remains fully permissible to represent female characters as victims of sexual abuse, while the MPAA "force[s] us to look away from a scene that shows a woman in a sexual scenario, which is both complicit and complex. It's misogynistic in nature to try and control a woman's sexual presentation of self."[34]

Gosling's advocacy for equitable gender treatment has associated him with memes that authenticate female fans' devotion to him. The most prominent of these is the "Hey Girl" meme that originated in 2008 on the Tumblr site "Fuck Yeah! Ryan Gosling." The common element of the "Hey Girl" postings is a photo of Gosling, often in close-up, and usually with head facing forward, eyes and smile directed toward his audience. The verbal solicitation "Hey Girl" accompanies the photo, with an off-handed comment or observation marking an intimate connection between the subject Gosling and the author of the meme. As with "Literally Me," "Hey Girl" uses a rhetorical strategy that diminishes emotional distance while reinforcing trust in the star. Here, however, the content creator's scripting of the text *as* Ryan Gosling, and then imagining the actor reciting this text back to the author, accentuates an even deeper intimacy between star and fan. Gosling is characteristically modest when confronted with the popularity of the "Hey Girl" phenomenon: in a 2014 episode of *MTV After Hours*, when host Josh Horowitz asks him to read some of the submissions aloud, the actor laughs in embarrassment, exclaiming: "This is so stupid" and "This is so dumb," not as an attempt to ridicule the authors, but as an expression of bewilderment at the close attention that the public pays him, as if he felt unworthy of such acclaim. Predictably, when Horowitz asks him to write a "Hey Girl" entry on the spot, Gosling refuses.[35]

The popularity of "Hey Girl" also attests to an interweaving of identification and desire that is not uncommon in online fan discourse. Danielle Henderson's collection of self-authored "Hey Girl" memes entitled *Feminist Ryan Gosling: Feminist Theory from Your Favorite Sensitive Movie Dude* mitigates her affective investment in the star by clarifying that she produced the collection to give her and her fellow gender studies graduate students a pleasurable way to remember the theories they were studying; unlike many of her friends, Henderson explains that she does not find Gosling sexually attractive, even as she positions the star as an advocate of feminism. Such entries as "Hey Girl. The Equal Rights Amendment hasn't been adopted, but thousands of people are taking to the streets for a FOOTBALL victory?" characterize Gosling as a man who empathizes with women's social and cultural subordination, and who is ready to expose the privileges associated with hegemonic masculinity.[36] On the other hand, the decoding of such entries as "Hey Girl. I know that Luce Irigaray is deeply into some Jacques Lacan-type stuff with regards to our critique of the masculine subject, but I thought she'd go out with me anyway" hedges on a toxic, heteronormative attitude toward women that risks registering as trivializing and arrogant, despite the photo of Gosling looking rejected, accented by two empty shot glasses on the bar in front of him.[37] Such internet memes complicate a star persona identification that thrives upon the actor's attentiveness to the politics of gender difference, by associating the elevation of his persona to feminist status with toxic heteronormativity. The "Hey Girl" phenomenon clearly enables some women to express their desire by identifying with the actor. The ability to imagine scenarios where Gosling is uniquely positioned to address his own fans with the voice of a female-authored text also registers as a sign of intimacy and trust.

As Shelley Cobb asserts, however, the growing cultural appeal of the "male celebrity feminist" (MCF)—a term applied to Gosling and other actors including Mark Ruffalo and Joseph Gordon-Levitt—comprises "a combination of their attractiveness, their decidedly un-macho heterosexuality, and their (often vague) statements about equality for men and women."[38] Cobb also draws critical attention to a "postfeminist logic" by which "men's appropriation of the term ["feminist"] . . . signals feminism's success."[39]

Earring Magic Ryan, or Gay Ken

The "Literally Me" Gosling does not have to *be* a lost loner seeking redemption for lost loner men to identify with him; all that is required is a focus upon film roles that *portray* him as a loner. While the "Hey Girl" Gosling relies more upon publicity about the actor's upbringing and political pronouncements than his prior character portrayals, the actor's connection with homosexuality operates quite differently. First, Gosling has never intimated any sexual attraction to men; indeed, his suggestion of women's superiority does nothing to form a basis for such desire. Second, although Gosling's shirtless body has been eroticized in such films as *Crazy, Stupid, Love* and *The Place Beyond the Pines*, the actor has never portrayed an openly or admittedly gay character.[40]

Yet it would be most inaccurate to suggest that the actor has distanced himself from the "gay community." Though constructed as heterosexual, Gosling's persona bypasses the terrain of toxic male heteronormativity by demonstrating his affective sociopolitical alliance with homosexuals. The popular press frequently mentions his "marriage equality" t-shirt, and gay publications highlight his prior residence in West Hollywood as a formative life experience. A writer for *BGAY* describes Gosling as "a symbol of the evolving narrative of masculinity, acceptance, and the beauty of being truly seen."[41] As the *BGAY* writer explains: "It's a performance that pays homage to the spirit of West Hollywood, a testament to the power of inclusivity, and a celebration of the journey from being a character in the background to one that stands proudly in the spotlight, much like the journey of many in the LGBTQ+ community."[42]

The actor's strongest connection to homosexuality, however, lies neither in the publicity about his upbringing, nor his West Hollywood past, nor any of his past film roles, but instead in his portrayal of a plastic product come-to-life as "Earring Magic Ken," interpreted as "gay" ever since Mattel released the platinum-haired, pastel-adorned doll in 1993. As Dan Savage notes, the doll's popularity among gay men stemmed from its appropriation of rave-oriented fashion trends rooted in late 1980s gay culture, including a single earring, black jeans, lavender vest draped over a transparent mesh shirt revealing a six-packed torso, and a silver chain from which hangs a pendant conspicuously resembling a cock ring.[43] Despite the preteenage girl sporting a Barbie charm and clip-on earring who is featured on the back of the box, the invitation to "Put Barbie and Ken charms on your earrings! Ken looks hip in his earring too!", and a Mattel representative's insistence that the necklace is *only* a necklace, and that "We're not in the business of putting cock rings into the hands of little girls!", the gay association remained strong enough to prompt Mattel to discontinue sales of the doll before the end of the same year that it was introduced.[44]

"Gosling is giving us face AND body, he looks just like a gay sex doll come to life," comments Mey Rude in an out.com article. "(That's what Ken is, right?)"[45] Yet Gosling does *not* portray Earring Magic Ken, a figure who even makes a brief appearance in the film. With his lean, firm, objectified body a product of the physical effort of tissue subtraction, and in the embrace of the pinks and pastels governing both his wardrobe and the film's color scheme, Gosling *revives* the Earring Magic version of Ken, sustaining a link between actor and archival playtime product that has continued to resonate with many gay men. The modesty and naivete with which Gosling inhabits his Ken identity is best illustrated in a segment of the film set in the Real World of patriarchal privilege. After Barbie remarks that men appear to be staring at her, Ken replies that "they're also staring at *me*," his observation immediately verified by a shot of two approaching gay men who are doing precisely *that*, with one of them sporting a pink t-shirt. The fact that Ken has done nothing to actively solicit this stare makes the exchange more resonant.

In Gerwig's *Barbie*, Ken traverses the territory of toxic masculinity and ultimately arrives at a place where he might begin to reflect and individuate. As a doll come to life, however, he finds it difficult to navigate this path on his own. Rather than serving as his own agent of change, things have just tended to *happen* to him. Reflection would involve coming to terms with the roles he has had to play: persistent suitor of someone who does not desire him; fierce competitor for her affection; unrelenting seeker of vengeance for having failed to gain it. Yet his experience of this succession of roles begins to register as transformative only after Barbie suggests that "Maybe all the things you thought were you aren't really you," a prompt to direct his search inward, toward his constitution as a discrete being: "I am Ken."

Figure 10.3 *"They are also staring at Me!" (*Barbie, *dir. Greta Gerwig, 2023).*

But *this* Ken is also Ryan Gosling, whose star persona makes it appear as if he were *meant* to portray Ken, confirming the actor's assertion in the *Variety* article that "in some ways, everything I've done led to it."[46] A modest, empathetic, sincere, and attractive heterosexual male with a record of attentiveness to the politics of gender and sexuality coupled with a critical understanding of patriarchy's insidious workings, Gosling possesses attributes that coalesce in a loner image that reinforces his identity as a man who upholds his own convictions. These attributes conglomerate to reveal Ken's ability to perceive his own descent into toxic masculinity as an aspect of performance rather than a behavior that defines him. Although he has never played a superhero, Ryan Gosling makes Ken emerge as an ideal companion to animate and embrace as an instrument of his audience's creation. Given these circumstances, what doll could be more fun to play with than Ken?

Part Four

The Polemics of *Barbie*

Barbie, *Feminism, and Consumerism: An Incoherent Combination*

GENEVIÈVE SELLIER
TRANSLATED BY ALISTAIR FOX

In an article widely read and cited in France, "Double speak. De l'ambiguïté tendancielle du cinéma hollywoodien,"[1] Noël Burch expands on Robin Wood's reflections on *Taxi Driver* (dir. Martin Scorsese, 1976) as an "incoherent text."[2] In this article, Burch describes the structural ambiguity of Hollywood cinema that results from its desire to appeal to audiences with divergent, if not contradictory, interests, with a view to a film's profitability. This ambiguity, which can verge on incoherence, has only deepened since the 1970s, due to a public that is increasingly and simultaneously polarized along political, gendered, racial, and sociocultural lines, enhanced and exacerbated by identity politics, national and international in scope.

Co-written by the female director Greta Gerwig with her partner Noah Baumbach, director of a number of independent films, among them *Marriage Story* (2019), *Barbie* presents the invention of the Mattel company's doll as a significant moment in the emancipation of girls, freeing them from their role as mothers. Combining narcissism, consumerism, and sisterhood (in a manner typical of post-feminism), the feminine world of Barbie is presented as self-sufficient, and the existence of men, symbolized by the Ken doll, regarded as the perfect accessory. The story of the film is constructed around the confrontation between the Real World (California), still ruled by the patriarchy, and the "ideal" world of the Barbie dolls, Barbie Land.

The ambivalence of the film as illustrated by its reception in France

The reception of *Barbie* in the mainstream and specialist press in France testifies to the ambivalence of the film, and how its ambiguity is inscribed in its screenplay and its *mise en scène*. The majority of critics acknowledge the challenge confronted by the director in her attempt to infuse a film financed by Mattel, the intention of which was to relaunch sales of the doll, with a feminist critique of Barbie. Sandra Onana in *Libération* opined: "Greta Gerwig had the almost impossible mission of dusting off Mattel's cheesy toy, despite a frankly aggressive marketing campaign—a bet that paid off for this charming satire, which did not allow itself to be eaten up by its paradoxes."[3]

Similarly, Étienne Sorin in *Le Figaro* remarked: "The chief strength of capitalism since its birth is to appropriate criticism and turn it into merchandise or entertainment. But that does not take anything away from the talent of the filmmaker, who without question goes beyond the requirements of Mattel (to dust off their doll) by taking the opportunity to settle her accounts with patriarchy in joyful good humor."[4] Cécile Mury in *Télérama* continued in a similar vein: "Greta Gerwig blows up the jaded, stereotyped image of the famous doll in a production that is funny and inventive. And above all super-effective in the placement of Mattel products."[5] Cyprien Caddeo writing in *L'Humanité* reported: "Can a film be both a barely disguised publicity stunt to sell toys and an inspiring feminist comedy? Yes, answers Greta Gerwig's most recent feature-length film, a colorful work that is both sincere and cynical, like a condensed version of this very epoch."[6]

It was, however, feminist critics, typically with academic credentials, writing in publications associated with "auteur" or art cinema, who were the most negative in their judgments of the film, dismissing its post-feminism along with the Mattel franchise. Murielle Jourdet, writing in *Le Monde*, proclaimed:

> Beneath its kitschy mockery, *Barbie* looks like the first assessment of post-Covid Hollywood, bundling several previously scattered trends—auteurism utterly devoured by the hegemony of franchises, permanent irony and postmodernity as narrative dead ends, "reassuring familiarity" as the safe haven of an industry in the throes of a moral crisis. Last, but not least, and undoubtedly the most distressing of all: the defence of a neoliberal, infantilizing feminism that has become the respectable façade of unabashed capitalism.[7]

Charlotte Garson, writing in *Cahiers du cinéma,* was equally condemnatory:

> Called a fascist by the teenager who put away her dolls—or duped by her manufacturers, Barbie sobs, but Robbie struggles to embody this "Coppélia,"[8] to convey the split that the film describes. Probably a problem with the screenplay: the costly and shiny artistic direction crushes any initiative for play … Faced with the total look of the brand, the didacticism of "empowerment" acts as an equally stifling discursive counterweight that prohibits the possibility of any future actions.[9]

Several weeks after the film came out in theaters, however, *Le Monde* published a number of columns by feminist researchers whose opinions were more diverse. In an article published on August 16, 2023, scholars Marjolaine Boutet and Hélène Breda praised the film:

> Never has the female gaze, the way a woman looks at the world through the eye of a camera, been imposed on hundreds of millions of spectators, both male and female, with such force … To consider Barbie as the (pop-) cultural object that she is, is to thwart the traditional dichotomies that tend to pit auteur cinema against mass culture and masculine productions (supposedly more legitimate) against socially devalued feminine cultures. Of course, *Barbie* alone cannot shake the foundations of the whole patriarchal society, and the many censures around the world show that the model is still solid. Nevertheless, the unprecedented success of this film may—we hope!—open the way for a new generation of blockbusters created by and for women.[10]

On August 18, 2023, Azélie Fayolle also defended the film in another article published in *Le Monde*:

> One of the strengths of the film is to reestablish the possibility of a deeper meaning, of which Barbie's tears are the hallmark. It is easier to imagine the end of the world than that of capitalism, and Greta Gerwig is not naive in showing that capitalism (here Mattel) extracts profit even from the criticism that is leveled against it. On and under the yoke of the firm, the director has made a film that is as feminist … as possible … Greta Gerwig shows how to put in place conditions that make new dreams for young girls possible, and which draw Barbies/women together into a single sisterhood, beyond diversity and generations. The mass production of interchangeable beings is thus transformed into feminist sharing and sisterhood.[11]

On the same day, *Le Monde* published a more critical interview with the sociologist Chiara Piazzesi, professor at the University of Quebec, Montreal:

> At the end of the day, according to Barbie and according to a certain rose-tinted feminism, all is well as long as women can do what they want, that they are not imposed with standards, expectations, or injunctions from the outside, and that they do what they do because it pleases them (and because they have chosen it). As Barbie has been saying since 1992: "You can be anything." But this response tends to make invisible the constraints and structural barriers that still exist for those, for example, whose body or appearance is too far removed from the prevailing beauty ideal. The solutions proposed by the film and by post-feminism are individual solutions, not collective ones; they do not seek to transform the way women and women's activities are perceived and negatively judged in the social space … The *Barbie* movie aims to sell Barbie dolls to little girls, and other toys to little boys. This reinforces the separation of gendered spheres in society and satisfies the many parents for whom it is important to see boys and girls each thrive in their own gendered sphere. This maintained segregation between the tastes, toys, and activities of each does not wish to disrupt the patriarchal order, in which a hierarchy of genders reigns that supports neither crossover, mixing, nor confusion.[12]

On August 26, 2023, again in *Le Monde*, Audrey Millet delivered a column denouncing the film:

> To the millions of people who wanted to make peace with their criticized childhood toy, Warner Bros. and Mattel made a promise: "She can do everything. He's just Ken." This is the feminism of Hollywood entertainment, that oppressors are silly and harmless. Above all, the film seems to say, in case of flat feet, invest in a pair of Birkenstocks. If you need to seduce Ken to channel his violence, whip out a Chanel outfit. In Barbie, brands are promoted to the rank of feminist weapons, and actresses—first and foremost Margot Robbie— to the rank of advertising muses … The *Barbie* movie shows how capitalism and white-collar workers swallow up political and social demands. Mattel and Warner Bros. gobble up the woke trend, distribute a second-rate feminist message, and present a vision of patriarchy as sweet as a marshmallow.[13]

This diversity of opinions held by feminist scholars illustrates both the ambivalence of the film and the different tendencies that operate today in the media and in academia—currents that emerged several decades later in France than in Anglophone countries. On the one hand, the materialist movement, the oldest, heir to the work of Christine Delphy and Nicole-Claude Mathieu, insists on capitalism as the "main enemy" of women's emancipation. This assumption is illustrated in France by the work of the essayist Mona Chollet, *Beauté fatale: Les nouveaux visages d'une aliénation féminine* [Fatal Beauty: The New Faces of Feminine Alienation] (published in 2012).[14] On the other hand, post-feminism, a more recent phenomenon, influenced by Anglophone cultural studies, highlights the agency of women, their individual autonomy, in a neo-liberal and consumerist context.[15]

In the light of the film's reception in France (of which I have offered a nonexhaustive review here), *Barbie* attests to the fact that the issue is no longer the denunciation or the defense of feminism, which we know has long remained a bogeyman for film critics and women filmmakers in France, but a debate on the nature of the kind of feminism that the film illustrates. In this sense, an important step has been taken, thanks to #MeToo. The very fact that *Le Monde* is largely echoing a debate that is taking place between feminist researchers is evidence of undeniable progress.

An assumed separation of the sexes

But this should not prevent us from looking a little closer at the story *Barbie* tells and how it tells it. The film offers a series of sequences that often resemble clips, and illustrate, on the one hand, the different feminist and post-feminist trends that have become popular in the Western world, and on the other, a vision of male/female relations that is inscribed in the American literary tradition analyzed by Leslie Fiedler,[16] who affirms the nonmixed nature of the American social world and the exclusion of women:

> Our great novelists, though experts on indignity and assault, on loneliness and terror, tend to avoid treating the passionate encounter of a man and a woman, which we expect at the center of a novel. Indeed, they rather shy away from permitting in their fictions the presence of any full-fledged, mature women, giving us instead monsters of virtue or bitchery, symbols of the rejection or fear of sexuality.

Even if *Barbie* illustrates this attitude in a reversed form, we find in it the same inability to deal with the encounter between a man and a woman.

The most striking feature of *Barbie* is, in fact, the nonmixed nature of these fictional worlds, which is claimed by the Barbies in Barbie Land as a condition of their happiness, where we see them organizing pajama parties from which they exclude the Kens. This nonmixing also characterizes the fictionalized Real World of the film (California), in which Barbie (Margot Robbie), in search of the person who has given her thoughts of death, meets cops who arrest her and students who reject her, before entering the Mattel building whose board of directors is exclusively male and white. Ken (Ryan Gosling), having returned from this Real World where, to his astonishment, he discovered male domination, converts all the other Kens into cowboys for whom horses are more important than women.

It is again in a context of nonmixedness that Gloria (America Ferrera)—the Mattel employee who is the source of Barbie's malfunction, and the mother of the teenager Sasha (Ariana Greenblatt), who is hostile to Barbie—intervenes. When she decides to accompany Barbie back to her world and discovers that the Kens have taken control of Barbie Land, she gives the Barbies a feminist speech on the contradictory injunctions that make life impossible for women. But this speech is in no way anchored in the world of the Barbies who, on the contrary, are convinced that they were perfectly happy so long as they were involved only with themselves. Moreover, we do not understand why Gloria and her daughter, as dark-haired as Barbie is blonde, belong to the Latina community, nor why they take up Barbie's cause after having expressed their hostility or discomfort with the doll. This ethnic inclusivity seems as artificial as Gloria's feminist speech.

While the Barbies do decide, on Gloria's advice, to regain power through trickery, by provoking the Kens' jealousy, what we see, in fact, is a series of all-male sequences accompanied by the melody of the song "I'm Just Ken," initially sung by Ryan Gosling in which the other Kens join in at various moments in the sequences. The Kens then brawl among themselves dressed in bright colors, before transforming into black shirts for an impeccably choreographed ballet performance, a reference to Fred Astaire and his doubles in *Top Hat* (dir. Mark Sandrich, 1935). The meaning of this long sequence is totally inconsistent with the narrative of the film, reinforcing the impression of a series of clips that aims to highlight alternately the performances of Margot Robbie and Ryan Gosling. The fact that Ryan Gosling triumphed at the Oscars by singing the song "I'm Just Ken," surrounded by his tuxedo-clad companions, once again in an impeccable all-male choreography, reveals the film's double discourse. Behind a "feminist" revaluation of the Mattel doll, there is hidden a reaffirmation of the difference between the sexes and the "artistic" superiority of men over women.

Next to this ballet, which occurs at the end of the film like an apotheosis, the choreographed sequences of the Barbies in the first part seem extremely poor: the camera angle is almost always the same, frontal in relation to the dance floor in front of Barbie's house, in a very busy setting, where the Barbies move in a rather disorderly manner, especially since they are all dressed differently. In contrast, the choreography of the Kens in identical black outfits, on an abstract dance floor where they form geometric figures recalling the musicals of Hollywood studio era,[17] evokes order and harmony, the mastery of bodies and rhythms.

In the few sequences where Barbie and Ken are together, it is always a question of enacting the desire of one gender to dominate or exclude the other.

Figure 11.1 *Battle formations: the Kens (Barbie, dir. Greta Gerwig, 2023).*

Even in the sequence showing the journey to the Real World, Ken imposes himself by surprise in Barbie's car, and she refuses to let him join her in the front seat. When they arrive together in California, their perceptions of the Real World are systematically opposed, and Ken soon leaves her to discover with amazement all the manifestations of male domination. Meanwhile, Barbie mentally evokes Sasha, the little girl who caused her dysfunction by abandoning her. She finds her at school where Sasha tries to "destroy" her, at the urging of her friends, with the traditional feminist arguments against the Mattel doll: "You've been making women feel bad about themselves since you were invented … You represent everything wrong with our culture: sexualized capitalism, unrealistic physical ideals … You set the feminist movement back fifty years, you destroy girls' innate sense of worth, and you're killing the planet with your glorification of rampant consumerism …"[18] Sacha ends her diatribe by calling her a "FASCIST"—which seems excessive in the face of poor Barbie in tears, and somewhat invalidates the diatribe. Indeed, the final "reconciliation" sequence at the end of the film presents itself as the resolution of the war between the sexes, showing the autonomy of each side in relation to the other: both will now live on their own terms without being subservient to the other.

A text that is incoherent to the point of cynicism

The fragmentation of the story into a series of sequences without narrative or aesthetic continuity feeds on a veritable referential frenzy, like so many winks to film buffs of all persuasions. Many commentators have had fun identifying these references, from the most obvious—*2001: A Space Odyssey*, (dir. Stanley Kubrick, 1968)—to the less explicit—Fred Astaire, Minelli, Powell and Pressburger, Jacques Demy, Jacques Tati, Monty Python, *The Matrix* (dir. the Wachowskis, 1999*)*, *Clueless* (dir. Amy Heckerling, 1995), *Top Gun* (dir. Tony Scott, 1986), etc. Should we rejoice in the fact that a female filmmaker is playing the same little game for *the happy few* as do her male colleagues Quentin Tarantino, Tim Burton, Wes Anderson? We can question this since this game is gratuitous in relation to the issue that the film attempts to resolve: how to give a feminist inflection to Barbie's world. The program initiated by the prologue—teaching little girls to take care of themselves rather than thinking of themselves as future mothers—also contradicts the epilogue, in which Barbie, having decided to integrate herself into the human world in order to become a woman, a real one, begins her new existence by going to an OB-GYN clinic, as if the essence of being a woman is her reproductive system. The insistence on portraying Barbie's designer, Ruth Handler, as a feminist ahead of her time, concerned above all with emancipating little girls, sweeps under the carpet a much less edifying story of plagiarism, illegal business practices, monstrous profits that the film is there to relaunch (which is what actually happened).[19] We do not understand why, after having found the Mattel building with relief, Barbie flees the management office, in a chase through the offices that seems to exist only to parody *Playtime* (dir. Jacques Tati, 1967), to a kitchen where Ruth Handler serves her tea before helping her escape. The turnaround of the teenager who agrees to follow Barbie and her mother to Barbie Land is also not very credible.

Rarely has a film seemed to me so disjointed in terms of narrative, so incoherent in the construction of the adventures and characters, so contradictory in the execution of its announced message. The ambiguity of the Hollywood women's films of the 1930s and 40s, mentioned by Noël Burch, derives from their description of women's suffering under patriarchy, a predicament, within the film, from which there is no escape—films such as *Stella Dallas* (dir. King Vidor, 1937), *Now Voyager* (dir. Irving Rapper, 1942), and *Gaslight* (dir. Thorhold Dickinson, 1944).[20] Instead, *Barbie* is constructed rather cynically around a desire to rehabilitate a flagship object from a fundamentally misogynistic consumer society, by adorning it with attributes borrowed from contemporary feminist movements, while carefully sparing male sensibilities. If, indeed, an escape from consumerist capitalism is not at issue, the alienation and suffering of women under patriarchy remain implicit in the discourse. Moreover, the film pretends to tick all the boxes of inclusivity—the Barbie President (Issa Rae) is black, the Barbie Diplomat (Nicola Coughlan) has curves, as does the Barbie Lawyer (Sharon Rooney), Ken has an Asian Ken and an African American Ken as sidekicks—without changing white supremacy and the tyranny of beauty one iota.

The Politics of "Always" and "Never":

The Monologue Heard Around the World—Race, Class, and Gender in Barbie

BRUCE ISAACS

Like so many other consumers of pop culture, I saw *Barbie* on its opening weekend in anticipation of what had evolved as a global cultural phenomenon.[1] Over the preceding six months, the film had exceeded its formal containment as "a film," or even a major Hollywood studio film, with the notoriety of the Mattel-Warner Bros. collaboration. During the U.S. summer of 2023, *Barbie* represented a complexly articulated global event: it was a film helmed by a contemporary director of distinction, a product within a global marketplace, a commodity, a style (with a distinctive color palette), a mediated spectacle, a way of thinking, and an identity formation. It was also an urgent feminist representation circulating at great speed, and without regional or national boundaries. And in this critical sense, *Barbie* arrived as a prepacked politics.

The presence of Greta Gerwig to helm a summer tentpole film signaled an artistic and cultural status usually reserved for alternative cinema, where Gerwig had cut her teeth as actor and then writer-director. The Mattel-Warner Bros. engagement of a distinctive, individualist artist (the auteur as branding) signaled prestige, seriousness, and artistic distinction. As a phenomenon, *Barbie* interpolated the spectator into a rich experiential world, calling on endlessly expanding audience demographics to form groups, speak to each other, and share their stories about *Barbie*/Barbie.[2]

Gloria's monologue

Viewed through these multifarious nodes of consumer engagement, on that single viewing (somewhat considered, but without the depth of formal sustained analysis), I confess to finding the film a condescending and vacuous fiction portending some form of concern for the individual, with an incoherent message of urgency for various collectives. I use the term "portend" deliberately because, ironically, in responding to criticism of its politics, filmmakers and commentators alike rose to *Barbie*'s defense by suggesting that the film was an entertainment, and thus should not be construed as a political message; that is, an entertainment in packaged form should not constitute a politics.[3] I take issue with this position on a number of fronts, but not least because the narrative and thematic turning point of the film—Gloria's (America Ferrera) monologue, "It is literally impossible to be a woman"—is expressed transparently as an articulation of a contemporary feminist politics. Ferrera tells us in a set of broad aphorisms about female life and identity:

> You have to be a career woman, but also always be looking out for other people. You have to answer for men's bad behavior, which is insane, but if you point that out, you're accused of complaining. You're supposed to stay pretty for men, but not so pretty that you tempt them too much or that you threaten other women because you're supposed to be a part of the sisterhood.

For Gloria, a woman's life is a political struggle for freedom, self-expression, and autonomy. In describing the female experience, she references labor conditions, domestic relationships, the expectations of the female as a mother, the female as a sexual object/spectacle, and the operation of patriarchy—"But never forget that the system is rigged." In my estimation, Ferrera's monologue explicitly encodes a political reality of oppression and subjugation through patriarchy. Thus, regardless of my interpretation of the film's fiction, that fiction is expressed as a politics of thought and action. And if that is the case, it is the responsibility of the spectator to engage the film not only as an entertainment spectacle, but as a political invocation. *Barbie*, no less than other explicit Hollywood critiques of patriarchy—*The Long Kiss Good Night* (dir. Renny Harlin, 1996), *The Silence of the Lambs* (dir. Jonathan Demme, 1991), and perhaps most notably, *Thelma and Louise* (dir. Ridley Scott, 1991)— asks precisely this of any spectator, regardless of their social, cultural, or gendered disposition.

A retrograde expression of a political project

In this chapter, I attempt to explain why I consider *Barbie*'s politics a retrograde expression of a political project that has at least gained some traction within a patriarchal Hollywood studio system. I see *Barbie* as an affirmation of a patriarchal industrial structure that defines and explains the institutional oppression of a system documented as far back as the first decade of its formation.[4] Of course, I am not suggesting that the studio system operated as an unchanging model of patriarchy across more than a century. Nonetheless, the exhaustive research of Hollywood historians has demonstrated the centrality and resilience of patriarchy to the operation of labor, and the contractual relationships between personnel and institutions that comprised the studio system. But beyond the industrial context of owners and workers that create a $140-million entertainment phenomenon, I argue that *Barbie* presents a strategic reduction of the complexity of contemporary social, cultural, economic, and political gender relationships. In crudest terms, *Barbie* makes lived experience—of gender, race, ethnicities, and categories of selfhood—simple, easy, and imminently packageable for a diversely articulated consumer base. In an era in which Hollywood cinema has interrogated the operation of patriarchy as a historical and social phenomenon, I find *Barbie* to be politically regressive and disingenuous, if not outright deceptive, in its presentation of a politics of political progressivism.[5]

In a contemporary media review I produced for the film, I argued: "You can't bring Mattel as the head of a major commodity corporation, idea, and brand, that has provided a relatively oppressive model of what it means to be a woman—white, middle class, usually subordinated within the patriarchal structure—and connect that to what you're going to try and convince me is progressive feminism."[6] While not explicit within the brevity of the review format, the position I adopted after that initial viewing was that any politics of identity had to engage with what has been described as the intersectionality of political discourse.[7] That is, *what is said* in the film takes form and makes meaning only through the multivalence of the mediated world through which the message is spoken. In my argument, I propose that *Barbie's* feminist hermeneutics operates only within, and in a subordinated relation to, the hermeneutics of internal contradiction identified by Frederic Jameson as the foundational "logic" of late capitalism.[8] *Barbie* is a product par excellence. And yet it is not merely a product, but a product in a highly mobile commodity form, stripped of much of its progressive political potential to counter, or even *critique*, patriarchy.

The inciting incident

Yes, there are moments in which the film gestures toward an authentic political encounter with patriarchy. One such moment occurs in what can be described as the "inciting incident" of the film's political narrative. Stereotypical Barbie's (Margot Robbie) matriarchal utopia—Barbie Land—is ruptured by a single thought:

> It is the best day ever. And so is yesterday and so is tomorrow and so is the day after … Do you guys ever think about dying?

Jacques Lacan might say that, in this stunning moment, the order of the "Barbie" symbolic is broken, and rudely intruded upon, by the order of the real. Gerwig is clearly a highly intellectual writer and seeks to display the philosophical foundations of her thinking.[9] In the simulacral utopia of Barbie Land, the world exists in what Jameson describes as a "perpetual present" of ahistorical, apolitical signs: colors and shapes, catchphrases, etc. of the commodity operation of the Barbie figure within a global, undifferentiated marketplace. In fact, Barbie Land could be read as a kind of virtual marketplace (as product organization and place of exchange) of symbolic identities, fashions, languages and idioms, and other social and economic markers. The Barbies' projection of a "yesterday," "today," and "tomorrow" requires only a single tense: the present. The Barbies inhabit, literally, a perpetually operating present time.

And then, suddenly, the simulacral commodity spell is broken with "Do you guys ever think about dying?," bringing in the subject that grounds Stereotypical Barbie in a history of existential inquiry. Her existentialist musing recalls Camus's elemental confrontation with the absurd, and also Hamlet's "To be or not to be" that frames the question of mortality in the infinitive. But Stereotypical Barbie's question recalls for me most emphatically that glorious moment in *Thelma and Louise*, in which the eponymous heroines, searching for a way out of patriarchy, realize the radicalism of their break from institutional oppression:

> Thelma: *OK, then listen. Let's not get caught.*
> Louise: *What are you talkin' about?*
> Thelma: *Let's keep going!*
> Louise: *What do you mean?*
> Thelma: *Go.*

Like Thelma and Louise, for Stereotypical Barbie, the contemplation of an ending, of a narrative coded through the operation of a patriarchal historicity, grounds Stereotypical Barbie as commodity in a lived, and thus *historicized*, subjectivity. In that moment, she acquires an internal life constituted through personal, subjective, and thus political memory. Almost as an afterthought— and Robbie's delivery is so casual, and so perfectly banal—the commodity is transformed into a thinking, feeling, being. The antinomy of the aesthetic design and the banality of the revelation shocks the spectator from what has thus far been a colorful, playful stupor. That single utterance—"Do you guys ever think about dying?"—is a radically emancipatory gesture, and so emphatically political in the way that feminists such as Judith Butler imagined the radicalism of female subjectivity within patriarchy.[10]

The spectacular commodity

And yet for the most part, and so disappointingly, I saw the subordination of the political to its spectacular commodity expression time and again in the film. Gloria's identification of the institutional and personal coordinates of patriarchy plays out as a set of clichés and stereotypical identity structures. Patriarchy is, metonymically, a building construction site, in which all laborers (who might just as easily have been aligned with the film's overt capitalist critique) are a predatorial "species" of toxic masculinity. I appreciate that Gerwig is working metonymically, using signs of patriarchy to stand in for the operation of patriarchy. But this is slippery territory in my opinion, and my sense is that *Barbie* veers too frequently—and too gleefully—into territory in which the sign not only stands in for the real thing, but in Jean Baudrillard's radical sense of the simulated sign within capitalist media structures effaces the operation, memory, and indeed, the thing-in-itself—of the real.[11]

This displacement of the real for the sign that structures the logic of *Barbie* renders a picture of identity and identity politics (identity is only ever a picture in *Barbie*) that is a simulation of the real rather than an organic expression of selfhood. Identities are understood in binary terms: this *or* that, this *while* that, this *in spite of* that—always *and* never. Experiences of power are set in ideal opposition to experiences of disempowerment. But surely even in the most banal sense of the operation of identity within social life, a progressive politics must acknowledge intersectionality and continuity as the foundational expression of selfhood. "Like, we have to always be extraordinary, but somehow we're always doing it wrong," suggests Gloria. And: "I'm just so tired of watching myself and every single other woman tie herself into knots so that people will like us." The terminological sleight of hand in Gloria's conception of woman undermines the political clout of her position (which I do not doubt at all). The oppression of the woman through the requirement to be "extraordinary" presumes a shared (universal) understanding of the "ordinary" operating outside of time and place, but also problematically outside of class, gender, ethnicity, or sexuality. "Doing it wrong" is correctly intoned by Gloria as a social, patriarchal cliché; Ferrera's delivery is deliberately performative and captures the stupidity and inherent oppressiveness of the sentiment. And yet Gloria herself appropriates the cliché as an ahistorical truth, diminishing its political potential as a critique of contemporary lived female experience. The binaristic formulation of the woman within patriarchy (*only* "this and that" rather than multitudinous) forges an essentialist, unchanging, and dehistoricized "truth."

Corporate capitalism

Barbie's overarching critique of corporate capitalism (also disingenuous if not outright deceptive) is undermined by a comic exchange that works as an emotional stew of 2000s Judd Apatow-era irony and sincerity.[12] Will Ferrell, once the voracious fashion CEO Jacobin Mugato in *Zoolander* (dir. Ben Stiller, 2001), is now redeemed as the CEO of Mattel: "Look, do you know how many times I've wanted to stand up in a board meeting and … and just say, 'can we just tickle each other?'" The image of the exploiting capitalist is whitewashed by revealing a repressed desire to tickle his employees; in the seriousness of the boardroom, where money is made to the detriment of laborers, the act of tickling the employee undermines the profit rationale of the corporation. "Thanks to the Barbies, I, too, can now relieve myself of this heavy existential burden (being a CEO) while holding on to the very real title of CEO." What are we to make of this ironic coding of Mattel as the creator-producer of all Barbies (but especially of Stereotypical Barbie as "the Barbie")? What are we to make of Mattel as a giant corporation who, in collaboration with Warner Bros., produced the film that proposes to function as a critique of that production itinerary?

Most troublingly, the film marginalizes the operation of an intersectional politics of class and racial identity when brought into the space of gendered experience. In the precursor to the famous final line of the film, a fierce politics of subaltern political identity is undermined by a commodity catchphrase that could neatly work as the next piece of Mattel branding. As Barbie prepares to visit a gynecologist for the first time, the film presents the following exchange between Gloria, Gloria's husband, identified in the credits as "El Esposo de Gloria" (The Husband of Gloria), and Sasha (Arianna Greenblatt), Gloria's daughter:

> Gloria's husband: *Sí se puede.*
> Gloria: *That's a political statement.*
> Sasha: *That's appropriation, Dad.*

Sí se puede

Sí se puede ("Yes, you can") is a political invocation to action. *Sí se puede* was for many political groups and grassroots activist communities an identification of a fight against class and racial oppression. Adam Hodges describes the way in which the term has been appropriated as a political call to action. Tracing the phrase from the United Farm Workers (the phrase's accepted point of origin) to César Chávez and Delores Huetra's use of *Sí se puede* to mobilize workers, to Obama's "Yes, you can" refrain to Kamala Harris's "No, you can't" retort to Biden (while Harris was still a senator), Hodges's piece reveals the way in which power is situated within linguistic phrases and their accompanying institutional uses.[13] Gerwig's "appropriation," however, is less a statement of political intent than, merely, a smart and catchy deferment of a signifier that represents appropriation as a depoliticized cultural signifier rather than appropriation as cultural critique.[14] For Sasha, appropriation is a playful linguistic catch cry; it is a contemporary mode of address bereft of historicity, of political intent, and thus feeling. What's at stake for Sasha in claiming "appropriation," as there is clearly something at stake for Gloria in challenging her husband's use of the phrase to which she bears some political lineage? For this reason, Greenblatt's delivery of the line, "That's appropriation, Dad," carries the affect of *disaffectedness.* Indeed, my disappointment with *Barbie*'s imagining of an anti-patriarchal politics stems less from the contours of its fictional narrative (which is relatively straightforward and formulaic) than from the way in which it eschews the value of political agitation for the ease and convenience of binarisms, catchphrases, clichés, and stereotypes. In *Barbie*, patriarchy is self-evident and unchanging, and patriarchy's institutional nuance is unquestioned and thus irrelevant to political progress. In this film that claims to be a feminist fiction, patriarchy can be experienced only as (as Stereotypical Barbie tells us) a "cognitive dissonance"; it isn't lived either by the Barbies of Barbie Land, nor the simulacral women of the Real World.

As I write this, we are two days past the Trump victory in the 2024 U.S. presidential election. Kamala Harris, the first female woman of color to run for the Presidency, has been defeated in terms more damaging to the Democratic Party, left U.S. politics, and female agency than had been anticipated even a day before the election. The Trump victory affirms what has been described as not only a rise in political conservatism, but what several commentators have recognized as the renewed vigor of a patriarchal right the *Independent* newspaper labeled "America's War on Women."[15] The polarization over abortion legislation is again front and center in the right's expression of the power of patriarchy to constrain the freedom of women as autonomous beings: the far right Trump supporter Nick Fuentes tweeted on X November 5, 2024: "Your body, my choice. Forever." This single statement in the media sphere has since received in excess of 100 million views and has been retweeted 35 million times.[16] The function of patriarchy to subjugate and oppress women within the new establishment of U.S. political life can and will only intensify.[17] And yet like so many critics and theorists of patriarchy, I would argue that the illumination of patriarchy, let alone the illumination of a social and political apparatus to dismantle it, requires situating patriarchy within historicized narratives in which people's real lives—and their lived experiences—exist in relation to what Foucault once described as the power dynamics of real institutions.[18] That is, we need our fictions that depict oppression to at least point back to something real—the power dynamics that structure lives—so that they might be dismantled. So that what Gloria calls "the system" is not merely "a system," an abstraction from the real thing, but a schematic, however vague, of how the thing works, and then how it might be broken down. This is why I admire a film like *Thelma and Louise*, which was so groundbreaking as a politics of the rejection of patriarchy within the domestic space, within small-town communities in the American Southwest, and within police and legal institutional shackles. Thelma and Louise *felt* such institutions for their material impact on their lived experience. Conversely, *Barbie* reduces power to an expression of commodity capitalism, emboldened by its refusal to engage in the actual history (past and present) of patriarchy that is surely required to take any steps toward activism and sustained political action.

The generality of political suffering: Can Barbie be an existentialist?

In what way does an identity politics in *Barbie* fail? And what might a progressive politics of identity look like? In his influential work on late modernity, Andreas Reckwitz writes:

> Whereas industrial modernity was based, in so many facets of life, on the reproduction of standards, normality, and uniformity—and one could say that "generality" reigned supreme—late-modern society is oriented toward the production of unique and singular entities and experiences, and it values qualitative differences, individuality, particularity, and the unusual … One could loosely describe late modernity as a society of radicalized individualism.[19]

It seems to me that the notion of a radicalized individualism precisely describes the political terrain of *Barbie*. The politics of radical individualism, however, is for Reckwitz not merely a matter of prioritizing the individual over the collective, but of affirming and then reproducing the social institutions that structure individualist identity. Radical individualism in its social and economic logic describes the "totality" (my term) of individualized experience. Reckwitz calls this *totalizable* discourse of the radical individual the unique "particularity" of late-modern society. Radical individualism for Reckwitz is, among other things, a way of doing the work of the self at a personal level; "particularity" describes a social and personal identity-making process of a society that requires the doing of this work for personal success and social recognition. Particularity is thus both a form of selfhood and a social, cultural, mediated, and commodified identity-formation.

I find Reckwitz's model for thinking about "late-modern" society so perfectly suited to the economic and political logic of *Barbie*. The individualized, subjective, personal (and, at some point in the simulacral past, political) self is reproduced as the radically individuated (particularized) expressive and reactive raw materials of selfhood: a "Barbie." The generality of suffering (the existential estrangement felt not only by Stereotypical Barbie in Barbie Land, but also by Gloria in recognizing the estrangement of her daughter) becomes the particular in so many clichéd, groundless, ahistorical brandings of lived experience; we should also note that the film concludes the Gloria–Sasha relationship arc with the reinstatement of the idyllic mother–daughter relationship. Again, it's an empty nostalgia that refuses to confront the reality of estrangement within, and in relation to, time. The particularity of identity branding reassures the spectator that the experience of "selfhood" is understood, that the trauma of selfhood is mastered, and that suffering is always allayed. This is not a politics of emancipation, or even progress. In Gerwig's utopia, the existential self is particularized and neatly branded as a universal categorical experience. And in this sleight of hand, and in an almost imperceptible shift in rhetorical address, the general (existential) becomes the particular (the female identity figuration). But further, the radical individualism of the particular effaces the generality of an intersectional political experience. *Barbie* populates its world with diverse figures. And yet while these figures represent difference, they do not act through—and thus *enact*—political difference. For its many diverse castings and characterizations, for me *Barbie* is a film bereft of class, color, and ethnicity, and certainly of the nuance of fluid and intersectional political identities.

Conclusion

The film in the most banal sense presents a reinstatement of "Barbie Land" as the utopia that encompasses simulation and real alike. *Barbie* offers the spectator-subject the identity figuration that facilitates the jingoism of "you do you" or "live your best life"; these are states of being and autonomy that can only be articulated (if not attained) in their packaged, commoditized, spectacular form.[20] It is a lifestyle of branded self-actualization.[21] *Barbie's* politics functions as the ironic excess of representation that precludes action, or even a language to enact. But it also muddies a hermeneutics of political progress within individual and collective life. Perhaps what offends most about *Barbie* is the free pass presented to capitalism in its purest form: the Mattel corporation headed by Will Ferrell. Mattel speaks a language of moral purpose and revelation—all multinational corporate CEOs wish to be relieved of the burden of that patriarchal mantle—and yet even the most cursory glance at the strategic identity curation of the Mattel-Warner Bros. collaboration (a capitalist venture that projects a future of larger collaborations as production studios seek out the packageable properties of other corporations)[22] demonstrates the social, cultural, and political impact of a corporate body bereft of political valence and social values.

Political agency, autonomy, and progress requires, first, political *estrangement* within a hegemonic structure. The generality of this estrangement is enacted in Stereotypical Barbie's revelation of the irreducible suffering of existence: "Do you guys ever think about dying?" But this revelation is fleeting, only to be packaged within the marketplace as "Barbie" in the latest Mattel advertisement:

> Kids, it's time to run out and get the new Depression Barbie! She wears sweatpants all day and night. She spent seven hours today on Instagram looking at her estranged best friend's engagement photos while eating a family-sized bag of Starbursts.

I appreciate the intrinsic humor value of such casually comic sentiments— these are familiar refrains in social media and popular culture exchanges on a myriad of platforms. But those mental states are comedic within the film precisely because such sentiments, repackaged as the "Depression Barbie" brand, efface the fundamental estrangement of those lived experiences. I confess to feeling at the very least ambivalent about the ironic excess of these representations of mental health and loneliness. Can we afford to tell stories

Figure 12.1 *"Get the NEW Depression Barbie" (Barbie, dir. Greta Gerwig, 2023).*

that critique the fetishizing of stereotypically beautiful white women with a glib aside sponsored by Mattel-Warner Bros.:

Stereotypical Barbie: *I'm not pretty anymore.*
Gloria: *What? You're so pretty.*
Stereotypical Barbie: *I'm not stereotypical Barbie pretty.*
Narrator: *Note to the filmmakers. Margot Robbie is the wrong person to cast if you want to make this point.*

The gag played very well in the theater in which I saw the film—like so much of Gerwig's ironic textual hijinks, its smart, self-aware, and reflexive. But it's an in-joke with an audience (myself included) compelled in the bravura moment to overlook the reality of what it's saying. The logic of a simulation obfuscates the experience of estrangement. The final betrayal is a natural conclusion in the film: that "ordinariness"—the existentialist—is particularized because it will make money. The production and consumption logic of Barbie and *Barbie* requires that identity be enacted in its radically particularized form—and, indeed, made visible in its commodity form. This is *Barbie's* spectacle of a politics rather than a politics: in "being ordinary," "being no-one"—simply "being" in the Sartrean sense—Stereotypical Barbie achieves an extraordinary, ecstatic, and imminently packageable identity. And of course, the same must therefore apply to Ken to affirm the political harmony of a future Barbie Land:

> Stereotypical Barbie: *You're not your girlfriend. You're not*
>   *your house. You're not your mink.*
> Ken: Ken is ... *me.*

Subjectivity is no less a brand than the mink, or the girlfriend, or "beach." I'm trying to imagine what Sartre might make of this simulacral plenitude.

Barbie, *the Feminist Mattel Ad*

REBECCA STRINGER

"We have to constantly defend ourselves from the poetry of the bards of conditioning—to jam their messages, to turn their rhythms inside out."[1]

ATTILA KOTÁNYI AND RAOUL VANEIGEM

The *Barbie* movie was marketed as a feminist film, and not a mere "Barbie puff piece" to advertise Mattel products.[2] Feminist media commentary on *Barbie*, however, largely described it in reverse terms: a brand loyal Mattel advertisement that is not meaningfully feminist.[3] In this chapter my reading of *Barbie* moves beyond this either/or to explore *Barbie* as an example of the cultural process Roland Barthes termed "inoculation," by which capitalism advances by incorporating the critiques directed against it, discursively remaking itself and depoliticizing the critiques in the process.[4] In medical inoculation we absorb a small dose of a virus, to protect against the more general threat it poses to our health. Barthes argued that in capitalist societies bourgeois institutions ward off threats to the market system in the same way: "One immunizes the contents of the collective imagination by means of a small inoculation of acknowledged evil; one thus protects it against the risk of a generalized subversion."[5] Focusing on the way feminist ideas and the Mattel corporation are co-staged and depicted in *Barbie*, I argue that, instead of representing either feminist critique or corporate interests, *Barbie* stages a merger of these through the recuperative process of inoculation, creating, as Barthes predicts, a "joint-stock company," in which the smaller shares (feminist ideas) "compensate the big ones" (Mattel and the wider market system).[6]

Before embarking on this reading, I lay the groundwork by discussing inoculation and its growing place in popular culture, drawing upon McKenzie Wark's account of the "spectacle of recuperative *détournement*,"[7] and feminist accounts of post-feminist media culture. Tracing inoculation in the recent history of Barbie marketing, I observe that Gerwig's *Barbie* marks a shift away from conventional post-feminism and toward the currently salient feminist iteration Andi Zeisler calls "marketplace feminism."[8] Reading *Barbie* as inoculative means focusing on the moments in *Barbie* that take the story into terrain that is "off-brand" and risky from Mattel's perspective. My discussion focuses on supporting character Sasha's (Ariana Greenblatt) speech to "destroy" Stereotypical Barbie (Margot Robbie), which voices feminist critiques of Barbie and provides the film's only mention of the wider context of climate emergency, at the risk of reminding environmentally conscious consumers of Mattel's off-putting status as a bulk manufacturer of single-use plastics. The exciting prospect of defying corporate interests by venturing into off-brand terrain itself became a lucrative selling point for *Barbie*, belying the film's actual narrowing of the scope for feminist critique of Mattel. In *Barbie* the inoculative process steers feminist dissent toward brand-tolerable existential matters of beauty stereotypes and personal self-esteem, and away from irredeemably off-brand terrain: environmental pollution, climate change, and the conditions for labor in Mattel factories.

Inoculation and the developing spectacle

In *Mythologies*, Barthes identified inoculation as one among a range of rhetorical figures that habitually recur within bourgeois discourse and together produce, in Cheva Sandoval's words, "a rhetoric of being that orders and regulates Western social space and consciousness."[9] As Barthes puts it, with inoculation a "class-bound institution" admits to "accidental evil … the better to conceal its principal evil," namely the scandalous perpetuation of systemic inequality in the form of class hierarchy.[10] Using affirmative action as her example, Sandoval observes that inoculation "provides cautious injections—in modest doses only—of dissimilarity": "by incorporating a small, tidy portion of difference, the good citizen-subject does not have to accept its depth or enormity, and thus s/he can remain as is."[11] Rendering difference and dissent as contained, controllable substances, inoculation immunizes individual consciousness and the "contents of the collective imagination."[12] Writing in the 1950s,[13] Barthes observes that historically bourgeois discourse was uncompromising and "stiff," but is now "much more supple" and "no longer hesitates" to inoculate against subversions as they arise.[14] In our time, accounts of contemporary bourgeois discourse suggest inoculation has only become a more defining feature. It underlies, for example, what Luc Boltanski and Eve Chiapello call the "new spirit of capitalism," referring to the making of a post-Fordist work culture, emblematized by casually dressed "cool capitalists," which disarms the left critique of alienation by incorporating it.[15] Inoculation is similarly dominant in popular culture, as shown in McKenzie Wark's account of our contemporary cultural environs as the spectacle of "recuperative *détournement*."[16]

Wark's account arises from her work on Guy Debord and the Situationist International and I will begin with the key term "*détournement*."[17] Favored by the Situationists and practiced in the 1990s as "culture jamming," *détournement* is a radical cultural practice that unsettles the private property arrangements constitutive of consumer capitalism's popular culture spectacle, doing so through the unauthorized appropriation of commodified cultural artifacts and their recontextualization in ways that contradict their intended meanings, giving voice to critique.[18] For example, in a famous *détournement* to which I will return, in 1993 the Barbie Liberation Organization set out to critique Mattel and Hasbro for deriving profit from marketing sexist gender stereotypes to children.[19] They *détourned* a large quantity of voice-box Barbies and GI Joes by swapping their voice-boxes and returning them for resale. The subsequent media storm about Barbies who bark "Dead men tell no lies" and GI Joes who declare "Math is too hard" comically exposed the constructedness of gender and corporate complicity in normalizing and commodifying sexism.[20] As Johanna Isaacson observes, *détournement* is a significant "feminist tactic," evident, for example, in the feminist punk aesthetics of Riot grrrl.[21]

Unauthorized *détournement* provides a powerful way to voice critique within the spectacle, and as such it is vulnerable to inoculation, or as Wark terms it, "recuperation."

Updating Debord's account of consumer capitalism as the "society of the spectacle,"[22] Wark explains that we are in the spectacle's later phase, that of recuperative *détournement*, where the spectacle has become "nothing but the recuperation of *détournement*," the scene of *détournement détourned*.[23] Corporate advertising and branding operates as a kind of cultural piracy in which radical political ideas and alternative, bohemian countercultures are routinely co-opted and *détourned*, creating cultural environs where it becomes unremarkable to repurpose protest songs to sell sneakers, or to hijack Martin Luther King's "I have a dream" speech to sell cellphones.[24] In corporate hands *détournement* becomes a means of securing rather than unsettling the dominant economic order, by appearing to be subversive—by absorbing and domesticating the appearance of being subversive. Through their looting of radical ideas, inoculative and recuperative cultural processes spell difficulty for radical praxis. As Nancy Fraser describes in her discussion of capitalism's "new spirit," with their discourses hijacked by their intended targets, social movements such as feminism are "increasingly confronted" with "strange shadowy" versions of themselves, "uncanny doubles" in media and political life that they "can neither simply embrace nor wholly disavow."[25] Even still, Wark's account suggests the spectacle of recuperative *détournement* remains always vulnerable to the power of unauthorized *détournement* to disturb private property and open on to a cultural commons—a place of collective belonging that "restores collective social 'authority' to meaning-making" and reimagines "the space of knowledge outside of private property."[26] She also points out that the generalization of unauthorized *détournement* in online sharing and popular practices of copying and remixing can unfold in different ways—as a weapon of mass distraction, or a lever of mass disruption: "Every kid with a BitTorrent client is an unconscious Situationist in the making."[27]

That inoculative and recuperative processes are pervasive in the contemporary spectacle is supported in the feminist critique of post-feminist media culture, where instead of being silenced or ignored, feminist dissent is subject to inoculation, or as Wark puts it, is recuperatively *détourned*.[28] In their classic essay "Survivor Discourse: Transgression or Recuperation?", Linda Alcoff and Laura Gray mark the early 1990s as a turning point in the mainstream reception of feminist dissent: "the dominant discourse has shifted its emphasis from strategies of silencing to the development of strategies of recuperation," demonstrating the capacity of dominant discourse, as per Barthes's "suppleness," to accommodate feminist dissent "while not significantly changing the underlying systems of dominance."[29] Post-feminist media texts ambivalently both "espouse and renege on feminist ideals," affirming feminism while marking it as no longer needed, and disappearing structural oppressions by recalibrating feminism around the neo-liberal values of personal responsibility, meritocracy, and individualism.[30] In recent years the spectacle's feminist inoculations have upscaled, moving away from post-feminist ambivalence and toward the embrace of feminism as "cool" by pop stars, celebrities, and aspiring social media influencers. Variously termed "marketplace feminism," "popular feminism," and "conspicuous feminism,"[31] this "glossy, feel-good feminism" is "probably feminism's most popular iteration ever."[32] Ill-equipped to meaningfully progress the feminist dismantlement of intersecting structural oppressions, it turns feminism into a selling point, trading on its increasing market value especially after the #MeToo movement,[33] in cultural productions that carry on the post-feminist reorganization of feminism around neo-liberal values, recalibrating feminist visions of collective movement for social change as lucrative brand slogans and market-friendly edicts of empowerment through self-improvement.

This outline of inoculation and its growing cultural presence in the developing spectacle maps directly onto Mattel's evolving strategies of Barbie marketing. Launched in 1959 by American entrepreneur Ruth Handler, Barbie dolls were born of the postwar consumerist spectacle Debord described, replacing the baby doll with a camera-ready teen fashion model who became one of the first children's toys to be advertised on television.[34] In later decades as feminist critiques arose and Barbie became "synonymous with all that is wrong with Western society's body-conscious culture,"[35] it became necessary to inoculate Barbie against feminist critique, as Mattel faced not only the Barbie Liberation Organization but also legal challenge for purveying socially harmful gender stereotypes.[36] Consistent with the spectacle's later phase,

Mattel's response was inoculative: the production of recuperative *détournements* that appropriate and recalibrate feminist themes, transforming the feminist critique from off-brand challenge to on-brand asset. Mattel's turn to movie-format televisual marketing gave rise to a "Barbie genre" characterized not only by its "allegiance to brand Barbie" but also its "post-feminist sensibility."[37] First aired in 1987, the earliest Barbie movies were soon classed as program-length commercials and banned from U.S. broadcast television, steering Mattel toward the growing and less tightly regulated home video market and the production of a fleet of typically post-feminist straight-to-DVD animated Barbie movies that follow the inoculative process, incorporating reference to "recent feminist discourse and gender politics" only to shut down "structural analysis of sexism, patriarchy, and male privilege."[38]

Gerwig's *Barbie* is the "proof of concept" for the next stage of Barbie marketing—that of leveraging company intellectual property to create a "cinematic universe based on Mattel toys" akin to the Marvel universe.[39] Marking a break from the Barbie genre's post-feminist ambivalence, *Barbie* reflects the current shift to marketplace feminism, its opening sequence conspicuously turning post-feminism's essential idea—that feminism is no longer needed because "all problems of feminism and equal rights have been solved"—into a satirical joke. As marketplace feminism, *Barbie* demonstrates how profitable embracing feminism can be. As my reading will show, *Barbie's* embrace of feminism is inoculative, and the job of inoculating Barbie has become a complex affair.

A feminist Barbie story

It is fitting that the release of *Barbie* coincided with the thirtieth anniversary of the Barbie Liberation Organization's unauthorized *détournement* of Mattel, for *Barbie* was marketed as a daring break with brand loyalty—a feminist Barbie movie instead of a Mattel advertisement, rippling with the possibilities of unauthorized feminist *détournement*. The media surrounding *Barbie* built hype by couching the film as a rumored feminist hijack of the Barbie story. It was anticipated that Gerwig would produce an "idiosyncratic, subversive, even feminist take on the doll, not just a commercial for Mattel,"[40] and that she indeed had was supported by an apparent scoop, repeated from *Time* in the *Hollywood Reporter*,[41] *Variety*,[42] the *New York Times*,[43] and beyond, providing "proof that the upcoming Barbie movie isn't just a sanitized love letter to the famous doll."[44] The scoop reported that the films' feminist content had caused conflict and lasting tension between the creatives and the corporation, with Mattel leadership flying from the United States to the scene of *Barbie*'s production in London to confront Gerwig and Robbie about concerning narrative detours into off-brand terrain, particularly the scene where supporting character Sasha "destroys" Stereotypical Barbie in her climactic speech voicing feminist and environmental critique of Barbie and Mattel.

Noticeably forecasting *Barbie*'s fictional Mattel leadership's journey to Barbie Land in an effort to rebox Stereotypical Barbie, the scoop framed Robbie and Gerwig as bravely culture jamming Mattel in a fight to publicly air feminist truths. Their reported response to Mattel's reprimand, however, clearly describes steering Mattel toward the inoculation of acknowledged evil. Robbie explained she and Gerwig had told Mattel: "we are going to honor the legacy of your brand, but if we don't acknowledge certain things—if we don't say it, someone else is going to say it … So you might as well be a part of that conversation."[45] *Barbie* will "say it"—give voice to critiques of Mattel that threaten to "destroy" its most iconic commodity by drawing attention to its social and environmental costs—not to make good on those critiques, but to repurpose them as acknowledged evil, shifting Mattel from being the derogated target of critique, into an immunized position as "part of the conversation," as per Barthes's "joint-stock company." In *Barbie*, the job of "saying it"—of voicing critique and thereby supplying the dose of difference needed for inoculation— is delegated primarily to Sasha, the discontented teenage daughter of Mattel employee Gloria (America Ferrera). In what follows I read Sasha's speech as an inoculation of acknowledged evil, then explore the "principal evil" it conceals— for Barthes, the reproduction of class hierarchy. In this light I examine *Barbie*'s depiction of Mattel employees in the Real World.

The journey Stereotypical Barbie takes in *Barbie* is initially sparked by Sasha's middle-aged mother Gloria, who works as the assistant to Mattel's CEO. Gloria's quiet midlife crisis, expressed in the drawings of *détourned* Barbies she produces alone at her desk at work, has consequences in Barbie Land after Gloria takes possession of Sasha's Barbie doll, having interceded on Sasha's plan to send the doll to goodwill. With depressed Gloria in command of Sasha's Barbie in the Real World, Stereotypical Barbie awakens in Barbie Land with flat feet, cellulite, and thoughts of death, triggering her journey to the Real World to find and cheer up the depressed person whose troubles are destroying her looks and peace of mind, as had happened to Weird Barbie. Assuming that person is a child, when she arrives in the Real World, Stereotypical Barbie mistakenly seeks Sasha rather than Gloria, finding Sasha and her friends gathered in their school cafeteria. The cafeteria scene contains the "off-brand" content that supposedly drew Mattel's ire. It begins with a student warning Barbie against talking to Sasha, signaling from the outset that Sasha is a threatening figure. As per her inoculative role, Sasha represents the virus—the embodiment of commercial threat to Mattel, and the only humorless character in this comedy. Ignoring the warning, Barbie introduces herself to Gothic black-wearing Sasha and friends, thinking she is their "favorite toy" and expecting instant adoration. Arranged like a mean consumer focus group in cynical times, unhappy customers Sasha and friends give their reactions to Barbie, with three including Sasha expressing hatred, and the fourth soon regretting confessing to loving Barbie. Sasha's friends encourage her to "destroy" Barbie by telling her how much she is hated and why.

Figure 13.1 *At her desk Gloria draws "irrepressible thoughts of death Barbie"; "all-body cellulite Barbie"; and "crippling shame Barbie"* (Barbie, *dir. Greta Gerwig, 2023*).

Figure 13.2 *Stereotypical Barbie receives a frosty reception from Sasha and friends* (Barbie, *dir. Greta Gerwig, 2023).*

Sasha's speech takes place early in the film and performs a double inoculation, against feminism, and against calls for climate justice. The speech would be a monologue like the celebrated speech her mother Gloria delivers later in the film, except for continual interruption by Barbie, marked below with ellipses. Throughout her speech, a series of beats follow her statements, marking each blow her words land on Barbie, underlining the threat her words pose to Barbie's and the brand's continued viability. But Sasha is a figure of inoculation, and her speech is acknowledged evil that wins immunity. As we would expect of recuperative *détournement*, the speech pirates actual feminist and environmental critiques that have been made of Barbie and Mattel, assuming control of how these critiques are articulated and contextualized:

> You've been making women feel bad about themselves since you were invented … You represent everything that's wrong with our culture. Sexualized capitalism, unrealistic physical ideals … you set the feminist movement back fifty years, you destroy girls' innate sense of worth, and you're killing the planet with your glorification of rampant consumerism …

Sasha's speech voices two critiques: a long-established *détourned* feminist critique that mentions "capitalism" but locates "the problem" with Barbie's impact on personal self-esteem, and secondly, a barely articulated environmental critique concerning Barbie's impact on the planet. In the remainder of the film the readily psychologized self-esteem critique diversely blooms as existential themes of self-making dominate this coming-of-age story. Meanwhile, the criticism that Mattel is "killing the planet" disappears as quickly as it is voiced. That feminism and environmentalism combine in Sasha's inoculative dose reflects the green turn in feminist politics. Mattel's tolerance to feminist critique has built up over decades of inoculative Barbie marketing, and *Barbie*'s updated inoculation controls for the green turn, furthering Mattel's inoculation to encompass the more recently emergent environmental critique.

Sasha's vague claim that Mattel is "killing the planet" refers to the company's status as a manufacturer of plastic goods and part of the "petrochemical empire" that arose in the 1950s with "the birth of a world composed of plastics and other synthetic products derived from petroleum."[46] Petrochemicals are now recognized as significant contributors to environmental pollution via air, water, and soil contamination, and to climate change via carbon emissions. Asked how she "got away" with including Sasha's speech in the film, Gerwig stressed the importance of giving "real estate" to "well-articulated, correct arguments from a really smart character given to Barbie against Barbie."[47] Not mentioned, however, is the correction of Sasha that takes place across the film. Reflecting her inoculative role, Sasha's story arc models "recovery." Steadily disabused of her critical position, she shifts from critiquing Barbie to joining Gloria in her rescue, and at the same time that the Barbies gain feminist consciousness at Gloria's behest, Sasha loses the feminist consciousness she began with, as we see her not only loving brand Barbie and wearing a complementary shade of lavender, but enthusiastically exclaiming: "Hell yes white savior Barbie!"—a designation Barbie immediately corrects. In *Barbie*, Ken (Ryan Gosling) destroys Barbie Land and drives Barbie to rock bottom, but it is Sasha who stands corrected, her inoculative role staging a political conversion from off-brand critic to on-side consumer. As inoculation, Sasha *does not* "destroy" Barbie, instead doing the opposite—welcoming her into her family and co-fostering her bright future at the film's conclusion.

As observed earlier, the process of inoculation Barthes describes enables an institution to survive critiques weighed against it, creating a spectacle of admitted evil that conceals the principal evil, namely the market system and its reproduction of class-stratified society. Having framed Sasha's speech as the key admitted evil in *Barbie*, before concluding I will consider the principal evil *Barbie* conceals, revealing further dimensions of the film's inoculative process. In *Barbie*, fictionalized Mattel staff feature for the first time in a Barbie movie, with corporate executives and their subservient underlings, Gloria and the ghost of Ruth Handler, and warehouse workers dispatching Ken's Mojo Dojo Casa House, all populating the film's depiction of Mattel in the Real World. In this depiction the corporate executives are singled out as bumbling sexist clowns, intertextually styled as Men in Black, who absurdly equate "female agency" with "sparkle." The resulting comedy presents another inoculation of admitted evil. As in Sasha's speech, the comedy surrounding *Barbie*'s sexist executives is pirated from actual feminist critique. For example, at the corporate headquarters when Barbie's earnest request to meet the "woman in charge" gains a comically defensive response from the man in charge (Will Ferrell), his words speak back to feminist critiques of the glass ceiling: "Listen, I know exactly where you're going with this and I have to say I really resent it … we had a woman CEO in the nineties and there was another one at [looking uncertain] some other time—so that's two right there!" Here, Mattel's admitted evil is vertical segregation by gender in corporate life, or the capture of the upper corporate echelon by sexist men. Meanwhile, the principal evil that remains concealed is the condition of labor in Mattel's lowest echelon.

Conspicuously absent from *Barbie*'s depiction of Mattel in the Real World are the working-class women who labor to produce Barbies and other products for Mattel in factories in China, Indonesia, Malaysia, Mexico, and Thailand.[48] In *Barbie*, Real World Mattel is visualized as the corporate headquarters or stock warehouse, not the factory floor, though the latter hosts the bulk of Mattel's employed workforce. Mattel is a multinational that maximizes profit by moving production offshore and thereby cutting labor costs. Just as Mattel's commodities have drawn critique, so too have its offshore labor practices. The late activist Marie-Claude Hessler systematically pursued Mattel and other toy manufacturers over the gap between their stated manufacturing principles and the actual conditions in their factories. Following Hessler's example, China Labor Watch recently investigated the circumstances in which Barbies are made in Mattel factories in China. On the factory floor, Mattel workers experience low wages, unsustainable workloads, harassment from line managers, an obligation to work overtime, and work with hazardous materials, such as glues and solvents, without adequate safety protocols, all in violation of local labor laws.[49] Mattel's factory workforce is primarily made up of working-class women, who report experiencing "an overall culture of sexual harassment" with inadequate reporting, the "absence of workplace accommodations for reproductive health needs," and "under-representation of women in leadership."[50] Barbies are made in the very conditions of sexist oppression the fictional Barbies triumphantly overcome in *Barbie*. While feminist and environmental critiques present off-brand terrain that can be managed into the inoculative process, the conditions of work of Barbie's direct producers mark out the off-brand terrain *Barbie* feared to tread, or in Barthes's terms, the principal evil its inoculations concealed.

Conclusion

As my discussion has sought to demonstrate, Barthes's concept of inoculation provides a useful lens for understanding what feminist ideas are "doing" in *Barbie*. Rather than being either politically sincere or mere window-dressing, feminist ideas arrive in this kind of text via hijack (removal from their social movement context) and are given a serious role to play in granting immunity to the power structures their social movement hopes to dismantle. The cultural pervasiveness of inoculative and recuperative processes in the spectacle of recuperative *détournement* poses a significant discursive challenge; however, as Alcoff and Gray observe, the dangers of recuperation are "not inevitable": "The nature of the discursive landscape involves enough indeterminacy and instability to resist absolute predictability or mono-dimensional effects."[51] The tactic of unauthorized *détournement* works with and deploys the indeterminacy of discourse, and I conclude my discussion of *Barbie*'s feminist inoculation with the example of an unauthorized *détournement* that publicly dismantled it.

Moving on from their earlier critique of sexist gender stereotypes in Mattel marketing, the Barbie Liberation Organization reformed in 2023 to culture jam the *Barbie* movie and underline the scandal of continuing to manufacture single-use plastics in the context of climate emergency. Fully elaborating the environmental critique that remains nascent in Sasha's inoculative speech, they disseminated a *détourned* Mattel advertisement for compostable mushroom-based Eco Warrior Barbies modeled on climate activists Greta Thunberg, Daryl Hannah, Julia Butterfly Hill, Phoebe Plummer, and Nemonte Nenquimo, and announced Mattel's intention to desist in plastics manufacturing and support a federal ban on single-use plastics.[52] Mattel's green turn was subsequently announced as real news in mainstream media outlets, and was then retracted, giving rise to further reports.[53] The action and subsequent media coverage accorded much-needed visibility to the climate activists Mattel is clearly competing with for young people's attention. It also powerfully undid Sasha's inoculation, forcing Mattel into involuntarily admitted evil. Mattel had no choice but to publicly confirm that the action was a hoax, thus owning up to the reputationally risky "planet killer" profile *Barbie* had so artfully managed.

Figure 13.3 *Eco Warrior Barbies. "Meet MyCelia™ EcoWarrior Barbie!", August 2, 2023, YouTube video, 1:02, https://www.youtube.com/watch?v=YBDvE21TeQc.*

Plastic, Kitsch: Ecologies of Barbie Land

SEÁN CUBITT

Barbie's much-commented opening sequence parodies the sequence in *2001: A Space Odyssey* (dir. Stanley Kubrick, 1968) when anthropoid apes first learn the use of tools by smashing skulls with a long bone. A monolithic Barbie inspires girls to smash their doll babies in an act intended to depict liberation from their toy ironing boards, cookers, and childcare, but it cannot entirely shed the violence Kubrick, perhaps cynically, associated with the fictionalized but, nonetheless, historical event of becoming human. It's hard to tell, and perhaps marginal, whether the breaking dolls and shattered teacups are made of plastic (perhaps an older, more frangible plastic) or ceramic. As the film transitions from the desert wilderness setting of this pre-credit sequence into the titles, it is very clear that whatever the evolutionary leap brought about by the Barbie apotheosis, it does not involve evolution beyond plastic. On the upside, the parody deflates Kubrick's grandiose vision, with the crescendo of the opening notes of Richard Strauss's *Also sprach Zarathustra* now matched to the giant Barbie in a swimsuit, winking over her ornamental, white-rimmed sunglasses. But a moment earlier, before we see the full body, one of the little girls tentatively touches her legs, which are manifestly plastic.

Plastic as material is clearly germane to the Mattel toy, but also to the look of Greta Gerwig's film, especially the work of production designer Sarah Greenwood and set decorator Katie Spencer. This chapter opens with the ugly

Figure 14.1 *A monolithic Barbie inspires girls to smash their doll babies in the film's pre-credit sequence (*Barbie*, dir. Greta Gerwig, 2023).*

side of plastic, tracking its involvement with many aspects of the film including cameras and postproduction, distribution, and product placement. Much of the film's iconography speaks from and to its origins in the petrochemical industry, sometimes obviously, as in the (imaginary) power driving the motorboat, rocket, and automobile shown in the road trip. There are also aesthetic properties to investigate, including the extensive use of physical effects where another film of comparable budget might have opted for digital—now more than ever a toolset with dramatic environmental consequences.[1] Unfortunately, even physical sets have carbon footprints.

Even uglier than the disavowed fossil fuels lurking beneath the film's plastic sheen, the film carries traces of "plastic" as a term of anti-women abuse. From the demeaning use of "doll" to describe stereotypically pretty women to the pressure to undergo plastic surgery, which is then open to mockery by men,[2] "plastic" as a term of abuse voices an implicit demand that women be natural, a state already brought into question in the opening sequence's rejection of maternity and domesticity as the natural fate of growing girls. As artifice, as artificial, "plastic" becomes an aggressive insult aimed at any attempt to remodel femininity, from hair care to makeup, foundation garments to fitness regimes. Though its name comes from molding figures and features, the phrase "plastic surgery" has become the target of tirades against dishonest, dissembling, and, most of all, unnatural body modifications.

The later phase of this chapter poses an alternative to plastic as a term of abuse. Recognizing the patriarchal source of demand for body modification communicated in part through popularization of impossible body form in Barbie dolls, it is also important to debate the validity of the impulse that drives people to remodel their bodies. It agrees that the plastic aesthetic is a mode of kitsch, but only as a preliminary move in an enquiry into the excessive, sentimental, and melodramatic aspects of kitsch, and how anxieties over nature and artifice lurking in the abusive use of "plastic" are not only strongly gendered but reveal satirical strategies emerging in Gerwig's film on the further side of postmodern pastiche, a return of irony after the "blank parody," in the form of an amused reverence for the early 1960s era of the doll's first mass popularity.[3]

Plastic, petrochemicals, and consumerism

About 430 million metric tons of plastic are produced a year. There are few signs that this rate of production will slow: production is set to reach 589 million metric tons a year in 2050.[4] The word "plastic," or more properly its plural "plastics," refers to polymers prized for the ease with which they can be molded into a variety of shapes and for their transparency, waterproofing, and low heat and electrical conductivity. The most common are polyethylene terephthalate (PET) and polyvinyl chloride (PVC) and trademarked types like Styrofoam and Perspex. *Encyclopedia Britannica* lists forty major types, each with their own production demands and uses. Though the industry started with naturally occurring animal- and vegetable-based resins like shellac and rosin, almost all contemporary plastics are synthesized from fossil fuels. The fundamental raw material in the polymer industry is petroleum: about 5 percent of global oil production went into the plastics business three decades ago,[5] but the 1995 number was already shaky: was that how much ended up in plastics, or did it include the amount wasted during production? Two decades later in 2015, when estimated annual production had risen from 150 to 400 metric tons, the U.S. Energy Information Administration (EIA) estimated about 2.7 percent of U.S. petroleum consumption went into plastics: 190

million barrels as feedstock (the semi-refined compounds used as the base for plastic production) and another million for power; while an additional 412 billion cubic feet of natural gas, or 1.7 percent of national production, provided power and a small amount of extra feedstock to the business. By 2023, the EIA was resisting giving figures for hydrocarbon gas liquids, key feedstock for propylene and other plastics, citing industry flexibility in what products they use and when (backed up in reports on naphtha and "other oils" from the same year that show enormous monthly fluctuations).[6] Fossil oils and gases are almost universal in the manufacture of plastics and plastic dyes. Yet no sign of the oil industry darkens the crystal skies and astroturf lawns of Barbie Land.

The two major petrochemicals in plastic polymer production are propylene and ethylene. Both are sourced from propane, a by-product of natural gas and petroleum refining, chemically "cracked" at temperatures around 850 degrees Celsius, a process which yields between 15 and 25 percent of the desired compounds. By-products include greenhouse gases methane and carbon dioxide. For polymer production, the ethylene and propylene have to be purified again, typically by distillation, leaving behind a mass of unused by-product. These purified "raw" materials are heated again with catalysts to create long-chain molecules (polymerization), and plasticizers, coloring agents, and stabilizers added before molding which, using any one of a number of techniques, requires the polymers be heated one more time, cooled, and excess removed. If the final product is thermoplastic, the excess can be sent back into production and molded again; if on the other hand, it is thermoset, the trimmings cannot be used. The amount of waste per batch may be small, but in a global market in excess of 400 million tons a year, the wastage of heat, finished material, and greenhouse gases is huge. Nothing in the panoramic vistas of Barbie Land suggests manufacture, nothing, that is, but the end-products. No dust or scratches mar the gleam of fresh new plastic molded into playhouses, fantasy airports, fairground rides, and randomly collected icons of U.S. cities: Las Vegas flamingos, New York's Statue of Liberty, Washington's Pink House, and what appears, in the mid-distance, to be a plastic 3D sign for Dunkin' Donuts. Like Barbie herself, the entire landscape seems the product of virgin birth.

Or indeed like at least one founding myth of the United States: that the land was "virgin" when the first Europeans arrived, and in the language of the eighteenth century, the settlers "improved" the nature they found.[7] The admirable multicultural gestures of the film's casting, grounded in Mattel's long-term policy of matching dolls to target demographics, do not extend to the fate of First Nations, only their assimilation—in the form of American Indian Barbie, for example—into the consumer fantasy of Barbie Land.[8] That fantasy includes the implication that, beyond being susceptible to the wishes of the dolls, everything in Barbie Land is inert—an unchanging perfect world whose denizens and very material are incapable of chemical or biological reactions. This is perhaps the most advanced aspect of the fantasy, or the most fantastical. The utopian playground of Barbie Land ignores not only the environmental "externalities" of extraction and waste but the new conditions of consumption in advanced economies: the real subsumption of consuming, which once was the final moment of the commodity-money-commodity cycle. Now, every act of consumption is also productive, generating information about payments, choices, places, times, and behaviors that retail back along the circuit to inform future production and marketing,[9] of the kind so much on display in the film. A beneficiary of the multimillion-dollar product placement industry that has grown up in the era of ad-blockers, skippable ads, and mute buttons, Barbie caused at least one viewer to roll her eyes "at the starring role played by a spotless Chevrolet 4x4, and [to laugh] aloud at the way the camera focused on Barbie's (empowering!) heart-shaped Chanel bag."[10] Ryan Gosling, as Ken, wears three TAG Heuer watches at once at one point, to the extent that TAG Heuer's CEO has claimed that customers are nicknaming one of its models the "Barbie watch."[11] Auto Trader reported a 120-percent increase in interest for Chevy Corvettes after the Barbie trailer dropped. The virginity of Barbie Land extends far beyond the gag at the end of the film when Barbie, with a sparkling smile, announces: "I'm here to see my gynecologist": its ambition is to absolve the entire dreamworld of original sin.

It is easy enough to accuse the film business and the media industries more generally of complicity in painting over the ugly realities of production and exploitation. It is perhaps less apparent that all industries, especially petrochemicals, participate in gulling their consumers into believing that their goods sprang whole, as the myth of intellectual property would have it, from the forehead of Minerva:[12] *Vorsprung durch Technik* ("progress through technology") as the long-running tagline for Audi automobiles has it, displacing biological evolution and factories with a mythos of work-free and dirt-free expertise. The plastic daisy chain Barbie wears around her neck references neither flowers nor the industry that produced the flowers, nor even the plastic they are made of, but childhood innocence, while at the same time celebrating both consumerism and suburban norms. In addition, as Anirban Gupta-Nigam puts it: "Plastic flowers played their part in articulating fictions of stability that lent permanence to a heterosexual, suburban order, the reproduction of which was critical for sustaining another fiction—that of an American way of life."[13] Margot Robbie's wide-eyed, blue-eyed portrayal of Barbie places her in the childishness of the dumb blonde stereotype,[14] a type whose naivety was always childlike, and yet sexualized and, ultimately, domesticated, like Jayne Mansfield in *The Girl Can't Help It* (dir. Frank Tashlin, 1956), in line with the American Dream. Gerwig's film sets up these tropes in order to subvert them and, yet, cannot entirely escape the powers of capital's account of its consumer products as infantile, innocent, and impenetrably superficial, wholly abstracted from their genocidal and patriarchal grounds.

Figure 14.2 *Barbie in her daisy chain necklace referencing a childhood innocence that celebrates consumerism and suburban norms (Barbie, dir. Greta Gerwig, 2023).*

Ken's admission that he doesn't know what he would like to do on a sleepover with Barbie is the perfection of fantasy as veneer.

Ken in Barbie Land

Barbie Land is also a place without work, true of many Hollywood films, though less so of television shows, many of which boast workplace settings, including kitchens, noticeably lacking or merely painted in *Barbie*. Although the film features Barbies as doctor, physicist, diplomat, judge, writer, lawyer, and journalist (as well as Dua Lipa's turn as mermaid Barbie), these professions are only roles played out and played with: fantasy role-plays. Even the presidential Pink House ("Seriously, no comment") is not a workplace like the fictional television White Houses of Jed Bartlett in *The West Wing* (NBC, 1999–2006), Mackenzie Allen in *Commander in Chief* (NBC, 2005–6), or the Underwoods in the U.S. version of *House of Cards* (Netflix, 2013–18). Likewise, as we learn when Ken and Barbie steal new clothes in the Real World, Barbie Land is a cashless economy, where goods are disposable yet sustainable, in a presumably circular economy (of the kind espoused in UNEP's 2023 report on plastic waste).[15] It is an economy without growth, without accumulation, displacing the modernist myth of progress, that foundational narratological driver of colonialism (as well as of capital). In this, it matches Patrick Wolfe's belief that "invasion is a structure, not an event," in the sense that history and narrative are no longer needed or possible after the catastrophe of colonization.[16] From a more utopian perspective, E. P. Thompson noted in his discussion of the then-likely transition from industrial time-discipline to an automated future that "men might have to re-learn some of the arts of living lost in the industrial revolution: how to fill the interstices of their days with enriched, more leisurely, personal, and social relations."[17] *Barbie*'s answer is not to adventure into creativity, science, and intellect. Instead, it celebrates the reduction of the child's play into manipulating miniature adults, a diminution of play that then provides a model for adults' childish toying with commodities rather than animating whatever comes to hand—transforming adult play from an endless duration of invented goals and narratives into, rather literally, the waste of time. The utopia that was previously the exclusive habitat of prepubertal children becomes available to adults only on the condition that it is no longer an experiment in remaking reality. Defusing Thompson's evocation of "personal and social relations" by making explicit that the condition of utopia is virginity, *Barbie's* utopia of play is denied a future and lies therefore beyond the reach of story.

One of the glories of *Barbie* is its titanic simplification of affect into the most obdurate of emotions. Ken's absolute fealty, his puppy love (condemned to sexlessness), is expressed in his showpiece song "I'm Just Ken" when he asks: "What will it take for her to see the man behind the tan?," Gerwig's pastiche of a hollow man who is nothing but his tanned surface. His song is a plea not so much for Barbie to recognize him as an attempt to gratify the (horribly sincere) desire for a self whose core is the simplest of all: a heart. To achieve love is his first and only aim, as if its achievement were the first necessity on the way to becoming complete. The first of many ironies in this plea is that Ken is a doll whose only task is to be so radically incomplete that *any* story can be told about and through him—to lack a heart so that children playing with him can transplant their own. Ken is plastic in the sense of being indefinitely malleable, capable of becoming whoever the child needs him to be. The needy Ken portrayed in the movie is the embodiment of that need. Its underlying truth is that Ken only exists to wrap his superficiality around the unanswerable need of the child-consumer.

As embodiment—the shell that Gerwig and her scriptwriters can pour need into—he is plastic also in the sense of surface without depth, sheen without brilliance. A doubled figure, a human animation of a doll that emulates a human, Ryan Gosling's character performs the role of a toy made from extruded petrochemicals, played on a disc also made almost entirely of plastic (with tiny amounts of metals sputtered over its surface between dye layers also derived from fossil hydrocarbons). The man behind the tan in these circumstances is an impossible illusion. There exists only the tan: the dyed plastic doll and the plastic disc reproducing the flat image of the animated plastic toy shown (on the majority of handheld and laptop displays) on plastic screens. And yet the illusion that a person, a psyche, lurks within the simulation is a true illusion in that it is an ironic emulation of a state of affairs that holds wherever either masculinity or personhood are performed, given to the world as plaything. Everyone in consumer capital is constrained to strive for a self-consistent self, despite the multiple roles each one of us is called on to act out in every institution we are hailed by. *Barbie*'s satire is all the more successful for demonstrating the foundational emptiness of the personae we adopt, up to and including the one our inner, commodified child plays out internally, for ourselves alone, when we are alone.

Short of revolution, the only cure the film offers to treat this true illusion or illusory truth of human selves is love, the adventure of the two that resolves the inadequacy of the lone self and its failure to exist.[18] Ken is lovable not only for his pecs but because his failure to *be* is such an accurate account of the common state, not only of those condemned to play the macho role but any idiot who pretends to exist, which is all of us humans. Bodybuilding is no different to plastic surgery. It is a way to recognize how unprepared any of us is to face the world, a determination, in many ways honorable, to change the body we have been born to and the biography that accumulates in it by substituting an ideal for the aggregation of wrinkles and folds that life provides. Precisely because he is plastic, Ken is a portrait of contemporary man: entirely technological, a derivative from a model he can never live up to, an effort to become in the face of the failure to be. Malleable and incomplete, during the denouement that follows the defeat of the Kens' attempted patriarchal coup, Ken learns he has to construct an identity for himself, a narratologically sound response to his vacuity and conformity to stereotype, but one that not only makes him a time-bound persona but forces him to embrace the fact that he has never been an achieved person. He learns he must accept his plasticity, even though that logically leads to and normalizes a post-narrative condition of perpetual incompletion.

Illusory narrative and impossible stories

Just before the film's conclusion, Barbie meets the spirit of Ruth Handler, widely credited as Barbie's inventor,[19] who explains that, similarly, there is no fixed goal for Barbies: their story goes on endlessly, without goal or teleology.

Only in the Real World is there work or money. The only way to generate a story of the kind Hollywood expects is to introduce the rupture that allows the invasion of Barbie's world by that Real-World regime where acts have consequences and, more particularly, events have meanings. In an inspired twist, Barbie Land's potential as an allegory for consumer capital is flipped so that the Real World becomes the allegorical double of Barbie Land. Its function is to displace the pervasive sense of absence to an elsewhere that, in time of need, can be visited. By re-creating lack as allegory, *Barbie* converts the psychoanalytic account of loss—the result of Oedipal trauma— into lack: an ongoing condition or, as Wolfe would say, a structure. Particularly by crediting Ruth Handler as the Real-World "creator" of the doll, the film absolves Barbie's world of the absence at source that, according to Lacanian psychoanalysis, all symbolization depends on. Noting in his book on dialectics that "in the shift from desire to drive, we pass from the lost object to loss itself as an object,"[20] philosopher Slavoj Žižek locates the drive to speak—to situate a self in the Symbolic domain of language and, among other symbol systems, movies—in the transformation of desire from something inherently personal into an "impersonal compulsion" mobilized by loss. As he explains, the personal loss pushing humans toward impersonal symbolization is the ground that consumer capital is built on:

> At the immediate level of addressing individuals, capitalism of course interpellates them as consumers, as subjects of desire, soliciting in them ever new perverse and excessive desires (for which it offers products to satisfy them) … the drive inheres in capitalism at a more fundamental, systemic level: the drive is that which propels forward the entire capitalist machinery, it is the impersonal compulsion to engage in the endless circular movement of expanded self-reproduction.[21]

Because, as the closing gynecology joke makes explicit, Barbie Land is without parturition, it is without the key moment of loss that creates the demand to access the Symbolic. In place of birth and separation from the mother's body, the allegory of the Real World literally displaces absence, places it elsewhere than in an originating past, as comedic incompetence, the perfect disguise for Mattel—as guiltless and guileless as the fantasy of its product.

The virginity of plastic, exempt in *Barbie* from the plastic waste that has become so important a trope of pollutant discourse in the 2020s,[22] is marked by cleanliness and hygiene. Associated as it is with pink, plastic becomes gendered, much as the pink becomes branded, working toward branding a certain mode of femininity. The infantilization of femininity in the film is, as the dumb blonde stereotype tells us, a long-familiar element of patriarchal culture and its constructions of looking at women. Not only does plastic virginity endow the prurient gaze with ethical permission, even an alibi (the site of the forbidden gaze does not exist): it re-creates a very specific image of infancy. Contrast this cleanliness with the dust, decay, and nameless fluids of Jan Švankmajer's *Alice* (1988), a vision of childhood at the brink of anxiety and disgust. *Barbie*, in contrast, comes across as a vision of childhood entering the American sublime,[23] without trepidation or awe and bereft of the simultaneously oppressed and sublimated nature that inspired poets and painters. Nature, in *Barbie*, is a brief traverse of the desert at the end of a montage of deliberately artificial dioramas of flower-fields, space, mountains, and sea, before arriving in "real" Los Angeles, where the aesthetics of anxiety in Švankmajer become, in the pastiche of the Mattel corporation as much as in Barbie Land itself, an anesthetic. The branded anesthetic of pink defangs a marshmallow storyworld that, for want of bite, lacks the wherewithal to generate the endlessly evolving stories promised by Ruth Handler. Perhaps there might be enough residual character dynamic to make a sequel or two, but the gambit that has made this film's narrative possible is sheer contingency—Ken's discovery of machismo. It is a rupture in the fabric of the fantasy but ultimately no more worth crying over than spilt milk. Barbie's diegetic world is only a foil, reflecting and amplifying Barbie but without the agency of locations that challenge their protagonists in so many other road movies and their colonial generic precursor, the wagon-train Western.

This difference also appears in the lack of back projections in the film, of the kind that appear so often in Westerns (the Ringo Kid framed against the desert sky in *Stagecoach* [dir. John Ford, 1939] for example). Unlike travel sequences in other movies, *Barbie* does not offer its viewers a montage of location footage, opting instead for mechanical dioramas separated by flamboyant horizontal wipes, reveling in their artificiality. Where other films seek invisible transitions

Figure 14.3 *Barbie's "virgin land," her prelapsarian "garden of the world," marked by plastic, cleanliness, hygiene, and pink (*Barbie, *dir. Greta Gerwig, 2023).*

Figure 14.4 Barbie *does not offer its viewers a montage of location footage, opting instead for mechanical dioramas (*Barbie, *dir. Greta Gerwig, 2023).*

from studio to location, *Barbie* makes that transition a central plot point. The film's marketing makes abundantly explicit that the film has no digital effects (barring standard postproduction jobs like editing, color-correction, and preparation for distribution formats). To understand the significance of this embrace of physical effects from the theatrical tradition is to grasp that Barbie Land is not just imaginary but illusory, an illusion showcased by the film's mechanical effects. The illusion separates the visual regime of Barbie Land from that of the Real World, a separation whose transgression makes it possible for narrative to enter the eternal present of Barbie Land.

At the same time, the stylistic commitment to the aesthetics of plastic— from the material base of the dolls animated by the actors, down to the polyester sheeting wrapped round painted water sets to give them sparkle— works by emphasizing the continuity, or at the very least the permeable borders, between living bodies and the products of the fossil fuel industries. This second aspect of *Barbie*'s aesthetics works in exactly the opposite direction to the formal divorce of artificial and natural we just observed, articulating, in visible forms, Heather Davis's observation that "plastic's rapid incursion into the environment intrudes on our notions of the separation of nature from culture."[24] Environmentalist conceptions of an ahistorical "nature" surrounding, even suffusing, but ultimately the other to historical "culture" cannot survive the ubiquity of plastic waste in every region of the planet and every living body. While the central narrative to-and-fro between Barbie Land and the Real World acts out the divorce between artifice and reality, the invitation to identify with a plastic doll, and the transmutation of plastic dolls into living actors, reorganize spectatorial orientation from the single axis of artifice-reality to include the ostensibly incompatible continuity of the living audience with the plastic universe that manifests itself with so much comedic celebration on their plastic displays.

At the time of writing, a particular group of organofluorine compounds known as PFAS (per- and polyfluoroalkyl substances) are in the news. Used for waterproofing, heat-resistance, and in cosmetics, and nicknamed "forever chemicals" because of their persistence in the environment, PFAS have been attracting headlines for their alleged health effects in humans, passed on through botanical and animal food chains, including chicken feed derived from human waste.[25] Understandably in the commercial context of news, a symptomatic *Guardian* report by Tom Perkins focuses on human "cancer, birth defects, liver disease, thyroid disease, plummeting sperm counts," as if everything in the world exists only to the extent that it ends up in a human body. The particular humanism of *Barbie* derives from its embrace of the plasticization of living bodies: if it is true that plastic Barbie comes to life as Margot Robbie, it is also the case that Margot Robbie becomes plastic for the duration of the film.

Meanwhile, the colonization of living humans by microplastics presents in physical, ecological form the successful overcoming of the division between humans, plastics, and world captured in the very first Mattel Barbie television commercial: "Beautiful Barbie, I'll make believe that I am you."

The make-believe that disavows the division between human and technical object has as its corollary the invasion of the human body by plastics, an invasion that is tempered and brought under the command of consumer capital again not by Latourian rituals of purification[26] but by embracing the body as plastic in the sense advanced by philosopher Catherine Malabou,[27] who concentrates on the concept of the plastic as formed or forming, as in "plastic arts." Her fascination with plasticity as dialectical mode of change exceeds the reversible flows praised by vitalist philosophies of becoming,[28] not least when she asserts: "A reasonable materialism, in my view, would posit that the natural contradicts itself and that thought is the fruit of this contradiction."[29] Neither a purely natural origin of humanity nor an imagined history of humanity's expulsion from some pre-technological Eden, the very idea of nature is self-contradictory. In practice, the impossibility of a self-identical nature is demonstrated by the incorporation of plastics into every human body, whether accidental or elected. The step from imagining to becoming Barbie promised by the commercial has become a very small one.

At the same time, identification with the doll, celebrated in the television spot, belongs to the symbolization process powered by ever-new desires outlined by Žižek. Ecomedia scholar Sy Taffel explains:

> If factory workers in the nineteenth and early twentieth centuries could be understood as cogs in the machine—solid metallic parts that served a single purpose—the contemporary information worker and precariat are perhaps better understood as plastic entities that are expected to remold themselves to occupy many niches throughout their working life.[30]

In this perspective, Malabou's neuroplasticity is not resistant to but an accommodation with contemporary labor, which requires not only conformance to each changing role in employment and continual upskilling in the arts of consumption (which today are wholly subsumed under capital as the production of data) but a constant renarrativizing of the always deficient self. Though the film abstracts itself from the world of work, work returns as the shadow parable of plasticity, much as *Barbie* depends on the rigorous separation of artifice from reality for its narrative premise, even though its aesthetic depends on their imbrication, at both material and psychic levels. Work-free (not to say work-shy), Barbie Land depends on the invisible labor of extraction, fabrication, and supply-chain workers, on historical labor buried in technologies, and the unpaid and externalized work of what economics demeans as "environmental services," actualities that, like the fictive "real-world" of the diegesis, disappear under its pristine superficies. These are some of the contradictions that make this film such a deceptively complex experience.

An *an*-ecological world

Various behind-the-scenes clips circulating online show that *Barbie* was almost entirely shot in studio but did not employ the virtual sets that have become so prevalent on contemporary studio shoots. Films that do surround actors with back projections or LED (light-emitting diode) cycloramas tend to give audiences the sense, via the performances they elicit, that such projections are watching the actors as much as the actors are observing and reacting to their virtual surrounds.[31] The purpose of virtual sets, apart from being quicker and cheaper than computer-generated imaging, is to provide actors with an environment that they can respond to and interact with. That interaction was not required for *Barbie:* Barbie Land is not a place that Barbie acts upon or that acts on her, only a setting that echoes her sunny existence.

The Barbies' endless and goalless play-acting of roles already mapped for them, along with the prohibition on work, does not require an ecology that they could work with or on. Beaches without swimming (the ecological transformation of land-based humans into aquatic mammals), kitchens without cooking, gardening without growing, Barbie Land models not only a plastic habitat but a profoundly *an*-ecological world. Both Ken's sense of inadequacy ("anywhere else I'd be a ten") and Barbie's fear of death are intrusions of ecological themes into a world that has no place for them. Ken's frustration is a joke at machismo's expense but also his legitimate response to a biology-free existence. Barbie's dread of mortality, however, is alien to a world that lacks the great facts of animal ecologies, hunger, sex, and death. It can only be traced to a parallel universe, a reality set obliquely to the otherwise completed universes of Barbie Land and Los Angeles.[32] Deprived of ecological demands to counter the self-centered ethos of consumption, Barbie's world has lost the option of plasticity in Malabou's malleable sense. Only risk imposed from without introduces the possibility of change. The gynecologist gag in the final scene reinforces Malabou's contention that "the natural contradicts itself" because it puts into play the radical instability of the self.[33] That self is structurally determined by consumer capital's insistence that there must be an identifiable person responsible for purchase and debt. Whatever splits or dispersals of subjectivity may hold of contemporary social life, economics still demands a name and formal identity, and it is that personal identity that is addressed as the target of data harvesting.

That "self" struggles to maintain itself between the opposing forces of neuroplastic demands for indefinitely malleable institutional, working, and consuming lives, on one side, and on the other, information capital's requirement of a fixed point of economic and informational accountability. Barbie's story is more than a convenient way of generating a narrative for a character lacking any motivation to start one. In her emergence from her self-centered multiplication of play-selves into the emotional frictions of her real mother and daughter operators, she is made to confront the radically split neuropathology, fluid yet fixed, that each of us, with varying degrees of failure, tries to adapt to. Played out as contradictions between necessarily virginal doll and ecologically connected biology, eternal youth and inevitable aging, a pseudo-community of endlessly reflected mirror images and the cruelty of intergenerational misunderstanding, the film veers off toward a satirical account of Barbie's eternal optimism in a twenty-first-century gloss on "the best of all possible worlds" of Voltaire's *Candide*.

Plastic surgery, if it were allowed to evade the prohibition on work in Barbie Land, would be a perfect fantasy for the workers Taffel describes, "plastic entities that are expected to remold themselves,"[34] this time not for gainful employment but for endless play. Because, however, there can be no labor of remolding, Weird Barbie marks a threshold that Barbie Land can only quarantine. It is left to Margot Robbie's Barbie to rebuild, not her body, which has already reached its sculpted apogee, but her affective connections to a world beyond the coherence and completion of the commodity. Where the task of cosmetic surgery, in the popular imagination and in sales pitches, is to counter the physical effects of time in favor of eternal youth and immortality without anxiety, Barbie's voyage to the Real World is a journey into durations and concerns that commodification excludes. But this account does not do justice to the secret utopianism behind elective surgery: the desire to make good the lack that commodification denies. When Barbie punches out the guy who tried to slap her butt, she makes clear that beauty is not pursued so others can desire, but so that she can be her own woman.

From kitsch to postmodernism and back again

Yet it has to be said in reply that the idea of beauty as therapy for the unhappy psyche that consumerism forces on her and her spectators is also a kind of retail therapy. Defining art's segregation from kitsch, archetypal modernist critic Clement Greenberg placed kitsch as commercial culture devised for newly urbanized proletarians whose older folk cultures no longer matched their new needs. "To fill the demand of the new market," Greenberg argued, "a new commodity was devised: ersatz culture, kitsch, destined for those who, insensible to the values of genuine culture, are hungry nevertheless for the diversion that only culture of some sort can provide."[35] The distinction from "genuine culture'" is characteristic of Greenberg's struggle to marry Trotskyism with inherited aesthetic elitism. Faced with the rise of fascism and its exploitative aesthetics in the late 1930s,[36] it may have seemed banal to Greenberg to derive commodified culture from "the debased and academicized simulacra of genuine culture."[37] Today, in the age of Hello Kitty, that genealogy feels less persuasive. Indeed, there are reasons to believe that the pop, postmodern, and conceptual turns in contemporary art have reversed the order,[38] so that art, in pursuit of autonomy, has abandoned the high Kantian ideals propounded by the last century's greatest aesthetician, Theodor Adorno,[39] in favor of the fantasized autonomy of the pure commodity. As gallery art and its attendant culture ascend toward an ever more obscure empyrean, kitsch is what is left by way of popular culture: not just a saleable culture, not only culture well-liked by many people, but in a reversal of Greenberg's belief that folk culture had lost its appeal, the realization of a new culture of the people.

Barbie is not a conspiracy to part children from their pocket money and brainwash them with capitalist ideology, or rather not limited to those crass roles, any more than a Picasso painting is pigment and paint at so many dollars a square meter. Nor is the film a critique of kitsch, although it does satirize Barbie as exemplary of commodity aesthetics. It is a critique of commodity aesthetics that mobilizes kitsch because kitsch is the only possible aesthetic adequate to the commodity form that *Barbie* sets out to satirize. Sharing the unanchored allegories and cognitive dissonance of the postmodern but no longer haunted by the ghosts of the avant-garde, kitsch is the available mode of critique after postmodernism.

Kitsch is the hollow shell sprayed with symbolic color, pink, in the establishing shots that kick off *Barbie*, or the shell filled with an attractive gel, like a chocolatier fills an empty chocolate with confections that, whatever their decorative savor, are always sweet. Postmodernism responded to this condition with the blank art of irony. But "irony is incompatible with kitsch,"[40] which superseded both modernist disdain for it and the efforts of the "post-" to overcome it when networks took over from factories. Kitsch emerges, after irony, as a new vehicle of satire. To escape postmodernity's ironic pastiche and reanimate parody as comedy, kitsch must reintegrate some kind of truth into its operation. Kitsch's peculiar form of truth is not solid belief. Rather, it operates in the void where belief once was so as to illuminate the truth of emptiness. Like truth itself, the absence of truth in *Barbie* provides consistency, presenting, as if it were continuous, an absent continuum connecting one role to another, and ultimately connecting the Barbie of the opening scene with the Barbie of the finale. This constellation of consistent nonexistence is an invitation to play with that sacrosanct idol, the self, turned this way and that, subjected to tribulations like Weird Barbie, but always the null economic vanishing point at the center of a turning world. A product of cyborg capital, blending petrochemicals with masquerades of humanity, kitsch is the true portrait of our age of enforced consumption, floated as an excessively obvious veil over the unrevealed, repressed world of workers, land, and the technologies it relies on. Beneath ubiquitous screens designed to hide them, intricate networks of general intellect and the workers that serve them churn unheeded. Kitsch is the superficial in the hour of its triumph, unable to reveal its infrastructure, but throwing its own spectacular shallowness into the spotlight. Kitsch is utopian not only because, like utopia, it does not exist, but because it encircles its void in sufficiently incoherent gloss to allow for the play of critical imagination. Even when it organizes itself in such a way that, like a double entendre, it can only be taken one way, kitsch portrays a world where selves are replete and self-moving but incapable of encountering the obstacle they present to their own desire.

Much of the narrative drive of the film comes from Barbie's affective transformation in the Real World. That she retains her meticulously performed vacuous grin demonstrates that the vacuum has not been filled, and yet she knows that she has a new purpose. This knowledge is what transforms her. The final joke tells us that even in her relationship with her adoptive family, technologically she is still a plastic doll. In the kitsch aesthetic of *Barbie's* plastic universe, the two are not incompatible. As Linda Hutcheon writes of parody, kitsch in *Barbie* "paradoxically both incorporates and challenges that which it parodies."[41] If audiences were not already aware, the voice-over tells us repeatedly that we are watching a movie designed to make money. But because it tells us so, we are also alert, as viewers, to the fractal folding of multiple messages inside one another, notably that the elementary, not to say patronizing feminism of the dialogue and the ostensible belief in deprogramming are sentimental fictions, the ostensible message lurking beneath the candy floss. The true irony, however, is that these more-or-less obvious messages betray a truth that, clearly stated, would make them impossible. Brecht's "realist" epic theater devoted itself to revealing the hidden truth beneath ideological appearances.[42] *Barbie* devotes itself to embroidering another, caricatural image over appearances, in such a way as to reveal, not the deep truth behind them, but that there is only a void. In Brecht's mid-century heyday, profit churned into investment, but today money is not only intangible but, accumulated in the obscene wealth of billionaires, it vanishes from the mundane world in the same way that, for us debtors, all the money we will ever earn has already vanished. There can be no depth aesthetic when the hidden truth is not reality but its vanishing.

Biology and technology are certainly not incompatible in the philosophy of Bernard Stiegler for whom "human knowledge is technological in its essence."[43] Not only are humans always tool-using animals but the accumulated wisdom of the dead comes alive again in technologies. At the same time, given the material base of plastics in the fossilized decay of ancient life and their spread through every vein of plant and animal across seven continents and five oceans, human technologies, the places where we store our knowledge, are also ecological. Yet knowledge, the accumulation of all human and ecological history, not only needs to breathe and metabolize, but it also needs its senses to invite the world across its vestibules if it is to know anything beyond self-reflexive calisthenics. Kitsch is devoted to entertainment and tied to surfaces. It cannot work up a new social realist dramaturgy on the Brechtian model, but that would be redundant in a time when the illusory nature of dominant culture is already common knowledge. Instead, in a reversal of Greenberg, *Barbie* exposes its own sentimentality; reversing postmodern critiques of the collapse of parody for lack of a shared system of values, it exposes exactly what we have been condemned to share as the paradise of consumerism—an endless cycle of depthless pleasures. As if seizing on another Brechtian maxim, *Barbie* seems to unfold in compliance with the axiom that cinema should "remain something entirely superfluous, though this indeed means that it is the superfluous for which we live. Nothing needs less justification than pleasure."[44] It is exactly this unjustified pleasure, elaborated over the emptiness of finance capital, that *Barbie's* kitsch exposes as vacuous. A surface that reveals itself as surface reveals the depthlessness of the screens we watch it on, and thus the unjustified pleasure that the film takes in itself (and we in it), as it inflates in the face of the vanishing of technological and ecological history and the disappearance of money as vehicle for good. The immaterial materiality of plastic may be all-too allegorical a medium but, by presenting the fiscal vacuum as vacuous, it serves to begin a reinvention of critique as entertainment.

Acknowledgment: With thanks to Hannah McCann, Janice Loreck, and Natalya Lusty.

Afterword

REBECCA STRINGER

After *Barbie*'s impressively bespoke credits rolled and I exited the sold-out cinema amid a sea of exhilarated spectators many of whom were clad in pink, I shared in the collective sense of uplift from *Barbie*'s adventurous story, kaleidoscopic beauty, cerebral comedy, and exercising intertextuality, even as lines of feminist critique of *Barbie* were forming in my mind. *Barbie* was shaping up as a culturally seismic event, and the next day I was to offer a feminist perspective on *Barbie* in media interviews. As I prepared, a friend sent me a link: more confident than I about *Barbie*'s feminism, alt right anti-feminist Ben Shapiro was burning Barbie dolls in protest against the film's feminist "wokeness." Mindful that when critiquing public expressions of feminism one must be wary not to encourage the forms of public anti-feminism arrayed against them, I resolved to avoid passing judgment on *Barbie*'s feminism. I used the media interviews instead to emphasize how *Barbie*'s popularity and appeals to feminism can, in turn, platform feminist debate about matters including and beyond those referenced in the film. My hope that the film would raise feminist voices has been borne out in the wealth of popular and academic feminist *Barbie* criticism produced in the film's wake, including this volume's collection of scholarly perspectives from film, cultural, and gender studies. This new archive of feminist *Barbie* criticism builds upon long-standing feminist engagement with Barbie as a site for cultural interrogation and critique, and spans a wide multiplicity of styles, approaches, and perspectives. It ensures Gerwig's extraordinary film enters history well attended by a thoughtful and expansive body of critical reflection, ready to be interpreted in evolving ways as Gerwig's career continues and as times change.

Appendices

Greta Gerwig: Biography

ALEX DICKIE

Born in Sacramento, California, in 1983, Greta Gerwig has become a rare generational talent in contemporary American cinema. Making her mark first as an actor and then as a writer and director, Gerwig has found success across a broad spectrum of film throughout her career, which so far spans two decades. After studying at Barnard College, Columbia University, Gerwig began collaborating with filmmakers Joe Swanberg and Mark Duplass in the mid-2000s on works that would be later grouped together under the banner of mumblecore. This form of independent film used commercial-grade digital video to capture the spontaneity of intruding on ordinary, domestic moments. Their flat aesthetics coupled with unaffected acting styles offered viewers a sense of amateur intimacy that stood apart from the increasingly commercial world of indie filmmaking.[1]

Gerwig received her first co-writing credit for *Hannah Takes the Stairs* (2007),[2] which was described by Mark Olsen in the *Los Angeles Times*[3] as the defining film of the mumblecore movement. She co-directed *Nights and Weekends* (2008) with Joe Swanberg and, following a memorable supporting role as an unceremoniously dispatched victim in Ti West's cult horror flick *The House of the Devil* (2009), Gerwig ventured into indie and studio films. Ranging from playing Natalie Portman's best friend in the hit romantic comedy *No Strings Attached* (2011) to the starring role in Whit Stillman's return to filmmaking *Damsels in Distress* (2011), Gerwig cemented herself as the go-to actress for savvy millennial women who were cool and literate but also goofy and aloof.[4]

During this period, Gerwig began her long-running creative partnership with indie dramedy director Noah Baumbach. Starting with a lead role in *Greenberg* (2010), for which she received an Independent Spirit Award nomination, Gerwig and Baumbach would continue their collaboration in his next two features: *Frances Ha* (2012), which secured Gerwig her first Golden Globe nomination, and *Mistress America* (2015). In addition to playing the lead in both films, Gerwig also shared screenwriting duties with Baumbach as they explored the lives of white, educated American millennial women pursuing creative careers.[5]

After a brief stint on the trendy television series *The Mindy Project* and collaborating with independent filmmakers Mike Mills and Rebecca Miller, Gerwig went behind the camera to write and direct her long-gestating low-budget, autobiographical coming-of-age feature *Lady Bird* (2017).[6] Her A24-backed solo directorial debut, conceived in part as a female perspective response to François Truffaut's *The 400 Blows* (*Les quatre cents coups*, 1959),[7] received rapturous reviews and saw Gerwig become the fifth woman to be nominated for the best director Oscar at the Academy Awards.

For her next feature, Gerwig revisited Louisa May Alcott's frequently adapted Hollywood staple *Little Women* (2019) for Sony Pictures Releasing. She successfully released the sumptuous mid-tier budget historical feature during a period when such films were becoming increasingly rare for studios.[8] While the versatile Gerwig has continued appearing sporadically in auteur-driven projects since her directing career gained traction, including performing voice-over in Wes Andersons' *Isle of Dogs* (2018), the multihyphenate film artist is dedicating more time on developing her own films.

In 2023, she shattered Hollywood's glass ceiling by directing and co-writing the global blockbuster *Barbie*, which made the summer of pink a cross-cultural phenomenon. Gerwig's confidence at navigating seemingly irreconcilable filmmaking spheres in the male-dominated American filmmaking environment while maintaining a cheerful sense of self-deprecation has enlivened Hollywood cinema during an era where films are undergoing considerable, perhaps permanent, transformations. As things stand, Gerwig is currently scheduled to adapt and direct C. S. Lewis's *The Chronicles of Narnia* series into multiple features and has returned to act in Noah Baumbach's *Jay Kelly* (2025), all backed by Netflix.[9]

Gerwig's earnest, lived-in portraits of women have situated her as an unlikely Hollywood corollary to British filmmaker Mike Leigh, one of the directors' major creative inspirations, who similarly shares empathetically embodying everyday realities.[10] As Gerwig enters the twentieth year of her career in film, her commitment to examining the interior lives of women, the everyday relationships between mothers and daughters, and coming-of-age stories with contemporary sensibilities have emerged as key thematic preoccupations across a wide array of screen works. Gerwig is one of the major millennial filmmaking figures in American cinema.

Filmography

COMPILED BY FRÉDÉRIC DICHTEL
AND ALEX DICKIE

LOL. Directed by Joe Swanberg. Written by Kevin Bewersdorf, Joe Swanberg, and C. Mason Wells. Starring Joe Swanberg, C. Mason Wells, Kevin Bewersdorf, and Greta Gerwig (as Greta). 2006.

Thanks for the Add! Directed by Joe Swanberg. Starring Greta Gerwig (as Girl), and Kent Osborne. 2006. [Short film.]

Hannah Takes the Stairs. Directed by Joe Swanberg. Written by Joe Swanberg, Greta Gerwig, and Kent Osborne. Starring Greta Gerwig (as Hannah), Kent Osborne, and Andrew Bujalski. 2007.

Baghead. Directed by Jay Duplass and Mark Duplass. Written by Jay Duplass, Mark Duplass, and John E. Bryant. Starring Ross Partridge, Steve Zissis, and Greta Gerwig (as Michelle). 2008.

I Thought You Finally Completely Lost It. Directed and written by Rod Webber. Starring Rod Webber, Irina Peligrad, Dede Webber, and Greta Gerwig (as Greta). 2008. [Short film.]

Nights and Weekends. Directed and written by Greta Gerwig and Joe Swanberg. Starring Greta Gerwig (as Mattie), Joe Swanberg, and Jay Duplass. 2008.

Quick Feet, Soft Hands. Directed and written by Paul Harrill. Starring Jason Von Stein, Ron Burnette, and Greta Gerwig (as Lisa). 2008. [Short film.]

Yeast. Directed and written by Mary Bronstein. Starring Mary Bronstein, Ignacio Carballo, and Greta Gerwig (as Gen). 2008.

Family Tree. Directed by Kentucker Audley. Written by Kentucker Audley and Timothy Morton. Starring Jessy Brodsky, Hallie Cooper-Novack, Lena Dunhamand, and Greta Gerwig (as Lena's Friend). 2009. [Short film.]

The House of the Devil. Directed and written by Ti West. Starring Jocelin Donahue, Tom Noonan, Mary Woronov, and Greta Gerwig (as Megan). 2009.

Une Aventure New-Yorkaise. Directed by Olivier Lécot. Written by Olivier Lécot. Starring Jonathan Zaccaï, Fanny Valette, Ebon Moss-Bachrach, and Greta Gerwig (as Tamera). 2009. [Television film.]

You Won't Miss Me. Directed by Russo-Young. Written by Russo-Young and Stella Schnabel. Starring Stella Schnabel, Simon O'Connor, Zachary Tucker, and Greta Gerwig (as Bridget). 2009.

Art House. Directed by Victor Fanucchi. Written by Kris Brown and Victor Fanucchi. Starring Greta Gerwig (as Nora Ohr), Chris Beier and Iggy Pop. 2010.

Greenberg. Directed by Noah Baumbach. Written by Jennifer Jason Leigh and Noah Baumbach. Starring Ben Stiller, Greta Gerwig (as Florence Marr), and Jennifer Jason Leigh. 2010.

Northern Comfort. Directed by Rod Webber. Written by Joseph James Bellamy, Greta Gerwig, and David T. Grophear. Starring Rod Webber, Greta Gerwig (as Cassandra), and Joseph James Bellamy. 2010.

Arthur. Directed by Jason Winer. Written by Peter Baynham and Steve Gordon. Starring Russell Brand, Helen Mirren, Jennifer Garner, and Greta Gerwig (as Naomi). 2011.

China, IL. Created by Brad Neely. Written by Brad Neely and eleven other writers, including Greta Gerwig (in 2015, ten episodes). Voice-over for the character of Pony Merks by Greta Gerwig. 2011–15.

Damsels in Distress. Directed and written by Whit Stillman. Starring Greta Gerwig (as Violet), Adam Brody, and Lio Tipton. 2011.

No Strings Attached. Directed by Ivan Reitman. Written by Elizabeth Meriwether and Michael Samonek. Starring Natalie Portman, Ashton Kutcher, Kevin Kline, and Greta Gerwick (as Patrice). 2011.

The Dish & the Spoon. Directed by Alison Bagnall. Written by Olly Alexander, Alison Bagnall, and Greta Gerwig. Starring Greta Gerwig (as Rose), Olly Alexander, and Eleonore Hendricks. 2011.

Frances Ha. Directed by Noah Baumbach. Written by Noah Baumbach and Greta Gerwig. Starring Greta Gerwig (as Frances), Mickey Sumner, and Adam Driver. 2012.

Jagoo. Directed by Hallie Cooper-Novack. Written by Hallie Cooper-Novack and Danielle Krudy. Starring Hale Appleman, Matt Burns, Emily Dorsch, and Greta Gerwig (as Olivia). 2012. [Short film.]

Lola Versus. Directed by Daryl Wein. Written by Zoe Lister-Jones and Daryl Wein. Starring Greta Gerwig (as Lola), Zoe Lister-Jones, and Hamish Linklater. 2012.

The Corrections. Directed by Noah Baumbach. Written by Noah Baumbach and Jonathan Franzen. Starring Ewan McGregor, Greta Gerwig, and Rhys Ifans. 2012. [Television film.]

To Rome with Love. Directed and written by Woody Allen. Starring Woody Allen, Penélope Cruz, Jesse Eisenberg, and Greta Gerwig (as Sally). 2012.

Making a Scene. Directed by Janusz Kaminski. Written by Lake Bell, Andrew Bujalski, J. C. Chandor, Greta Gerwig et al. Starring Cate Blanchett, Bradley Cooper, Chiwetel Ejiofor, and Greta Gerwig (as woman). 2013. [Short film.]

Eden. Directed by Mia Hansen-Løve. Written by Mia Hansen-Løve and Sven Hansen-Løve. Starring Félix de Givry, Pauline Etienne, Vincent Macaigne, and Greta Gerwig (as Julia). 2014.

The Humbling. Directed by Barry Levinson. Written by Buck Henry, Michal Zebede, and Philip Roth. Starring Al Pacino, Greta Gerwig (as Pegeen), and Nina Arianda. 2014.

"Doug Becomes a Feminist." In *Portlandia*, season 5, episode 7. [Television series: 2011–18.] Directed by Daniel Gray Longino. Starring Fred Armisen, Carrie Brownstein, and Greta Gerwig (as Mermaid). 2015.

Maggie's Plan. Directed by Rebecca Miller. Written by Rebecca Miller and Karen Rinaldi. Starring Ethan Hawke, Greta Gerwig (as Maggie), and Julianne Moore. 2015.

Mistress America. Directed by Noah Baumbach. Written by Noah Baumbach and Greta Gerwig. Starring Greta Gerwig (as Brooke), Lola Kirke, and Shana Dowdeswell. 2015.

"Freedom Tower Women's Health." *The Mindy Project*, season 4, episode 24. [Television series: 2012–17.] Created by Mindy Kaling. Directed by Linda Mendoza. Starring Mindy Kaling, Chris Messina, Ed Weeks, and Greta Gerwig (as Sarah Branum). 2016.

"Homewrecker." In *The Mindy Project*, season 4, episode 26. [Television series: 2012–17.] Created by Mindy Kaling. Directed by Michael Spiller. Starring Mindy Kaling, Chris Messina, Ed Weeks, and Greta Gerwig (as Sarah Branum). 2016.

20th Century Women. Directed and written by Mike Mills. Starring Annette Bening, Elle Fanning, and Greta Gerwig (as Abbie Porter). 2016.

Jackie. Directed by Pablo Larraín. Written by Noah Oppenheim. Starring Natalie Portman, Peter Sarsgaard, and Greta Gerwig (as Nancy Tuckerman). 2016.

Wiener-Dog. Directed and written by Todd Solondz. Starring Greta Gerwig (as Dawn Wiener), Keaton Nigel Cooke, and Tracy Letts. 2016.

Lady Bird. Directed and written by Greta Gerwig. 2017.

Isle of Dogs. Directed by Wes Anderson. Written by Wes Anderson, Roman Coppola, and Jason Schwartzman. Starring Bryan Cranston, Koyu Rankin, Edward Norton, and Greta Gerwig (voice-over as Tracy Walker). 2018.

Little Women. Directed and written by Greta Gerwig. 2019.

White Noise. Directed and written by Noah Baumbach. Starring Adam Driver, Greta Gerwig (as Babette), and Don Cheadle. 2022.

Barbie. Directed by Greta Gerwig. Written by Greta Gerwig and Noah Baumbach. 2023.

Snow White. Directed by Marc Webb. Written by Erin Cressida Wilson and Greta Gerwig et al. (uncredited). 2025.

The Chronicles of Narnia (exact title TBA). Directed by Greta Gerwig. Written by Matthew Aldrich, Greta Gerwig, and C. S. Lewis. In production.

Barbie *(dir. Greta Gerwig, 2023)*

Summary in Three Acts

HILARY RADNER AND REBECCA STRINGER

Preamble

A group of little girls play with baby dolls in a desert landscape. The narrator (Helen Mirren) announces the arrival of Barbie, who appears as a giant figure dressed in a one-piece swimsuit, strapless with black-and-white stripes. With the arrival of Barbie, the little girls smash their baby dolls. Mirren's voice-over extolls Barbie in all her various avatars, proclaiming: "Barbie is all of these women, and all of these women are Barbies."[1]

Act One: The Problem

Stereotypical Barbie has her "best day ever," in Barbie Land, in which women "hold every kind of job," and where Barbie "has a great day every day." Dominated by women, Barbie Land might be termed a gynocracy, rather than a matriarchy, as there are no mothers, grandmothers, or social hierarchy. Barbies are presented as enjoying complete equality; notwithstanding,

Stereotypical Barbie, the film's heroine, is inevitably the center of attention, while the Kens' role is largely decorative.

At the end of the day, during a block party for Barbies and Kens, which Barbie describes as "a giant blow-out party with all the Barbies, with planned choreography and a bespoke song," Barbie experiences "thoughts of death." After the party she sends Ken home, as it is girl's night at Barbie's Dreamhouse, where "every night is girl's night."

The next day nothing goes right for Barbie—her appliances malfunction and, more notably, she develops bad breath, flat feet, and eventually cellulite, recalling the "thoughts of death," which had afflicted her the previous day. The Barbies determine that she herself is malfunctioning and must seek the advice of Weird Barbie, who informs Barbie that her owner has played with her too much, creating a "rip in the continuum that is the membrane between Barbie Land from the Real World." The movie's crisis is clear: Barbie must return to the Real World and "find the girl who is playing with you" who "must be sad" or she, Barbie, will not recover. Weird Barbie explains that Stereotypical Barbie and the girl "are becoming inextricably intertwined." Barbie "must help her to help" herself. At first, Barbie is reluctant and wishes everything will stay the same (represented by a pink Manolo Blahnik high-heeled pump in Weird Barbie's presentation of her conundrum) such that she can continue to live "her best life ever." Eventually, directed by Weird Barbie, she realizes that she must save herself (represented by a Birkenstock in this same presentation) and that her only option is to travel to the Real World. At Barbie's goodbye party, a banner reads: "Bon voyage to reality and good luck restoring the membrane that separates our world from theirs so you don't get cellulite."

Act Two: The Unraveling

Barbie travels to the Real World, accompanied by Ken, who "pops up in the backseat" of her car during the course of her journey, which proceeds from "sportscar, to speed boat, to rocket ship, to tandem bike, to camper van, to snowmobile, to rollerblades"—until the two arrive in Los Angeles. They find the Real World confusing and are arrested twice. Ken discovers, to his great joy, that the Real World is governed by men, mobilizing a form of patriarchy or, more accurately, androcracy. Barbie has a hallucinatory experience in which she experiences what it is to be human. Tears roll down her cheeks, a sign of her growing understanding. Next to her on a park bench is an "older woman," new to Barbie as Barbies do not grow old. Barbie tells her that she is beautiful; she replies: "I know."

Ken and Barbie reunite. Ken informs Barbie: "Men rule the world." Barbie inexplicably "knows" the location of the young girl who, she thinks, is her owner. The FBI alerts Mattel that there are two "genital-less" dolls at large in the Real World. Barbie finds the young girl (Sasha) at her high school and confronts her, while Ken seeks out the library in order to do more research on patriarchy. Sasha and her friends reject Barbie. Sasha brands Barbie a "Fascist," reducing her to tears again. Barbie realizes that she is neither loved nor respected in the Real World.

Barbie's despondency is disrupted when she is abducted by men sent from the Mattel Corporation headquarters. Ken returns to Barbie Land with the intention of establishing patriarchy. Sasha and her mother Gloria witness her abduction. Gloria recognizes her, revealing that it was she, Gloria, who had been playing with Barbie the doll, which she had retrieved when Sasha, as a teenager, discarded her childhood toys. It was Gloria, and not Sasha, who had infected Barbie with her sadness.

The abductors deliver Barbie to the CEO of Mattel, who attempts to put her back in her box, but she escapes with the help of the ghost of her maker, Ruth Handler, who has an office on the seventeenth floor of the Mattel building. Sasha and Gloria, who followed her abductors to Mattel headquarters, rescue Barbie as she leaves the building, fleeing the leadership group. With Gloria driving, they (Gloria, Sasha, and Barbie) undertake the journey back to Barbie Land, with the Mattel leadership group in hot pursuit. The film reaches the point of no return: Mattel and Ken must be stopped, or the destruction of Barbie Land and Barbie herself will follow.

Act Three: Order Restored

Barbie Land has been transformed by Ken into a patriarchy—or, rather, an androcracy, as Barbie Land includes no fathers, only what Ken calls "bro-homies." The new Kendom Land culture resembles a nonstop American frat party without the alcohol or sex (neither Barbies nor Kens have genitals). All the Barbies have been brainwashed, performing like zombies or Stepford wives, serving at the command of the Kens. Ken has permanently set up residence in Barbie's Dreamhouse, now his "Mojo Dojo Casa House." Completely dispossessed of her house and identity in her absence, Barbie becomes hysterical as Ken throws out her clothes telling her to "take your lady fashions with you." Barbie collapses in despair saying: "This is the lowest I've ever been. Emotionally AND physically." Weird Barbie picks her up and has her transported to Weirdhouse, a refuge for all those who do not fit the Kendom-Land norms. The Mattel leadership team continues its journey to Barbie Land.

Gloria and Sasha leave Barbie Land, now variously described as Ken Land, Kendom, or Kendom Land, with Allan, who reveals himself as a stowaway. Gloria, overcome with guilt, turns the car around and returns to Barbie Land and Weird Barbie's house. Here, she saves the day, rousing the Barbies out of their trance by pointing out the contradictions of their current position, inducing "cognitive dissonance," which miraculously deprograms the Barbies. The now radicalized Barbies spread the word and the fight begins. The Barbies triumph over the Kens by tricking them, using their seductive skills and feminine wiles to provoke jealousy among the Kens, with the result that the Kens fight among themselves to the tune of "I'm Just Ken." While the Kens brawl, Barbie Land's original Constitution is confirmed, and the Barbies return to power. Barbie and Ken make peace with each other, while agreeing to go their separate ways. The Mattel Corporation, having arrived in Barbie Land during the Kens' battle, is satisfied that order has been restored and resolve to create a new Barbie, Ordinary Barbie, at the suggestion of Gloria, and to restore the portal.

Denouement

Barbie no longer feels she has a role in Barbie Land and no longer knows who she is. Helped by Ruth Handler, or her ghost, who magically appears and advises her, ultimately telling her to "Now … feel," Barbie chooses to become human (while Billie Eilish sings "What Was I Made For?"). She abandons, in the words of Helen Mirren's voice-over, "the pastels and plastic of Barbie Land for the pastels and plastic of Los Angeles." The story concludes, then, with what appears to be Barbie's first visit, shod in pink Birkenstocks, to her OB-GYN. She proudly announces: "I am here to see my gynecologist."

Notes

Foreword

1 Tagline in "*Barbie*|Trailer Main Trailer," Warner Bros., May 26, 2023, YouTube video, 2:41, https://www.youtube.com/watch?v=pBk4NYhWNMM.

2 Geneviève Sellier, "*Barbie*: Une opération commerciale de blanchiment féministe," *le genre & l'écran*, July 30, 2023, https://www.genre-ecran.net/?barbie. Translated into English by Alistair Fox and Hilary Radner as: Geneviève Sellier, "*Barbie*: A Marketing Exercise in Laundering Feminism," in "Forum: Barbenheimer," ed. Audrey Mitchell, *Australasian Journal of American Studies* 43, no. 1 (2024): 135–7, https://www.jstor.org/stable/48787093.

3 Andi Zeisler, *We Were Feminists Once: From Riot Grrrl to Covergirl®, the Buying & Selling of a Political Movement* (New York: PublicAffairs, 2016).

4 Richard Brody, "'Barbie' Is Brilliant, Beautiful and Fun as Hell," *New Yorker*, July 21, 2023, https://www.newyorker.com/culture/the-front-row/barbie-is-brilliant-beautiful-and-fun-as-hell.

5 Richard Brody, "The Oscars are more Barbie than they'll admit," *New Yorker*, March 11, 2024, https://www.newyorker.com/culture/the-front-row/the-oscars-are-more-barbie-than-theyll-admit/.

6 Geneviève Sellier, "*Barbie*, Feminism, and Consumerism: An Incoherent Combination," in *Greta Gerwig's* Barbie, ed. Hilary Radner and Rebecca Stringer (London: Bloomsbury, 2026), 179.

7 For a contemporary, extended, and influential discussion of neo-liberal feminism, see Catherine Rottenberg, *The Rise of Neoliberal Feminism* (New York, NY: Oxford University Press, 2018).

Introduction

1 Grant Harvey, "Hello, BarbieGPT . . . ," theneurondaily.com, June 13, 2025, https://www.theneurondaily.com/p/hello-barbiegpt. All references to the film, *Barbie*, DVD, directed by Greta Gerwig, 2023 (Burbank, CA: Warner Brothers Entertainment,

2023). References to the script, Greta Gerwig and Noah Baumbach, "Barbie," *Deadline*, https://deadline.com/wp-content/uploads/2024/02/Barbie-Read-The-Screenplay.pdf.

2 Hilary Radner, *The New Woman's Film: Femme-centric Movies for Smart Chicks* (London/New York: Routledge, 2017), 81. See Appendix A in this volume, 237–42.

3 Yannis Tzioumakis, "After the 'Great Studio Pullback of '08': Late Indiewood and American Independent Film Theatrical Distribution in the Age of Streaming (2008–2019), *Media Industries* 10, no.1 (2023), https://journals.publishing.umich.edu/mij/article/id/1482/, https://doi.org/10.3998/mij.1482. See, in particular, endnote 8.

4 Hilary Radner, *Neo-Feminist Cinema: Girly Films, Chick Flicks and Consumer Culture* (London/New York: Routledge, 2010). See also Hilary Radner, "Introduction: What Do Women Watch," 1–6, and "After Woman's Picture: The New Woman's Film and the Chick Flick," 7–25, in Radner, *The New Woman's Film*. Schatz in this volume, 22–3.

5 For a contemporary, extended, and influential discussion of neo-liberal feminism, see Catherine Rottenberg, *The Rise of Neoliberal Feminism* (New York: Oxford University Press, 2018). For a discussion of neo-liberalism and film theory, see also Mari Ruti, *Feminist Film Theory and* Pretty Woman (New York/London: Bloomsbury, 2016).

6 Hilary Radner, "Barbenheimer: An Unholy Alliance?," in "Forum: Barbenheimer," ed. Audrey Mitchell, *Australasian Journal of American Studies* 43, no. 1 (2024): 132–5, https://www.jstor.org/stable/48787093.

7 Some of the material informing this introduction was included (in a very different format) as Hilary Radner, "Barbenheimer: An Unholy Alliance?," and Hilary Radner, "Response to Geneviève Sellier," Forum: Barbenheimer," ed. Mitchell, 132–5; 138–9.

8 David Fear, "'Barbie' may be the most subversive blockbuster of the 21st century," *Rolling Stone*, July 18, 2023, https://www.rollingstone.com/tv-movies/tv-movie-reviews/barbie-review-margot-robbie-ryan-gosling-greta-gerwig-1234784040/; Richard Brody, "'Barbie' Is Brilliant, Beautiful and Fun as Hell," *New Yorker*, July 21, 2023, https://www.newyorker.com/culture/the-front-row/barbie-is-brilliant-beautiful-and-fun-as-hell.

9 Behlil and Erdede in this volume, 143–55.

10 Hilary Radner, "Hit Movies for 'Femmes'" in Radner, *Neo-Feminist Cinema*, 117–33.

11 Shelley Stamp, *Movies-Struck Girls: Women and Motion Picture Culture after the Nickelodeon* (Princeton: Princeton University Press, 2000).

12 See Jeanine Basinger, *A Woman's View: How Hollywood Spoke to Women 1930-1960* (Hanover, NH/London: University Press of New England/Wesleyan University Press, 1993); Mary Ann Doane, *The Desire to Desire: The Woman's Film of the 1940s* (Bloomington/Indianapolis: Indiana University Press, 1987), esp. 1–37; Molly Haskell, *From Reverence to Rape: The Treatment of Women in in the Movies* (New York: Penguin, 1975).

13 See Thomas Schatz, quoted in Radner, "Hit Movies for 'Femmes,'" 132.

14 Rob Schaap, "No Country for Old Women: Gendering Cinema in Conglomerate Hollywood," in *Feminism at the Movies: Understanding Gender in Contemporary Popular Cinema*, ed. Hilary Radner and Rebecca Stringer (New York/London: Routledge, 2011), 151–62.

15 Timothy Corrigan, "The Commerce of Auteurism," in *Film and Authorship*, ed. Virginia Wright Wexman (New Brunswick, NJ: Rutgers University Press, 2002), 101.

16 Gaylyn Studlar and Kevin S. Sandlar, "Introduction," in *Titanic: Anatomy of a Blockbuster*, ed. Gaylyn Studlar and Kevin S. Sandlar (New Brunswick, NJ: Rutgers University Press: 1999), 9.

17 Schatz in this volume, 21–35.

18 Thomas Schatz, "How 2 Companies Came to Dominate the Media Business," *thenation. com*, December 13, 2023, https://www.thenation.com/article/society/netflix-disney-media-consolidation/.

19 The inclusion of high-end iconic cars, such as the 2024 Chevy Blazer SS EV driven by Gloria (America Ferrera), working woman, mom, and Barbie's savior in the film, underlines the efforts to reach Ryan Gosling's "literally me" fans. See, for example, Jet Sanchez, "'Barbie' movie features at least five GM vehicles," *drivencarguide.co.nz*, August 3, 2023, https://www.drivencarguide.co.nz/news/barbie-movie-features-at-least-five-gm-vehicles/.

20 Laine Priestly, "Barbie's movie but Gosling fans are in it for Ken," *Otago Daily Times*, July 20, 2023, https://www.odt.co.nz/news/dunedin/barbie's-movie-gosling-fans-are-it-ken.

21 See, for example, discussion in "What is going on with the 'Ryan Gosling is literally me' memes?", *reddit.com*, 2 yr. ago, https://www.reddit.com/r/OutOfTheLoop/comments/16g1ejn/what_is_going_on_with_the_ryan_gosling_is/.

22 De Angelis in this volume, 157–71.

23 Alicia Van der Meer, "What the 'Barbie' Movie Taught Influencer Marketing about Man-hating," *prnewsonline.com*, November 14, 2023, https://www.prnewsonline.com/what-the-barbie-movie-taught-influencer-marketing-about-man-hating/#:~:text=The%20stats%20indicate%20that%2C%20in,the%20film%20to%20stratospheric%20heights.

24 Charlotte Brunsdon, *Screen Tastes: Soap Opera to Satellite Dishes* (London/New York: Routledge, 1997), 101. See also Radner, *Neo-Feminist Cinema*; Radner, *The New Woman's Film*.

25 Box Office Mojo, "Top Lifetime Grosses," *boxofficemojo.com*, https://www.boxofficemojo.com/chart/top_lifetime_gross/?area=XWW; Box Office Mojo, "Top Lifetime Grosses," *boxofficemojo.com*, https://www.boxofficemojo.com/chart/top_lifetime_gross/?area=XWW&offset=200, accessed September 27, 2025.

26 Rebecca Rubin, "'Barbie' Is Officially the Highest-Grossing Release of the Year With $1.36 Billion Globally," *Variety*, September 2, 2023, https://variety.com/2023/film/box-office/barbie-highest-grossing-worldwide-movie-year-1235705510/; Willa Paskin, "Greta Gerwig's 'Barbie' Dream Job," *New York Times*, July 17, 2023, https://www.nytimes.com/2023/07/11/magazine/greta-gerwig-barbie.html; "Pretty Woman (1990)," *the-numbers.com*, https://www.the-numbers.com/movie/Pretty-Woman#tab=summary; reneleclair, "1990–Top 10 Movies," *imdb.com*, https://www.imdb.com/list/ls062544325/; "What is $14,000,000 in 1989 worth in 2025," *amortization.org*, https://www.amortization.org/inflation/amount.php?year=1989&amount=14000000.

27 See also Dickie, in this volume, 71–85; Hilary Radner, "Creating Female Audiences: The Decline of the 'Girly' Heroine and the Return of the Formidable 'Femme,'" *Comunicazioni sociali* no. 3 (2014): 357–67, https://www.vitaepensiero.it/autore-hilary-radner-196327.html.

28 Perkins in this volume, 87–99.

29 See Hilary Radner, "After the Woman's Picture: The New Woman's Film and the Chick Flick," in Radner, *The New Woman's Film*, 7–25. See also Rob Schaap, "No Country for Old Women," 151–62.

30 A less successful prequel *The Hunger Games: The Ballad of Songbirds & Snakes* (dir. Francis Lawrence) was released in 2023. A sequel to this film is planned for a 2026 release.

31 Hollywood uses a coarse model to understand its audiences, which are divided into four quadrants: males under 25; males over 25; females under 25; and females over 25. While increasingly refined demographic models are used by various agencies, public discussion continues to focus on the four quadrants.

32 Laura Corollo, "*Wonder Woman* Audience Share in the U.S. 2017, by Gender," *statistica.com*, December 10, 2024, https://www.statista.com/statistics/807534/wonder-woman-audience-gender/#:~:text=The%20statistic%20shows%20the%20audience,of%20the%20audience%20was%20female.

33 "2017 Worldwide Box Office," *boxofficdmojo.com*, https://www.boxofficemojo.com/year/world/2017/.

34 For a more extended discussion of *Wonder Woman* and the growing feminist awareness that characterizes the second decade of the twenty-first century, see Hilary Radner, trans. Geneviève Sellier, "Une Renaissance féministe?: Le cinéma populaire contemporain et la culture de consommation," *genre-ecran.net*, January 5, 2018, https://www.genre-ecran.net/?Une-renaissance-feministe.

35 "*Avatar*, 2009," *the-numbers.com*, https://www.the-numbers.com/movie/Avatar#tab=summary.

36 "Top 25 Movies at the Worldwide Boxoffice," *the-numbers.com*, https://www.the-numbers.com/box-office-records/worldwide/all-movies/cumulative/released-in-2025.

37 For an extended discussion of toys and the event film, see Dana Polan, *The Lego Movie* (Austin: University of Texas Press, 2020).

38 Sinwell in this volume, 118.

39 Sinwell in this volume, 117.

40 W. B. Yeats, "The Second Coming," in *Michael Robartes and the Dancer*, ed. John Marck Ockerblom, February 1998, using the 1921 Cuala Press edition, https://www.theotherpages.org/poems/yeats02.html#second; Church Gibson and Zamboni in this volume, 54, 57–58.

41 "Trans pride flag color picked from Bibble from Fairytopia," #bibble #barbie #barbiefairytopia #fairytopia #trans," *tumblr.com*, https://www.tumblr.com/barbie-pride-flags/651737852356558848/trans-pride-flag-color-picked-from-bibble-from.

42 Skjerseth and Young in this volume, 129.

43 John Berger, *Ways of Seeing* (London: British Broadcast Corporation and Penguin Books, 1972), 47.

44 Church Gibson and Zamboni in this volume, 62.

45 Brittany Schultz, "Barbie's memento mori teaches that reckoning with death shows us how to live," *National Catholic Reporter*, July 29, 2023, https://www.ncronline.org/culture/barbies-memento-mori-teaches-reckoning-death-shows-us-how-live.

46 In the Walt Disney animated film *The Little Mermaid* (dir. John Musker and Ron Clements, 1989), Ariel in the title role becomes human so that she can marry another man, following the classic marriage plot. *Barbie* offers, then, a departure from this model.

47 For a more detailed account of the film's narrative, see Appendix B in this volume, 243–7.

48 Amy Burge and Jodi McAlister, *The Bonkbuster: Women's Popular Reading in the Long 1980s* (New York/London: Bloomsbury, 2025).

49 White in this volume, 37–51; Ferriss in this volume, 101–14.

50 White in this volume, 40–3.

51 White in this volume, 47–50.

52 See Julianne Pidduck, *Contemporary Costume Film: Space, Place and the Past* (London: Bloomsbury, 2004).

53 White in this volume, 48.

54 Ferriss in this volume, 101–14.

55 Chloe Mac Donnell, "Birkenstocks One of Most Purchased Fashion Items of 2022," *Guardian*, December 25, 2022, https://www.theguardian.com/business/2022/dec/25/birkenstocks-one-of-most-purchased-fashion-items-of-2022.

56 Katie Van Sycle, "'Hip-Looking,' 'Unusually Quotidian': 13 Fashion People on Birkenstocks," *thecut.com*, June 3, 2014, https://www.thecut.com/2014/06/13-fashion-people-on-birkenstocks.html.

57 Sinwell in this volume, 122.

58 Cubitt in this volume, 230.

59 Perkins in this volume, 87–99; Kim Wilkins, *American Eccentric Cinema* (New York: Bloomsbury, 2019).

60 Sellier in this volume, 175–84.

61 Isaacs in this volume, 186.

62 Cubitt in this volume, 215–19; Stringer in this volume, 209–10.

The Barbenheimer Phenomenon and the Post-Pandemic Streaming-Era Movie Industry

1 For a detailed survey of media consolidation since 1989, see Thomas Schatz, "New Hollywood, New Millennium," *Film Theory and Contemporary Hollywood Movies* (New York: Routledge, 2009). For the impact of streaming on Conglomerate Hollywood, see Schatz, "How 2 Companies Came to Dominate the Movie Business," *The Nation*, December 13, 2023, https://www.thenation.com/article/society/netflix-disney-media-consolidation/. See also Schatz, *Power Surge: Conglomerate Hollywood and the Studio System's Last Hurrah* (Berkeley: University of California Press, 2026).

2 The financial data throughout this chapter are culled from two online data services, The Numbers and Box Office Mojo, as well as the annual reports of the Motion Picture Association of America, which are also available online (and by request).

3 Quoted in Alex Barasch, "After 'Barbie,' Mattel is raiding its entire toybox," *New Yorker* July 2, 2023, https://www.newyorker.com/magazine/2023/07/10/after-barbie-mattel-is-raiding-its-entire-toybox.

4 Clayton Davis, "Oscar shakeup: 'Barbie' moved to adapted screenplay by Academy despite WGA classification as original," *Variety*, January 3, 2024, https://variety.com/2024/film/awards/barbie-moved-adapted-screenplay-oscars-1235848136/.

5 Bryn Sandberg, "Making of 'Little Women': Greta Gerwig gives modern take on 1868 novel for big screen," *Hollywood Reporter*, November 29, 2019, https://www.hollywoodreporter.com/news/general-news/making-little-women-greta-gerwig-gives-modern-take-1868-novel-big-screen-1256879/.

6 Quoted in Sandberg, "Making of 'Little Women.'"

7 Kate Arthur, "Greta Gerwig on 'Little Women's' Oscar nominations—and That One Big Snub," *Variety*, February 4, 2020, https://variety.com/2020/film/news/greta-gerwig-oscars-directing-snub-little-women-1203491117/.

8 On the film's development, see Elizabeth Wagmaister, "'This is not about selling toys!': Mattel Bosses on 'Barbie's' Long Development, Needing a Female Director, and More," *Variety*, July 20, 2023, https://variety.com/2023/film/news/barbie-movie-mattell-execs-toy-adaptations-1235674597; Kyle Buchanan, "Greta Gerwig on the Blockbuster 'Barbie' Opening (and How She Got Away with It)," *New York Times*, July 25, 2023, https://www.nytimes.com/2023/07/25/movies/greta-gerwig-barbie-movie.html.

9 Angelique Jackson, "Greta Gerwig to Direct 'Barbie' with Margot Robbie, Filming to Start in 2022," *Variety*, July 9, 2021, https://variety.com/2021/film/news/greta-gerwig-barbie-movie-director-margot-robbie-noah-baumbach-1235015427/.

10 Greta Gerwig quoted in Buchanan, "Greta Gerwig on the Blockbuster 'Barbie' Opening."

11 Tim Gray, "Oscar expands best pic noms to 10," *Variety*, June 24, 2009, https://variety.com/2009/film/awards/oscar-expands-best-pic-noms-to-10-1118005322/. This came to be known as the "Dark Knight rule."

12 Borys Kit, "Inside the Studios' (and Apple's) Frenzy to Get Christopher Nolan's Next Film," *Hollywood Reporter*, September 15, 2021, https://www.hollywoodreporter.com/movies/movie-news/christopher-nolan-pitch-to-studios-including-apple-seeking-his-next-film-1235014132/; Rebecca Rubin and Brent Lang, "How Universal Beat Other Studios (and Apple) to Land Christopher Nolan's WWII epic," *Variety*, September 14, 2021, https://variety.com/2021/film/news/christopher-nolan-universal-deal-1235064461/.

13 Matt Donnelly, "Margot Robbie's 'Barbie' Sets 2023 Release Date, Unveils First-Look Photo," *Variety*, April 26, 2022, https://variety.com/2022/film/news/margot-robbie-barbie-release-date-1235241864/.

14 Jeremy Fuster, "Behind 'Operation Barbie Summer,'" *thewrap.com*, July 24, 2023, https://www.thewrap.com/barbie-movie-marketing-box-office-warner-bros-plan/.

15 Anthony D'Alessandro, "'Barbie' struts to No. 2 in *Deadline*'s 2023 most valuable blockbuster tournament," *deadline.com*, May 6, 2024, https://deadline.com/2024/05/barbie-movie-profits-1235902885/.

16 Claire Moses, "Mark your calendars: 'Barbenheimer' is coming," *New York Times*, June 28, 2023, https://www.nytimes.com/2023/06/28/movies/barbie-oppenheimer-release-day.html.

17 Rebecca Rubin, "Box Office: 'Barbie' opens to record-setting $155 million, 'Oppenheimer' shatters expectations with $80 million debut," *Variety*, July 23, 2023, https://variety.com/2023/film/box-office/box-office-barbie-oppenheimer-opening-weekend-shatter-records-1235677601/. Both of these totals were later adjusted upward.

18 Nicole Sperling, "'Barbie' ruled the box office, but 2023 was tough for women in Hollywood," *New York Times*, March 5, 2024, https://www.nytimes.com/2024/03/05/business/media/academy-oscars-women.html#:~:text=121-,'Barbie'%20Ruled%20the%20Box%20Office%2C%20but%202023%20Was%20Tough,at%20a%20considerably%20slower%20rate; Josh Rottenberg, "UCLA diversity report finds women and minorities drove Hollywood's biggest successes," *Los Angeles Times*, March 7, 2024, https://www.latimes.com/entertainment-arts/movies/story/2024-03-07/ucla-diversity-report-women-minorities-drove-2023-box-office-success#:~:text=While%20the%20box%20office%20continued,were%20more%20than%2040%25%20women.

19 Justin Chang, ""Wicked" and "Gladiator II" Offer Nostalgic, Half-Satisfying Showdowns," *New Yorker*, November 20, 2024, https://www.newyorker.com/magazine/2024/12/02/wicked-movie-review-gladiator.

20 Owen Gleiberman, "Is Hollywood's addiction to sequels cannibalizing its future?", *Variety* November 30, 2024, https://www.google.com/search?client=safari&rls=en&q=Owen+Gleiberman%2C+%E2%80%9CIs+Hollywood%E2%80%99s+addiction+to+sequels+cannibalizing+its+future%3F%E2%80%9D%2C+Variety&ie=UTF-8&oe=UTF-8.

21 Rubin, "Box Office." See also Rubin, "Imax scores $106 billion globally, second-largest year in company's history, thanks to 'Oppenheimer,'" *Variety*, January 9, 2024, https://variety.com/2024/film/news/imax-box-office-second-biggest-year-history-oppenheimer-1235865457/.

22 Tatiana Siegel, "Netflix lost Margot Robbie's 'Wuthering Heights' to Warner Bros. despite $150 million offer—has the streamer lost its deal-making mojo?", *Variety*, November 6, 2024, https://variety.com/2024/film/news/margot-robbie-wuthering-heights-warner-bros-netflix-1236202619/.

23 Wendy Lee and Samantha Masunaga, "Netflix might put Greta Gerwig's 'Narnia' in Imax theaters. Will it create a streaming blockbuster?," *Los Angeles Times*, October 29, 2024, https://www.latimes.com/entertainment-arts/business/story/2024-10-29/netflix-might-put-narnia-in-theaters-will-it-create-a-streaming-blockbuster.

The Americanization of Feminine Culture: Female Authorship and the Culture Industry from Alcott to *Barbie*

1 Kirsten Acuna, "'Barbie' painted the town pink," *Business Insider*, July 28, 2023, https://www.businessinsider.com/how-much-did-barbie-spend-marketing-box-office-success-explained-2023-7#:~:text=The%20film%20has%20a%20reported%20production%20budget%20of%20%24145%20million; "*Barbie* (2023)," *boxofficemojo.com*, https://www.boxofficemojo.com/title/tt1517268/, consulted June 27, 2025; Brent Lang, "'Barbie' Broke Records, but Studios Employed Fewer Female Directors on 2023's Top Film,"

variety.com, January 1, 2024, https://variety.com/2024/film/news/barbie-precentage-female-directors-employment-2023-study-1235859152/.

2 Ann Douglas, *The Feminization of American Culture* (New York: Knopf, 1977).

3 Nina Baym *Woman's Fiction: A Guide to Novels by and about Women in America, 1820-1870* (Ithaca, NY: Cornell University Press, 1978); Shelley Stamp, *Movie-Struck Girls: Women and Motion Picture Culture after the Nickelodeon* (Princeton: Princeton University Press, 2018); Tania Modleski, *Loving with a Vengeance: Mass-Produced Fantasies for Women*, 2nd ed. (New York: Routledge, 2008); Mary Ann Doane, *The Desire to Desire: The Woman's Film of the 1940s* (Bloomington: Indiana University Press, 1987); Hilary Radner, *Neo-Feminist Cinema: Girly Films, Chick Flicks, and Consumer Culture* (New York: Routledge, 2011); Michele White, *Producing Women: The Internet, Traditional Femininity, Queerness, and Creativity* (New York: Routledge, 2015); Elana Levine, ed., *Cupcakes, Pinterest, and Ladyporn : Feminized Popular Culture in the Early Twenty-First Century* (Champaign: University of Illinois Press, 2015); Susan J. Douglas, *Where the Girls Are: Growing up Female with the Mass Media* (New York: Times Books, 1994); Patty Ahn et al., *Bangtan Remixed: A Critical BTS Reader* (Durham, NC: Duke University Press, 2024).

4 Lauren Berlant, *The Female Complaint: The Unfinished Business of Sentimentality in American Culture* (Durham, NC: Duke University Press, 2008).

5 Eve Sedgwick, "Queer Performativity: Henry James's *The Art of the Novel*," *GLQ* 1, no. 1 (1993): 1–16, https://doi.org/10.1215/10642684-1-1-1.

6 Richard Dyer, "Entertainment and Utopia" (1977) in *Only Entertainment*, ed. Richarch Dyer, 2nd ed. (New York: Routledge, 2002) 19–35.

7 Gerwig was involved in independent film as an actor and writer since 2006, and this work informs her authorial persona. Her first director credit was with Joe Swanberg on *Nights and Weekends* (2008); the two also co-wrote the script.

8 Susan Cheever, *Louisa May Alcott* (New York: Simon & Schuster, 2010).

9 Meghan O'Rourke, "American Girlhood Culture Is Really Strange," *The Atlantic*, July 26, 2023, https://www.theatlantic.com/ideas/archive/2023/07/barbie-movie-review-girlhood-greta-gerwig/674821/.

10 M. G. Lord, *Forever Barbie: The Unauthorized Biography of a Real Doll* (New York: Morrow and Co., 1994). One of the most memorable visual and cultural jokes of the *Barbie* phenomenon is Gerwig's cheeky reference to the alien monolith of *2001: A Space Odyssey* (1968) to represent the monumentality of Handler's innovation. Gerwig's citation deflates Kubrick's hubris, not least by luxuriating in the "trivial" delights of the widescreen technicolor aesthetic that the male director was determined to exalt in his film.

11 See Erica Rand's wonderful *Barbie's Queer Accessories* (Durham, NC: Duke University Press, 1995).

12 Max Horkheimer and Theodor W. Adorno. *Dialectic of Enlightenment* (New York: Continuum, 1999).

13 Sarah Banet Weiser, "What's Your Flava: Race and Postfeminism," in *Interrogating Postfeminism*, ed. Yvonne Tasker and Diane Negra (Durham, NC: Duke University Press, 2007), 201–26. For work on Barbie, race, and globalization, see, among others, Ann DuCille, *Skin Trade* (Cambridge, MA: Harvard University Press, 1996) and Frances Negrón-Muntaner "Barbie's Hair: Selling Out Puerto Rican Identity in the Global Market," in *Boricua Pop* (New York: New York University Press, 2022), 206–27.

14 Wendy Goldman Getzler, "With profits up, Mattel launches in-house studio Playground Productions," *kidscreen.com*, October 16, 2013, https://kidscreen.com/2013/10/16/with-profits-up-mattel-launches-in-house-studio-playground-productions/; David Ng, "Mattel creates new film division to turn toys into movies," *Los Angeles Times*, September 6, 2018, https://www.latimes.com/business/hollywood/la-fi-ct-mattel-film-division-20180906-story.html.

15 Richard Dyer, "Believing in Fairies: The Author and the Homosexual," in *Inside/out: Lesbian Theories, Gay Theories*, ed. Diana Fuss (New York: Routledge, 1991), 185–201.

16 Radner, *Neo-feminist Cinema*.

17 Willa Paskin, "Greta Gerwig's 'Barbie' Dream Job," *New York Times Magazine*, July 11, 2023, https://www.nytimes.com/2023/07/11/magazine/greta-gerwig-barbie.html.

18 Roland Barthes, "Myth Today: The Inoculation," *Mythologies*, trans. Annette Lavers (New York: The Noonday Press/Farrar, Straus & Giroux, 25th printing, 1991), 151–2. Originally published in French as: Roland Barthes, *Mythologies* (Paris: Éditions du Seuil, 1957).

19 Nathaniel Hawthorne, "Letter to William D. Ticknor, January 19, 1855," in Nathaniel Hawthorn, *The Letters, 1833–1856,* ed. Thomas Woodson et al., *The Centenary Edition of the Works of Nathaniel Hawthorne*, Vol. 16 (Columbus: Ohio State University Press, 1987), 304.

20 Timothy Corrigan, "The Commerce of Auteurism: A Voice without Authority," *New German Critique* 49, Special Issue on Alexander Kluge (Winter 1990): 43–57.

21 Patricia White, "Sentimental Miseducation: Women Directors Coming of Age," *Cinema, Media, and Human Flourishing*, ed. Timothy Corrigan (Oxford: Oxford University Press, 2023) 118–33.

22 Parts of the discussion of *Little Women* appear in Patricia White, "Ambidextrous Authorship: Greta Gerwig and the Politics of Women's Genres," *Los Angeles Review of Books*, February 7, 2020, https://lareviewofbooks.org/article/ambidextrous-authorship-greta-gerwig-and-the-politics-of-womens-genres/ with thanks to editor Anna Shechtman.

23 Previous adaptations of *Little Women* include George Cukor (1933), Mervy LeRoy (1949), and Gillian Armstrong (1994).

24 Louisa May Alcott to Elizabeth Bond, March 20, 1869, Swarthmore College Friends Historical Library, https://digitalcollections.tricolib.brynmawr.edu/object/sc213057.

25 Greta Gerwig, Directors Guild of America podcast, quoted in White, "Ambidextrous Authorship."

26 For an influential argument, see Angela McRobbie "Post-Feminism and Popular Culture," *Feminist Media Studies* 4, no. 3 (2004): 255–64.

Fake Feminism and Strident Pink Spectacle: Fashion, Celebrity Culture, and the Marketing of Greta Gerwig's *Barbie*

1 Julia Neel, "Barbie: The Designer's Doll," *Vogue* (UK), January 9, 2009, https://www.vogue.co.uk/gallery/barbies-designer-looks.

2 See John Izod, *Hollywood and the Box Office, 1895-1986* (Basingstoke: Macmillan, 1988).

3 See Rachel Lubitz, "Where did that stereotype between Birkenstocks and lesbians really come from," *mic.com*, June 30, 2017, https://www.mic.com/articles/181069/where-did-that-stereotype-between-birkenstocks-and-lesbians-really-come-from.

4 See, for example, *TERF Wars: Feminism and the Fight for Transgender Futures* (London: Sage Publications, 2020).

5 See, for example, Jeanine Basinger, *A Woman's View: How Hollywood Spoke to Women, 1930–1960* (New York: Knopf, 1993) and Marcia Landy and Amy Villarejo, *Queen Christina* (London: British Film Institute, 1995).

6 Charles Eckert, "The Carole Lombard in Macy's Window," *Quarterly Review of Film Studies* 3, no. 1 (1978): 1–21, doi:10.1080/10509207809391376.

7 Sophie Caraan, "Burger King Brazil Unveils a 'Barbie' Burger with Pink Sauce," *hypebeast.com*, July 17, 2023, https://hypebeast.com/2023/7/burger-king-brazil-barbie-burger-announcement-info.

8 See, for example, Rosalind Gill, "Post-Post-Feminism?: New Feminist Visibilities in Postfeminist Times," *Feminist Media Studies* 16, no. 4 (2016): 610–30, https://doi.org/10.1080/14680777.2016.1193293.

9 See, for example, Diane Negra, *What a Girl Wants: Fantasizing the Reclamation of Self in Postfeminism* (London: Routledge, 2009); Catherine Rottenberg, *The Rise of Neoliberal Feminism* (New York: Oxford University Press, 2018); Angela McRobbie, *Feminism and the Politics of Resilience: Essays on Media, Gender and the End of Welfare* (Cambridge: Polity Press, 2020); Rosalind Gill, "From Sexual Objectification to Sexual Subjectification: The Resexualisation of Women's Bodies in the Media," *Feminist Media Studies* 3, no. 1 (2003): 100–6.

10 Matthew Velasco, "Greta Gerwig's Margiela Couture Dress Sent Cannes (and Fashion Twitter) Into a Frenzy," *wmagazine.com*, May 16, 2024, https://www.wmagazine.com/fashion/greta-gerwig-couture-stripe-corset-dress-cannes-film-festival.

11 Julia Guerra, "A History of Barbiecore Fashion, From the Early Aughts to Today," *instyle.com*, June 17, 2024, https://www.instyle.com/barbiecore-5397428.

12 Cady Lang, "The Long, Complicated, and Very Pink History of Barbiecore," *TIME*, June 27, 2023, https://time.com/6290606/barbiecore-trend-history/.

13 Stephen Gundle, *Glamour: A History* (Oxford: Oxford University Press, 2009), 251.

14 Ashley Mears, "Discipline of the Catwalk," *Ethnography* 9, no. 4 (2008): 429–56, https://doi.org/10.1177/1466138108096985; Mears, "Discipline of the Catwalk," 430.

15 In fact, as pointed out by Silvia Grasso, author of the book *Filosofia di Barbie*: "Barbie is a copy of another doll known as Bild Lilli. Bild Lilli originated as a comic strip, first appearing on June 24, 1952, on the front page of the pilot issue of *Bild Zeitung*, the famous German newspaper founded by Axel Springer . . . Bild Lilli embodies both representational codes: the erotic and the domestic 'angel of the home'; reflecting the aesthetic canon that had been established some years earlier, during the National Socialist regime, as the sole ideal of beauty—fair skin, blonde hair, voluptuous curves, and a compliant, servile character." See Silvia Grasso, *Filosofia di Barbie* (Genoa: Nuovo Melangolo, 2024), 57, 59.

16 Caroline Reilly, "Hyperfemininity Isn't a Trend—It's a Movement: Hyperfemininity by Girly Girls, for Girly Girls," *nylon.com*, February 20, 2024, https://www.nylon.com/life/hyperfemininity-tiktok-feminism-movement.

17 Danya Issawi, "Yes, Another Year in Y2K Fashion," *thecut.com*, November 14, 2023, https://www.nylon.com/life/hyperfemininity-tiktok-feminism-movement.

18 Cady Lang, "The Long, Complicated, and Very Pink History of Barbiecore," *Time*, June 27, 2023, https://time.com/6290606/barbiecore-trend-history/.

19 Madeleine Schulz, "How Long Can the Barbiecore Craze Last?," *voguebusiness.com*, July 19, 2023, https://www.voguebusiness.com/fashion/how-long-can-the-barbiecore-craze-last.

20 BOF, "Livia Firth," *businessoffashion.com*, https://www.businessoffashion.com/people/livia-firth/.

21 Livia Giuggioli Firth, @liviafirth, *instagram.com*, August 19, 2023, https://www.instagram.com/liviafirth/p/CwHVHHntoJ9/?img_index=1.

22 Elizabeth Castaldo Lundén, *Fashion on the Red Carpet: A History of the Oscars®, Fashion, and Globalisation* (Edinburgh: Edinburgh University Press, 2021), 2.

23 Georg Simmel, "Fashion," *International Quarterly* 10, no. 1 (1904): 130–55, repr. in *American Journal of Sociology* 62, no. 6 (1957): 541–58; Ted Polhemus, *Street Style: From Sidewalk to Catwalk* (London: Thames & Hudson, 1994).

24 Margot Robbie and Andrew Mukamal, with Fabien Baron, Craig McDean, Edward Enninful, Margaret Zhang, and Greta Gerwig, *Barbie™: The World Tour* (New York: Rizzoli International Publications, 2024).

25 Elizabeth Wissinger, *This Year's Model: Fashion, Media, and the Making of Glamour* (New York: New York University Press, 2015), 57.

25 Laird Borelli-Persson, "What Barbie-core Looked Like Before Barbie-core," *Vogue*, July 18, 2022, https://www.vogue.com/article/what-barbiecore-looked-like-before-barbiecore.

27 See Mary Ann Doane, *The Desire to Desire: The Women's Film of the 1940s* (Bloomington: Indiana University Press. 1987).

28 Caroline Evans, "The Enchanted Spectacle," *Fashion Theory* 5, no. 3 (2001): 271–310, https://doi.org/10.2752/136270401778960865; Evans, "The Enchanted Spectacle," 306.

29 Daniel J. Boorstin, *The Image: A Guide to Pseudo-Events in America* (New York: Atheneum, 1962).

30 See, for example, Stuart Cunningham and David Randolph Craig, *Social Media Entertainment: The New Intersection of Hollywood and Silicon Valley* (New York: New York University Press, 2019).

Greta Gerwig: From Indiewood to Conglomerate Hollywood—New Iterations of the Contemporary Auteur

1 Kyle Paoletta, "The Rise and Fall of the Marvel Cinematic Universe: How a movie studio and its head honcho redefined moviemaking for the worst," *The Nation*, July 11, 2024, https://www.thenation.com/article/culture/mcu-marvel-studios-reign-review/.

2 Nancy Mills, "Plight of Women Directors Improved—But Not Much," *Los Angeles Times*, November 17, 1986, http://articles.latimes.com/1986-11-17/entertainment/ca-3890_1_women-directors.

3 Judith Mayne, "Female Authorship Reconsidered (The Case of Dorothy Arzner)," in *Auteurs and Authorship: A Film Reader*, ed. Barry Keith Grant (Malden, MA: Blackwell Publishing, 2008), 265–6.

4 Yvonne Tasker, "Vision and Visibility: Women Filmmakers, Contemporary Authorship, and Feminist Film Studies," in *Reclaiming the Archive: Feminism and Film History*, ed. Vicki Callahan (Detroit: Wayne State University Press, 2010): 219, 226.

5 Timothy Corrigan, "The Commerce of Auteurism: a Voice without Authority," *New German Critique* 49 (1990): 50.

6 Thomas James Wardak, "Author Functions, Auteur Fictions Understanding Authorship in Conglomerate Hollywood Commerce, Culture, and Narrative," PhD diss., University of Sheffield (2017), 304.

7 Deb Verhoeven, *Jane Campion* (London/New York: Routledge, 2009), 11, 16.

8 "Barbie," *Box Office Mojo,*, https://www.boxofficemojo.com/release/rl1077904129/.

9 Linda Badley, Claire Perkins, and Michele Schreiber, "Introduction," in *Indie Reframed: Women's Filmmaking and Contemporary American Independent Cinema*, ed. Linda Badley et al. (Edinburgh: Edinburgh University Press, 2016), 2–3.

10 Umberto Gonzalez, "Sundance Isn't Just a Festival for Indie Film—It's Also a Talent Farm for Marvel," *The Wrap*, February 2, 2023, https://www.thewrap.com/marvel-directors-who-made-sundance-movies/.

11 Brent Lang, "Major Studios' Pledges to Hire More Female Filmmakers and People of Color Were 'Performative,' Study Finds," *Variety*, January 2, 2024, https://variety.com/2024/film/news/major-studios-hiring-female-filmmakers-people-of-color-barbie-cocaine-bear-1235859366/.

12 Thomas Schatz, "How 2 Companies Came to Dominate the Media Business," *The Nation*, December 13, 2023, https://www.thenation.com/article/society/netflix-disney-media-consolidation/.

13 Pamela McClintock, "Warner Bros. Discovery Chief David Zaslav at CinemaCon: 'We are in no rush to bring movies to Max,'" *Hollywood Reporter*, April 25, 2023, https://www.hollywoodreporter.com/movies/movie-news/warner-bros-discovery-david-zaslav-cinemacon-1235399752/.

14 Thomas Schatz, "New Hollywood, New Millennium," in *Film Theory and Contemporary Hollywood Movies*, ed. Warren Buckland (London: Routledge, 2009), 25.

15 "Collectively, this group of companies on average managed a 6.46 percent market share in 2009–2019, a figure that is remarkably similar to the 6.91 percent of the studio specialty film divisions in the 1998–2008 timeframe. I would like to suggest then that it is this group of companies that became the dominant force in the industry's middle tier in the 2010s, at least when it comes to the theatrical film market." Yannis Tzioumakis, "After the 'Great Studio Pullback of '08': Late Indiewood and American Independent Film Theatrical Distribution in the Age of Streaming (2008–2019)," *Media Industries* 10, no. 1: 15.

16 "[L]ate indies' lack of a collectively strong commitment to Indiewood films suggest that Indiewood is slowly giving way to more commercial mid-range budget films." These changes have brought specialty films into closer orbit with "the Hollywood mainstream, blurring the lines between the two even more" (Tzioumakis, "Great Studio Pullback," 18, 22).

17 Rebecca Rubin, "Inside 'Barbie's' Pink Publicity Machine: How Warner Bros. Pulled Off the Marketing Campaign of the Year," *Variety*, July 23, 2023, https://variety.com/2023/film/box-office/barbie-marketing-campaign-explained-warner-bros-1235677922/.

18 Mia Galuppo, "'Lady Bird': How Greta Gerwig Re-Created 2002 to Tell Her Coming-of-Age Story," *Hollywood Reporter*, November 10, 2017, https://www.hollywoodreporter.com/movies/movie-features/lady-bird-how-greta-gerwig-created-

2002-tell-her-coming-age-story-1055561/; "Little Women," *Box Office Mojo*, https://www.boxofficemojo.com/release/rl218596865/

19 Tzioumakis, "Great Studio Pullback," 19.

20 Eliana Dockterman, "Why It Took 64 Years to Make a Barbie Movie," *Time*, June 29, 2023, https://time.com/6289787/barbie-movie-history-mattel/.

21 Pamela McClintock, "'Barbie' Becomes Biggest Warner Bros. Movie Ever at Global Box Office," *Hollywood Reporter*, August 28, 2023, https://www.hollywoodreporter.com/movies/movie-news/barbie-biggest-warner-bros-movie-globally-box-office-1235575786/.

22 Janet Staiger, "The Package-Unit System: Unit Management After 1955," in *The Classical Hollywood Cinema: Film Style & Mode of Production to 1960*, ed. David Bordwell et al. (London: Routledge & Kegan Paul, 1985), 330.

23 Justin Kroll, "Greta Gerwig, Noah Baumbach to Co-Write 'Barbie,'" *Variety*, July 15, 2019, https://variety.com/2019/film/news/greta-gerwig-noah-baumbach-barbie-write-margot-robbie-1203267621/.

24 Gerwig on turning in the first draft: "They probably won't let us make this, but maybe it will turn into some nice Hollywood lore about scripts that never came to be.'" Quoted in Seija Rankin, "The Making of 'Barbie,'" *Hollywood Reporter*, January 4, 2024, https://www.hollywoodreporter.com/movies/movie-features/margot-robbie-greta-gerwig-ryan-gosling-making-barbie-movie-1235766454/.

25 Kyle Buchanan, "Greta Gerwig on the Blockbuster 'Barbie' Opening (and How She Got Away with It)," *New York Times*, July 25, 2023, https://www.nytimes.com/2023/07/25/movies/greta-gerwig-barbie-movie.html.

26 "I assembled that team before I had a greenlight at all. I guess I'm sort of a believer, and maybe this comes from working on independent films, that in a way you just have to start making the movie. If you wait for permission all the time, you'll never get there." Gerwig quoted in "In The Conversation with 'Barbie' Director Greta Gerwig," *Critics Choice*, January 5, 2024, YouTube video, 14:51, https://www.youtube.com/watch?v=zS6vwMbcDUI.

27 Alex Moshakis, "'It had to be totally bananas': Greta Gerwig on bringing Barbie to life," *Guardian*, July 9, 2023, https://www.theguardian.com/film/2023/jul/09/it-had-to-be-totally-bananas-greta-gerwig-on-bringing-barbie-back-to-life.

28 Dockterman, "It took 64 years."

29 "It's about showing the work. I wanted to see that it was authentically artificial. Really fake." In "Greta Gerwig: The 60 Minutes Interview," aired on CBS December 3, 2023, available as "Greta Gerwig|Sunday on 60 Minutes," through the streaming service Paramount Plus.

30 "How would they do this in 1959? . . . To me, I wanted to give myself the constraints of what a movie world is." Quoted in "Greta Gerwig explains how Carole Lombard and Katharine Hepburn inspired 'Barbie,'" *Turner Classic Movies*, July 27, 2023, YouTube video, 14:16, www.youtube.com/watch?v=1ugNIPus_FU.

31 Zoe Mutter, "Adventures in Barbie Land," *British Cinematographer* 119 (2023): 42–9.

32 These included CGI-set extensions, Volume, a virtual production soundstage that enables filmmakers to generate 360-degree scenery with control over variable lighting, and the Farsight, a viewfinder that populates or blocks stages with digital characters.

33 "Greta Gerwig: The 60 Minutes Interview."

34 McClintock, "'Barbie' Becomes Biggest Warner Bros. Movie Ever at Global Box Office."

35 Moshakis, "'It had to be totally bananas.'"

36 Mutter, "Adventures in Barbie Land."

37 "Greta Gerwig's Adventures in Moviegoing," *Criterion Channel*, n.d., video, 24:15, https://www.criterionchannel.com/greta-gerwig-s-adventures-in-moviegoing.

38 James Kendrick, "What is the Criterion? The Criterion Collection as an Archive of Film as Culture," *Journal of Film and Video* 53, nos. 2/3 (2001): 126.

39 "Bringing Barbie to the Big Screen," *Warner Bros. Entertainment*, March 10, 2024, YouTube video, 5:19, https://www.youtube.com/watch?v=l7i98T3Mq2s.

40 Brian Hiatt, "The Brain Behind 'Barbie': Inside the Brilliant Mind of Greta Gerwig," *Rolling Stone*, July 3, 2023, https://www.rollingstone.com/tv-movies/tv-movie-features/barbie-greta-gerwig-interview-margot-robbie-ryan-gosling-superhero-movie-1234769344/.

41 Gerwig noted: "It was the most control I've had" and that working on an IP "gave us permission to do things I certainly wouldn't have done if I was originating the idea," in "'Barbie': Jane Campion in conversation with Greta Gerwig and Noah Baumbach," February 9, 2024, YouTube video, 29:24, https://www.youtube.com/watch?v=_nOX7_a2Scg.

42 Michael Z. Newman, *Indie: An American Film Culture* (New York: Columbia University Press, 2011), 61–2.

43 "Greta Gerwig, Jury President of the 77th Cannes Film Festival," *Festival Cannes*, December 4, 2023, https://www.festival-cannes.com/en/press/press-releases/greta-gerwig-jury-president-of-the-77th-cannes-film-festival/.

Barbie, Irony, and Post-Indie Cinema

1 Shirley Li, "The Surprising Key to Understanding the Barbie Film," *The Atlantic*, July 21, 2023, https://www.theatlantic.com/culture/archive/2023/07/barbie-movie-america-ferrera/674781/.

2 David Fear, "Barbie may be the most subversive blockbuster of the 21st Century," *au.rollingstone.com*, July 19, 2023, https://au.rollingstone.com/music/music-news/barbie-review-margot-robbie-ryan-gosling-greta-gerwig-48612/.

3 Alison Willmore, "We shouldn't have to grade *Barbie* on a curve," *Vulture*, July 21, 2023, https://www.vulture.com/article/barbie-review-we-shouldnt-have-to-grade-this-on-a-curve.html.

4 Fear, "Barbie May Be."

5 Jeffrey Sconce, "Irony, Nihilism and the New American 'Smart' Film," *Screen* 43, no. 4 (2002): 349–69; Claire Perkins, *American Smart Cinema* (Edinburgh: Edinburgh University Press, 2012).

6 Willa Paskin, "Greta Gerwig's 'Barbie' Dream Job," *New York Times Magazine*, July 11, 2023, https://www.nytimes.com/2023/07/11/magazine/greta-gerwig-barbie.html.

7 Linda Hutcheon, *Irony's Edge: The Theory and Politics of Irony* (London: Routledge, 1995), 11.

8 John Biguenet, "Double Takes: The Role of Allusion in Cinema," in *Play It Again Sam: Retakes on Remakes*, ed. Andrew Horton and Stuart Y. McDougal (Berkeley: University of California Press, 1998).

9 Hannah Reich, "Barbie is opening after much fanfare, so what's the deal with Margot Robbie and Greta Gerwig's fantasy comedy?", *abc.net.au*, July 19, 2023, https://www.abc.net.au/news/2023-07-19/barbie-movie-margot-robbie-ryan-gosling/102591364.

10 Alex Moshakis, "'It had to be totally bananas': Greta Gerwig on Bringing Barbie to Life," *Guardian*, July 9, 2023 https://www.theguardian.com/film/2023/jul/09/it-had-to-be-totally-bananas-greta-gerwig-on-bringing-barbie-back-to-life.

11 Rachel Treisman, "Is Barbie a feminist icon? It's complicated," *npr.org*, July 27, 2023, https://www.npr.org/2023/07/27/1189987314/barbie-movie-feminist-history; Diana Reid, "Left-wing propaganda or anti-feminist? What Barbie is really trying to say," *Sydney Morning Herald*, August 1, 2023, https://www.smh.com.au/culture/movies/barbie-shows-how-modern-feminism-became-the-perfect-accessory-20230731-p5dsop.html.

12 Caetlin Benson-Allot, "Greta Gerwig's Girlhood Trilogy," *Film Quarterly* 77, no. 2 (2023): 67–72.

13 Claire Perkins, "My Effortless Brilliance: Women's Mumblecore," in *Indie Reframed: Women's Filmmaking and Contemporary American Independent Cinema*, ed. Linda Badley, Claire Perkins, and Michele Schreiber (Edinburgh: Edinburgh University Press, 2016).

14 Nicolas Rapold, "Greta Gerwig and Little Women," *The Film Comment Podcast*, January 2, 2020, https://www.filmcomment.com/blog/the-film-comment-podcast-greta-gerwig-and-little-women/.

15 Hilary Radner, *The New Woman's Film: Femme-centric Movies for Smart Chicks* (London/New York: Routledge, 2017).

16 Aisha Harris, "Greta Gerwig on *Lady Bird*, John Hughes, and Being 'Ready' to Step Behind the Camera," *Slate*, December 8, 2017, https://slate.com/culture/2017/12/greta-gerwig-on-em-lady-bird-em-john-hughes-and-being-ready-to-step-behind-the-camera.html.

17 Perkins, *American Smart Cinema*.

18 John Fleury, Bryan Hikari Hartzheim, and Stephen Mamber, eds., *The Franchise Era: Managing Media in the Digital Economy* (Edinburgh: Edinburgh University Press, 2019), 2.

19 Sarah Sinwell, *Indie Cinema Online* (New Brunswick, NJ: Rutgers University Press, 2020), 5.

20 Nicolas Bourriaud, *Postproduction: Culture as Screenplay: How Art Reprograms the World* (New York: Lukas & Sternberg, 2002), 13.

21 Constantine Verevis, "New Millennial Remakes," in *Media of Serial Narrative*, ed. Frank Kelleter (Columbus: Ohio State University Press, 2017), 128.

22 Claire Perkins and Michele Schreiber, "Independent Women: From Film to Television," *Feminist Media Studies* 19, no. 7 (2019): 919–27; James Lyons and Yannis Tzioumakis eds., *Indie TV: Industry, Aesthetics and Medium Specificity* (Abingdon: Routledge, 2023).

23 Jessica Ford, "Women's Indie Television: the Intimate Feminism of Women-centric Dramedies," *Feminist Media Studies* 19, no. 7 (2019): 928–43.

24 Perkins and Schreiber, "Independent Women."

25 Taylor Nygaard and Jorie Lagerwey, *Horrible White People: Gender, Genre, and Television's Precarious Whiteness* (New York: New York University Press, 2020).

26 Brené Brown, *The Gifts of Imperfection: Let Go of Who You Think You're Supposed to Be and Embrace Who You Are* (Center City, MN: Hazelton Publishing, 2010).

27 Lauren Berlant, *Cruel Optimism* (Durham, NC: Duke University Press, 2011).

28 Meg Walters, "Are we all Depression Barbie now? In Greta Gerwig's film, depression and anxiety are an intrinsic part of womanhood," *glamourmagazine.co.uk*, August 3, 2023, https://www.glamourmagazine.co.uk/article/depression-barbie-margot-robbie.

29 Nora Dominick, "This one scene in *Barbie* is making everyone feel 'called out' by how accurate it is," *buzzfeed.com*, July 25, 2023, https://www.buzzfeed.com/noradominick/barbie-depression-barbie-scene-reactions.

30 Angela McRobbie, "Notes on the Perfect: Competitive Femininity in Neoliberal Times," *Australian Feminist Studies* 30, no. 83 (2015): 3–20.

31 Andrew Freund, @andrewfreund, "If you go to see #Barbie this weekend you'll notice a homevideo montage scene," *tiktok.com*, July 22, 2023, https://www.tiktok.com/@andrewfreund/video/7258383808687328554?lang=en.

"Authentically Artificial": Embodying the Self in *Barbie*

1 Willa Paskin, "Greta Gerwig's 'Barbie' Dream Job," *New York Times*, July 17, 2023, https://www.nytimes.com/2023/07/11/magazine/greta-gerwig-barbie.html.

2 Stephen Greenblatt, *Renaissance Self-Fashioning: From More to Shakespeare* (Chicago: University of Chicago Press, 2005), 2.

3 Fred Davis, *Fashion, Culture, and Identity* (Chicago: The University of Chicago Press, 1992), 25.

4 Joanne Entwistle, *The Fashioned Body: Fashion, Dress and Modern Social Theory*, 2nd ed. (London: Polity Press, 2015), 35.

5 Jennifer Craik, *The Face of Fashion: Cultural Studies in Fashion* (New York: Routledge, 1994), 16.

6 Hilary Radner, *The New Woman's Film: Femme-centric Movies for Smart Chicks* (New York/London: Routledge, 2017), 131, 142.

7 As Radner observes, the film's aesthetics are equally retro. Filmed in black and white, it nods to European art cinema. The film's look is "specifically designed to counter the glamour and 'bling' of chick flicks such as the *Devil Wears Prada*." See Radner, *New Woman's Film*, 146.

8 Kyle Buchanan, "How Those 'Barbie' Dreamhouses Came to Life: 'We All Had to Believe in It,'" *New York Times*, July 26, 2023. On Barbie's cars, see Chris Lezotte, "Pink Power: The Barbie Car and Female Automobility," *The Journal of American Culture* 46, no. 3 (2023): 197–208. Her pink convertible is a modified pre-facelift C1 Corvette.

9 Marjorie Garber, "Introduction," *Vested Interests: Cross-Dressing and Cultural Anxiety* (New York: Routledge, 1992), 1–3. See also Cady Lang, "The Long, Complicated, and Very Pink History of Barbiecore," *Time*, June 27, 2023, https://time.com/6290606/barbiecore-trend-history/; Carol M. Dole, "The Return of Pink: Legally Blonde, Third-wave Feminism, and Having It All," *Chick Flicks: Contemporary Women at the Movies*, ed. Suzanne Ferriss and Mallory Young (New York: Routledge, 2008), 58–78.

10 Laurie Pressman, "Beyond Barbie: An Homage to Pantone Pinks," *Pantone.com*, August 22, 2023, https://www.pantone.com/articles/colors/beyond-barbie-an-homage-to-pantone-pinks. The set decorators used Rosco's fluorescent pink paint. See Kase Wickman, "It Was the Year of Barbie Pink, but Whose Color Is It Anyway?" *Vanity Fair*, November 27, 2023, https://www.vanityfair.com/style/2023/11/the-year-of-barbie-pink.

11 Michael Ordoña, "How Margot Robbie Overcame a 'Palpable and Debilitating' Panic to Make 'Barbie,'" *Los Angeles Times*, February 5, 2024.

12 Isabelle McNeill, "'That Reality-Challenged Woman': Dreams and Matter in Barbie," *Feminist Media Studies* (July 3, 2024).

13 Gia Kourlas, "The Dance Delight in 'Barbie' Belongs to the Kens," *New York Times*, July 26, 2023, https://www.nytimes.com/2023/07/28/arts/dance/ken-dance-barbie-movie.html.

14 Quoted in Lang, "The Long, Complicated, and Very Pink History of Barbiecore."

15 Carol Spencer, *Dressing Barbie: A Celebration of the Clothes that Made America's Favorite Doll, and the Incredible Women Behind Them* (New York: Harper Design, 2019), 29–30.

16 For an introduction to the significance of authenticity in contemporary philosophy, see Somogy Varga and Charles Guignon, "Authenticity," in *Stanford Encyclopedia of Philosophy*, ed. Edward N. Zalta and Uri Nodelman, February 20, 2020, https://plato.stanford.edu/entries/authenticity/.

17 "There was no black, white, or chrome allowed" in Barbie Land. See Jocelyn Silver, "How Barbie's Production Designers Created the Plastic, Fantastic World of Barbie Land," *Vogue*, July 21, 2023, https://www.vogue.com/article/barbie-production-designer-interview.

18 It later became a backlot for 20th Century Fox, adding to the film's Hollywood satire. Barbie and Ken think they are going to the State of Los Angeles in the Country of California.

19 Emily Cameron, "The Unexpected Influence of Sylvester Stallone on Greta Gerwig," *Far Out*, September 26, 2024, https://faroutmagazine.co.uk/unexpected-influence-of-sylvester-stallone-on-greta-gerwig/.

20 Stacy Gillis, "A Proposal in Plastic: Jane Austen in Barbie Land," *Feminist Theory* 25, no. 4 (2024): 585.

21 Mia Vicino, "Greta Gerwig's Official Barbie Watchlist," *Letterboxd*, July 13, 2023, YouTube video, 15:28 https://www.youtube.com/watch?v=s2rNnOGfmv0&list=PL6iyk30XguJj70lQUT0vCdbhZJghMuAtX&index=1&t=17s.

22 Greta Gerwig and Noah Baumbach, *Barbie* (London: Faber & Faber, 2023), 24.

23 McNeill notes that both Barbie Land and the Real World are cinematic constructs. See McNeill, "'That Reality-Challenged Woman': Dreams and Matter in Barbie."

24 McNeill, "'That Reality-Challenged Woman': Dreams and Matter in Barbie."

25 On the film's engagement with issues of reproductive justice, see Della J. Winters, Courtney A. Grimm, and Raveena Bola, "'I'm Here to See My Gynaecologist': Reproductive Justice and the Deleuzian Becoming of Barbie," *Feminist Theory* 25, no. 4 (2024): 665–8.

26 Greenblatt, *Renaissance Self-Fashioning*, xi.

Queer Barbie, Weird Barbie, and Greta Gerwig's Many Queer Kens

1 "Barbie (2023)," *boxofficemojo.com*, https://www.boxofficemojo.com/title/tt1517268/, consulted June 27, 2025; "Greta Gerwig makes history as Barbie has biggest opening weekend for film directed by a woman," *Guardian*, July 24, 2023, https://www.theguardian.com/film/2023/jul/24/barbie-movie-box-office-greta-gerwig-records-highest-grossing-woman; "2023 Worldwide Box Office," *boxofficemojo.com*, https://www.boxofficemojo.com/year/world/2023/, consulted June 27, 2025; "All Time Worldwide Box Office Warner Bros Movies," *the-numbers.com*, https://www.the-numbers.com/box-office-records/worldwide/all-movies/theatrical-distributors/warner-bros, consulted June 27, 2025.

2 One could argue that this centering of Mattel and Warner Bros. also puts into question Greta Gerwig's authorship of *Barbie*.

3 Significantly, the repetition of this opening within the trailer for the film, along with the proliferation of pink and bright fluorescent hues, and the ubiquity of rollerblading and Indigo Girls lyrics, suggested the queerness and campiness of the film to future audiences.

4 In 1993, a group of performance artists in New York City switched out the voice boxes of Teen Talk Barbie with GI Joe dolls so that she might say things like "Attack!" and "Vengeance is Mine!"

5 Erica Rand, *Barbie's Queer Accessories* (Durham, NC: Duke University Press, 1996), 4–5.

6 James Factora, "The Queerest Barbie Moments of All Time: Bring back Earring Magic Ken, You Cowards." *Glamour UK*, August 4, 2023, https://www.glamourmagazine.co.uk/article/barbie-lgbtq-moments.

7 Samantha Puc, "Queer Barbies Go Back Further Than You Might Think," *The Mary Sue*, August 2, 2023, https://www.themarysue.com/queer-barbies-go-back-further-than-you-might-think/.

8 Clara Bradbury-Rance, "Butch Barbie," *Feminist Media Studies* (July 25, 2024): 1–5.

9 Alexander Doty, *Making Things Perfectly Queer: Interpreting Mass Culture* (Minneapolis: University of Minnesota Press, 1993), 70.

10 Adrienne Rich, "Compulsory Heterosexuality and Lesbian Existence," *Signs* 5 (1980): 631–60; Gayle Rubin, "Thinking Sex," in *The Gay and Lesbian Studies Reader*, ed. Michelle Aina Barale, Henry Abelove, and David M. Halperin (New York: Routledge, 1993) 3–44; Eve Sedgwick, *Epistemology of the Closet* (Berkeley: University of California Press, 1990); Michael Warner, "Introduction," in *Fear of a Queer Planet: Queer Politics and Social Theory* (Minneapolis: University of Minnesota Press, 1993) vii–xxxi; Judith Butler, *Gender Trouble: Feminism and the Subversion of Identity* (New York/London: Routledge, 1990); Judith Butler, *Undoing Gender* (New York/London: Routledge, 2004);

David Halperin, *Saint Foucault: Towards a Gay Hagiography* (Oxford: Oxford University Press, 1995); Annamarie Jagose, *Queer Theory: An Introduction* (New York: New York University Press, 1996); Lee Edelman, *No Future: Queer Theory and the Death Drive* (Durham, NC: Duke University Press, 2004); Sara Ahmed, *Queer Phenomenology* (Durham, NC: Duke University Press, 2006); José Esteban Muñoz, *Cruising Utopia: The Then and There of Queer Futurity* (New York: New York University Press, 2009); Kara Keeling, *Queer Times, Black Futures* (New York: New York University Press, 2019); and Eliza Steinbock, *Shimmering Images: Trans Cinema, Embodiment, and the Aesthetics of Change* (Durham, NC: Duke University Press, 2019).

11 Alexander Doty, *Flaming Classics; Queering the Film Canon* (New York/London: Routledge, 2000), 7.

12 Lisa Laman, "Margot Robbie Wasn't the Original Choice for Barbie," *Collider*, January 21, 2024, https://collider.com/barbie-movie-casting/.

13 Rand, *Barbie's Queer Accessories*, 2.

14 Rand, *Barbie's Queer Accessories*, 46.

15 According to *Esquire,* Ken's designers "advocated for Ken to have some sort of genitalia, 'if no actual penis, then at least a "bulge" in his trousers . . . The squeamish male executives at Mattel' did not agree. Ken's smooth groin area was the compromise the two parties reached." See "The History Behind Ken," *Time Magazine*, July 20, 2023, https://time.com/6296386/barbie-ken-history/.

16 Elizabeth Freeman, "Queer Belongings: Kinship Theory and Queer Theory," in *A Companion to Lesbian, Gay, Bisexual, Transgender, and Queer Studies*, ed. George Haggerty and Molly McGerry (Malden/Oxford: Blackwell Publishing, 2007), 298.

17 Laura Mulvey, "Visual Pleasure and Narrative Cinema," *Screen* 16, no. 3 (1975): 6–18, https://doi.org/10.1093/screen/16.3.6.

18 Lisa Henderson, *Love and Money: Queers, Class and Cultural Production* (New York: New York University Press, 2013).

19 Nicholas de Villiers, "Glancing, Cruising, Staring: Queer Ways of Looking," *Bright Lights Film Journal,* August 1, 2007, http://brightlightsfilm.com/glancing-cruising-staring-queer-ways-looking/#.Wp2U_JPwbaZ.

20 Dan Savage, "Ken Comes Out," *Chicago Reader*, July 22, 1993, https://chicagoreader.com/news-politics/ken-comes-out/.

21 Clara Bradbury-Rance, "Butch Barbie," *Feminist Media Studies* (July 25, 2024): 3, https://www.tandfonline.com/doi/full/10.1080/14680777.2024.2372015.

22 Mark Ronson and Andrew Wyatt, "I'm Just Ken," *Barbie the Album*, Atlantic, 2022, Spotify.

23 Mel Stanfill, "Where the Femslashers Are: Media on the Lesbian Continuum," "Symposium," *journal.transformativeworks.org*, https://journal.transformativeworks.org/index.php/twc/article/download/959/829?inline=1. See also Mel Stanfill, "Where

the Femslashers Are: Media on the Lesbian Continuum," in "Queer Female Fandom," ed. Julie Levin Russo and Eve Ng, special issue, *Transformative Works and Cultures* 24 (2017), http://dx.doi.org/10.3983/twc.2017.959.

24 Stanfill, "Where the Femslashers Are."

25 David Opie, "Life in Plastic: A Gay History of Barbie's Journey to the Big Screen," *Gay Times*, July 21, 2023, https://www.gaytimes.com/culture/life-in-plastic-a-gay-history-of-barbies-journey-to-the-big-screen/.

26 Kimberlé Crenshaw quoted in Bradbury-Rance, "Butch Barbie," 2.

27 The 1989 cult song "Closer to Fine," written and performed by the iconic lesbian duo Indigo Girls, is heard on multiple occasions throughout *Barbie*. For a more extended discussion of the significance of the song to the film, see Skjerseth and Young in this volume, 129–142. Indigo Girls, "Indigo Girls—Fine Live at The Fillmore," September 1, 2018, YouTube video, 4:12, https://www.youtube.com/watch?v=IQCFwaAQijI.

"What Was I Made For?" and "I'm Just Ken": The Musical Binary of *Barbie*

1 See DeAngelis in this volume, 157–71.

2 Zack Sharf, "Ryan Gosling said '100% no' when first asked to sing 'I'm just Ken' live at the Oscars because 'there's a lot of ways that could go wrong,'" *Variety*, April 12, 2024, https://variety.com/2024/film/news/ryan-gosling-said-no-im-just-ken-oscars-performance-1235969101/.

3 The worldwide *Barbie* audience was 66.2% female, 33.8% male, according to Statista. See *statista.com*, https://www.statista.com/statistics/1401677/gender-distribution-of-barbie-oppenheimer-worldwide/.

4 See Anahid Kassabian, *Hearing Film: Tracking Identifications in Contemporary Hollywood Film Music* (New York: Routledge, 2001), and Julie Hubbert, "The Compilation Soundtrack from the 1960s to the Present," in *The Oxford Handbook of Film Music Studies*, ed. David Neumeyer (Oxford: Oxford University Press, 2013), 291–318. For a more sustained discussion of the use of the soundtrack as a promotional tool in Conglomerate Hollywood, see Peter Stapleton, "Music and the Woman's Film: *Sex and the City: The Movie* (2008)," *Feminism at the Movies: Understand Gender in Contemporary Popular Cinema*, ed. Hilary Radner and Rebecca Stringer (New York/London: Routledge, 2011), 163–77.

5 For an elaboration of the term and usage of "diegesis," see, for example, Robynn J. Stilwell, "The Fantastical Gap Between Diegetic and Nondiegetic," in *Beyond the Soundtrack*, ed. Daniel Goldmark, Lawrence Kramer, and Richard Leppert (Berkeley: University of California Press, 2007), 184–202.

6 Greta Gerwig and Noah Baumbach, "Barbie," *deadline.com*, https://deadline.com/wp-content/uploads/2024/02/Barbie-Read-The-Screenplay.pdf.

7 To explore the gendering of Classical Hollywood scoring before John Williams, see Heather Laing, *The Gendered Score: Music in 1940s Melodrama and the Woman's Film* (Aldershot: Ashgate, 2007).

8 Rick Altman, *The American Film Musical* (Bloomington: Indiana University Press, 1989), 63.

9 Altman, *The American Film Musical*, 62.

10 Ian Biddle and Freya Jarman-Ivens, "Oh Boy! Making Masculinity in Popular Music," in *Oh Boy!: Masculinities and Popular Music*, ed. Freya Jarman (New York: Routledge, 2007), 7.

11 Biddle and Jarman-Ivens., "Oh Boy!," 3.

12 Biddle and Jarman-Ivens, "Oh Boy!," 7.

13 Lucia Kramer, "From Glam Rock to Cock Rock: Revis(it)ing Rock Masculinities in Recent Feature Films," in *Performing Masculinity*, ed. Rainer Emig and Antony Rowland (Basingstoke: Palgrave Macmillan, 2010), 166.

14 Kramer, "From Glam Rock to Cock Rock," 170.

15 Mekado Murphy, "'Barbie' | Anatomy of a Scene," *New York Times*, March 4, 2024, video, 4:34, https://www.nytimes.com/video/movies/100000009341480/barbie-scene.html.

16 "Mark Ronson Says Greta Gerwig Wanted the 'Most Maximalist Thing' on 'I'm Just Ken' | The Breakdown," *Rolling Stone*, February 22, 2024, YouTube video, 14:53, https://www.youtube.com/watch?v=mzwdvD67WcY.

17 Murphy, "'Barbie' | Anatomy of a Scene."

18 Lloyd Whitesell, "Expressive Thresholds and Anomalous Utterances," in *The Oxford Handbook of the Hollywood Musical*, ed. Dominic McHugh (Oxford: Oxford University Press, 2022), 7.

19 Kelly Kessler, *Destabilizing the Hollywood Musical* (London: Palgrave Macmillan, 2010), 8.

20 Billie Eilish in "How Billie Eilish and FINNEAS Created Oscar-Winning 'What Was I Made For,'" *Vanity Fair*, December 7, 2023, YouTube video, 18:34, https://www.youtube.com/watch?v=mewdcHIvMmA.

21 Jilly Boyce Kay, *Gender, Media and Voice: Communicative Injustice and Public Speech* (Cham: Springer, 2020), 3.

22 Billie Eilish quoted in Brittany Spanos and Yana Yatsuk, "Billie Eilish and the Pursuit of Happiness," *Rolling Stone*, June 17, 2023, https://www.rollingstone.com/music/music-features/billie-eilish-new-album-happier-than-ever-tour-1183156/.

23 Eilish in "How Billie Eilish and FINNEAS Created Oscar-Winning 'What Was I Made For.'"

24 Eilish in "How Billie Eilish and FINNEAS Created Oscar-Winning 'What Was I Made For.'"

25 Kate McQuiston, "Some Assembly Required: Hybrid Scores in *Moonrise Kingdom* and *The Grand Budapest Hotel*," in *The Routledge Companion to Screen Music and Sound*, eds. Miguel Mera, Ronald Sadoff, and Ben Winters (London: Routledge, 2017), 478.

26 Kate McQuiston, "Some Assembly Required."

27 Jessica Wang, "Barbie's moving montage features real women from the lives of cast and crew," *Entertainment*, July 24, 2023, https://ew.com/movies/barbie-montage-explained-real-women/#:~:text=Director%20Greta%20Gerwig%20has%20confirmed,scope%20of%20womanhood%20and%20humanity.

28 Chris Willman, "Billie Eilish and Finneas on 'Barbie' and the Benefits of Writing from a Doll's POV: 'You Say Something You Maybe Weren't Brave Enough to Say about Yourself,'" *Variety*, December 2, 2023, variety.com/2023/music/news/billie-eilish-finneas-barbie-interview-what-was-i-made-for-1235815815/.

29 "I'm Just Pete - SNL," October 15, 2023, YouTube video, 3:42, https://www.youtube.com/watch?v=O-UfkZKKGc0.

30 Atlantic Records, "Ryan Gosling, Mark Ronson, Slash & The Kens—I'm Just Ken (Live From The Oscars 2024)," March 11, 024, YouTube video, https://www.youtube.com/watch?v=fo6T5BwxFh0.

31 Eilish in "How Billie Eilish and FINNEAS Created Oscar-Winning 'What Was I Made For.'"

32 Mikael Wood, "What Billie Eilish learned from her own 'Barbie' song, 'What Was I Made For?'," *Los Angeles Times*, November 14, 2024, https://www.latimes.com/entertainment-arts/awards/story/2023-11-14/billie-eilish-what-was-i-made-for-barbie-greta-gerwig.

33 Billie Eilish quoted in Angie Marticoccio, "Billie Eilish Would Like to Reintroduce Herself," *Rolling Stone*, April 24, 2024, https://www.rollingstone.com/music/music-features/billie-eilish-hit-me-hard-and-soft-mental-health-fame-1235003585/.

34 See Elena Nicolaou, "'Barbie' brought new fans to the Indigo Girls' discography," *Today*, March 14, 2024, https://www.today.com/popculture/music/indigo-girls-barbie-interview-rcna143185; Lydia Polgreen, "Why is everyone suddenly listening to a staple of my angsty adolescence?," August 8, 2023, *New York Times*, https://www.nytimes.com/2023/08/08/opinion/indigo-girls-barbie-cringe.html.

35 Billboard Staff, Joe Lynch, Stephen Daw, and Hannah Dailey, "70 Top LGBTQ+ Anthems of All Time," *Billboard*, June 6, 2024, https://www.billboard.com/lists/lgbtq-anthems-queer-pride-songs/.

36 Trish Bendix, "How the Indigo Girls Brought Barbie 'Closer to Fine,'" *New York Times*, July 24, 2023, https://www.nytimes.com/2023/07/24/arts/music/barbie-indigo-girls-closer-to-fine.html.

37 Polgreen, "Why is everyone suddenly listening to a staple of my angsty adolescence?".

38 Willa Paskin, "Greta Gerwig's 'Barbie' Dream Job," July 17, 2023, *New York Times*, https://www.nytimes.com/2023/07/11/magazine/greta-gerwig-barbie.html.

39 Mary Louise Kelly, Amy Ray, and Emily Saliers, "The Indigo Girls on How Their Song Ended Up in 'Barbie,' Which Is Up for 8 Oscars," *NPR*, February 28, 2024, https://www.npr.org/2024/02/28/1234645051/the-indigo-girls-on-how-their-song-ended-up-in-barbie-which-is-up-for-8-oscars.

40 "Closer to Fine," *genius.com*, https://genius.com/Indigo-girls-closer-to-fine-lyrics.

"Barbieist vs. Oppenheimerist": A Gender-Based Reception Study of *Barbie* in Turkey

1 Audrey Mitchell, ed., "Forum: Barbenheimer," *Australasian Journal of American Studies* 43, no. 1 (2024): 119–50, https://www.jstor.org/stable/48787093.

2 Cate Alexander and Camille Intson, "Bimbos and Bombs: The Barbenheimer Phenomena," *Imaginations: Journal of Cross-Cultural Image Studies* (March 2024), https://doi.org/10.17742/IMAGE29701.

3 Rebecca Rubin, "Inside *Barbie*'s Pink Publicity Machine: How Warner Bros. Pulled Off the Marketing Campaign of the Year," *Variety*, July 23, 2023.

4 Aidan Kelley, "*Oppenheimer* Budget Breakdown: How Christopher Nolan's Historical Epic Became a Break Out Hit," *Collider*, September 8, 2023, https://collider.com/oppenheimer-box-office-budget/.

5 Elise Shafer, Patrick Frater, and Naman Ramachandran, "*Barbie* and *Oppenheimer* Global Box Office Numbers by Country," *Variety*, August 1, 2023, https://variety.com/lists/barbie-oppenheimer-global-box-office-numbers/.

6 Box-office data, *boxofficemojo.com*, https://www.boxofficemojo.com/showdown/sd205125124/.

7 Box office data for India, collected by sacnilk.com, shows that in the first nine weeks Oppenheimer was a "superhit," grossing over $15 million, while Barbie was a "hit," grossing approximately $5.5 million. "Oppenheimer Box Office Collection," *sacnilk.com*, December 5, 2023, https://www.sacnilk.com/news/Oppenheimer_2023_Box_Office_Collection_Day_Wise_Worldwide; "Barbie Box Office Collection," *sacnilk.com*, December 5, 2023, https://www.sacnilk.com/news/Barbie_2023_Box_Office_Collection_Day_Wise_Worldwide.

8 Soo-Mee Park, "Why Did *Barbie* Bomb in South Korea?," *Hollywood Reporter*, August 10, 2023.

9 Abid Rahman, "China Box Office: *Barbie* Gains Foothold, Crosses $25M," *The Hollywood Reporter*, July 31, 2023, https://www.hollywoodreporter.com/movies/movie-news/china-box-office-barbie-1235547738/.

10 Raphael Rashid, "'The Fear of Being Labelled Feminist Is Real': *Barbie* Movie Flops in South Korea," *The Guardian*, August 2, 2023, https://www.theguardian.com/world/2023/aug/02/barbie-movie-flops-south-korea-feminism; Park, "Why Did *Barbie* Bomb in South Korea?".

11 Zack Sharf and Patrick Frater, "Warner Bros. Apologizes after 'Barbenheimer' Posts Spark Criticism from Studio's Japan Unit," *Variety*, August 1, 2023, https://variety.com/2023/film/news/warner-bros-japan-criticizes-barbie-twitter-barbenheimer-posts-1235683885/.

12 Akira Mizuta Lippit, "A Scholarly Look at Oppenheimer in Japan," *Deadline*, May 29, 2024, https://deadline.com/2024/05/oppenheimer-japan-reaction-guest-column-1235942666/.

13 Nabih Bulos, "The *Barbie* Movie's Arab World Rollout Hits a Snag," *Los Angeles Times*, August 31, 2023, https://www.latimes.com/world-nation/story/2023-08-31/barbie-arab-world-middle-east-censorship-lgbtq-feminism-mothers.

14 Melis Behlil, "Turkey: Transnational Dimensions of a Large National Film Industry," in *Contemporary Balkan Cinema: Transnational Exchanges and Global Circuits*, ed. Lydia Papadimitriou and Ana Grgić (Edinburgh: Edinburgh University Press, 2020).

15 Turkish box office data from https://boxofficeturkiye.com/tum-zamanlar/seyirci-rekorlari/tum-filmler. Records have been kept since 1989, so these numbers do not include Turkish popular cinema's "golden age," the Yeşilçam era from the mid-1950s to the late-1970s. Hollywood productions in the top fifty are *Titanic* (dir. Cameron, 1997) at #31; *Furious 7* (dir. Wan, 2015) at #32; *Spider-Man: No Way Home* (dir. Watts, 2021) at #34; *Avatar: The Way of Water* (dir. Cameron, 2022) at #41; *The Fate of the Furious* (dir. Gray, 2017) at #42; *Avatar* (dir. Cameron, 2009) at #45; and *Avengers: Endgame* (dir. Russo and Russo, 2019) at #49.

16 According boxofficeturkiye.com, from 17.10 Turkish Lira (TRL) in 2020 to 185.05TRL in 2025, *boxofficeturkiye.com*, https://boxofficeturkiye.com/yillik.

17 Şenay Aydemir, "Barbie'sin Sen Barbie Kal," *Evrensel*, July 22, 2023, https://www.evrensel.net/yazi/93346/barbiesin-sen-barbie-kal.

18 Müjde Işıl, "Mükemmel Olmana Gerek Yok," *Milliyet*, July 21, 2023, https://www.milliyet.com.tr/kultur-sanat/mukemmel-olmana-gerek-yok-6979216.

19 Sevda Dursun, "Barbie LGBT Mi Oldu? Rüya Evinde Erkeğin Adı Yok," *Yeni Şafak*, July 20, 2023, https://www.yenisafak.com/hayat/barbie-lgbt-mi-oldu-ruya-evinde-erkegin-adi-yok-4546587.

20 Çisil Demir and Haber Merkezi, "*Barbie* Tartışması," *Milliyet*, July 20, 2023, https://www.milliyet.com.tr/dunya/barbie-tartismasi-6978705.

21 Hazal Deniz Kaya, "Pembe Balondan Gözükenler: Bir Barbie Filmi," *Kaos GL*, August 7, 2023, https://kaosgl.org/gokkusagi-forumu-kose-yazisi/pembe-balondan-gozukenler-bir-barbie-filmi.

22 Ezgi Zorba, "Nasıl Da Ters Köşe Olduk," YouTube video, July 21, 8:07, https://www.youtube.com/watch?v=EvYOV4zqiZA.

23 Başak Can, "Barbie Film İncelemesi!," July 18, 2023, YouTube video, 8:07, https://www.youtube.com/watch?v=7l7Vbg41Lz0.

24 Kenneth MacKinnon, *Love, Tears, and the Male Spectator* (Vancouver: Fairleigh Dickinson University Press, 2002).

25 Zeynep Ocak and Kaan Karsan, "*Barbie*: İnceleme," July 26, 2023, YouTube video, 28:33, https://www.youtube.com/watch?v=WhvMJ-ogeGU.

26 "Barbie'ci vs. Oppenheimer'cı," *Ekşi Sözlük*, July 14, 2023, https://eksisozluk.com/barbieci-vs-oppenheimerci--7682884. Ekşi Sözlük is a platform unique to Turkey, akin to a social and informal Wikipedia.

27 Peker Dural, "The Social Construction of Masculinity on New Media: Ekşi Sözlük and Interpretative Repertoires," *NesneDergisi* 9, no. 21 (2021): 511–33.

28 Melis G. Laebens and Aykut Öztürk, "Partisanship and Autocratization: Polarization, Power Asymmetry, and Partisan Social Identities in Türkiye," *Comparative Political Studies* 54, no. 2 (2021): 245–79, https://doi.org/10.1177/0010414020926199.

29 For example, the user "deli the smooth talker" writes: "This is a binary that separates straight men from f*****s. For someone whose gender is listed as male and who heard the phrase 'my lion son' at least once in their life to go watch . . . on such a day is nothing short of being a f*****, is it? I intentionally left the film title blank so that if the reader cannot automatically fill it in, they should confront their own gayness." *Ekşi Sözlük*, July 27, 2023, https://eksisozluk.com/barbie-vs-oppenheimer--7678166.

30 Murat Soner, "Pembesi Gitti Tozu Kaldı – *Barbie* Eleştirisi," YouTube video, August 9, 2023, 28:33, https://www.youtube.com/watch?v=tAmqNSdB5yM.

31 Ali Yaşar, "Barbie'ler ve SJW'ler İçin Detaylı *Barbie* İNCELEMESİ [A Detailed *Barbie* ANALYSIS for Barbies and SJWs]," YouTube video, July 26, 2023, 28:33, https://www.youtube.com/watch?v=D6BR9RiIRkg. Identfying as a "Video creator, scriptwriter, and film critic," Ali Yaşar runs the YouTube channel Filmograf.

32 Adrienne L. Massanari and Shira Chess, "Attack of the 50-Foot Social Justice Warrior: The Discursive Construction of SJW Memes as the Monstrous Feminine," *Feminist Media Studies* 18, no. 4 (2018): 525–42, doi:10.1080/14680777.2018.1447333.

33 The *Oxford English Dictionary* defines "feminazi" as "A person (typically a woman) regarded as holding extreme feminist views. The term was popularized by the United

States talk show host Rush Limbaugh." *Oxford English Dictionary*, s.v. "feminazi (*n.*),"
September 2024, https://doi.org/10.1093/OED/1230073465.

34 Taha Ulukaya, "Barbenheimer - Eleştirel Parodi," August 5, YouTube video, 11:56,
https://www.youtube.com/watch?v=2HApjzJ2_0k.

35 Bob Pease, "The Rise of Angry White Men: Resisting Populist Masculinity and
the Backlash against Gender Equality," in *The Challenge of Right-Wing Nationalist
Populism for Social Work: A Human Rights Approach*, ed. Carolyn Noble and
Goetz Frank Ottmann (New York/London: Routledge, 2021); Joseph Jay Sosa,
"Backlash," *Feminist Anthropology* 3, no. 2 (2022): 198–205, https://doi.org/10.1002/
fea2.12087.

36 Cagla Diner and Şule Toktaş, "Waves of Feminism in Turkey: Kemalist, Islamist and
Kurdish Women's Movements in an Era of Globalization," *Journal of Balkan and Near
Eastern Studies* 12, no. 1 (2010): 41–57, doi:10.1080/19448950903507388.

37 Nil Uzun-Weidner and Aksu Bora, "Women's and Feminist Movements," in
*Authoritarianism and Resistance in Turkey: Conversations on Democratic and Social
Challenges*, ed. Esra Özyürek, Gaye Özpınar, and Emrah Altındiş (Cham: Springer,
2018).

38 Ayşe Güneş and Ezikoğlu Çağlar, "Legal and Political Challenges of Gender Equality
and Crimes Against Women in Türkiye: The Question of Istanbul Convention," *Women
& Criminal Justice* 33, no. 1 (2022): 14–27, doi:10.1080/08974454.2022.2040695.

39 Tuğba Bayar, "Turkey's Withdrawal from Istanbul Convention: International Human
Rights Regime Vis-à-Vis Authoritarian Survival," *Turkish Studies* 25, no. 1 (2023):
22–42, doi:10.1080/14683849.2023.2262721.

40 Ersin Çelik, "İstanbul Sözleşmesi'ndeki LGBT Kodları Nelerdi?," *Yeni Şafak*, March 24,
2021, https://www.yenisafak.com/yazarlar/ersin-celik/istanbul-sozlesmesindeki-lgbt-
kodlari-nelerdi-2057995.

41 Recep Tayyip Erdoğan, quoted in "Recep Tayyip Erdoğan, Women Not Equal to Men,"
Guardian, November 24, 2014, https://www.theguardian.com/world/2014/nov/24/
Türkiyes-president-recep-tayyip-erdogan-women-not-equal-men.

42 Recept Tayypip Erdoğan, quoted in "Recep Tayyip Erdoğan, A Woman Is Above
All Else a Mother," *Guardian*, March 8, 2016, https://www.theguardian.com/
world/2016/mar/08/recep-tayyip-erdogan-a-woman-is-above-all-else-a-mother-
turkish-president.

43 Deniz Kandiyoti, "Locating the Politics of Gender: Patriarchy, Neo-Liberal Governance
and Violence in Turkey," *Research and Policy on Turkey* 1, no. 2 (2016): 103–18, doi:10.
1080/23760818.2016.1201242; Funda Hülagü, "Anti-Feminism in Türkiye: A Critical
Political Economy Perspective," *Gender: Zeitschrift für Geschlecht, Kultur und
Gesellschaft* 6 (2021): 25 –41, http://dx.doi.org/10.25595/2290.

44 Luke, Turner, *Men at War: Loving, Lusting, Fighting, Remembering 1939–1945*.
(London: Weidenfeld & Nicolson, 2024).

45 Tuba Kancı, Buşra Çelik, Yavuz Bülent Bekki, and Umutcan Tarcan, "The Anti-Gender Movement in Turkey: An Analysis of Its Reciprocal Aspects," *Turkish Studies* 24, no. 5 (2023): 882–904, doi:10.1080/14683849.2022.2164189.

46 Ayşe Akalın, "'We Don't Want to Die': Diffuse Feminism against Femicide inTurkey," *Third World Quarterly* (October 2024): 1–17, doi:10.1080/01436597.2024.2413847.

Deeper into Ken: The Accessibility of Ryan Gosling

1 Valvour, "Why Masculinity Is in Crisis (and What We Can Do about It)," *medium.com*, September 7, 2024, https://valvour.medium.com/why-masculinity-is-in-crisis-and-what-we-can-do-about-it-2906289eec11 [no longer available].

2 Stephanie Pappas, "APA issues first-ever guidelines for practice with men and boys," APA.org 50, no. 1 (2019), https://www.apa.org/monitor/2019/01/ce-corner.

3 Pappas, "APA."

4 Richard V. Reeves, *Of Boys and Men: Why the Modern Male Is Struggling, Why It Matters, and What To Do About It* (Washington, DC: Brookings Institution Press, 2022), 21–32.

5 Michael Kimmel and Lisa Wade, "Ask a Feminist: Michael Kimmel and Lisa Wade Discuss Toxic Masculinity," *Signs: Journal of Women in Culture and Society* 44, no. 1 (2018), https://doi.org/10.1086/698284.

6 Pappas, "APA issues first-ever guidelines for practice with men and boys."

7 Ramin Setoodeh, "Ryan Gosling on Nearly Turning Down Ken, Singing Live at the Oscars and Wanting a 'Beach-Off' Over Those 'Barbie' Snubs," *variety.com*, February 7, 2024, https://variety.com/2024/film/features/ryan-gosling-barbie-oscars-performance-snubs-ken-1235898750/.

8 Claire Sisco King and Isaac West, "This Could Be the Place: Queer Acceptance in *Lars and the Real Girl*," *QED: A Journal of GLBTQ Worldmaking* 1, no. 3 (2014): 78.

9 Susan Jeffords, *Hard Bodies: Hollywood Masculinity in the Reagan Era* (New Brunswick, NJ: Rutgers University Press, 1994).

10 Logan Hill, "Building a Bigger Action Hero: Inside Hollywood's Muscle Factory," *Men's Journal*, December 4, 2017, https://www.mensjournal.com/health-fitness/building-a-bigger-action-hero-20140418.

11 Max Olesker, "The Rise and Rise of the Spornosexual," *esquire.com*, January 12, 2015, http://www.esquire.co.uk/culture/features/7588/the-rise-and-rise-of-the-spornosexual.

12 Michael DeAngelis, "Soft and Hard: Accessible Masculinity, Celebrity, and Post-Millennial Cuteness," in *The Aesthetics and Affects of Cuteness*, ed. Joshua Paul Dale,

Joyce Goggin, Julia Leyda, Anthony P. McIntyre, and Diane Negra (New York/London: Routledge, 2017), 194–215.

13 David Greven offers an insightful analysis of this scene in *Ghost Faces: Hollywood and Post-Millennial Masculinity* (Albany: SUNY Press, 2016), 27–9.

14 Team Lehren, "Ryan Gosling Reacts To Fans Viral Response To His Shirtless Ken Photo From Barbie Movie," *lehren.com*, July 2, 2022, https://lehren.com/entertainment/hollywood/ryan-gosling-reacts-viral-shirtless-ken-photo-barbie-movie/139092/.

15 Jacob Osborne, "Ryan Gosling's Ken Workout & Diet Plan," *Man of Many*, July 17, 2023, https://manofmany.com/lifestyle/fitness/ryan-goslings-ken-workout-diet-plan.

16 Osborne, "Ryan Gosling's Ken Workout & Diet Plan."

17 "Ryan Gosling On Waxing His Whole Body for 'Barbie': 'That's the Ken Life,'" *Access Hollywood*, July 14, 2022, YouTube video, 1:55, https://www.youtube.com/watch?v=P1kXpyT2bj8.

18 "Ryan Gosling on his 'fake' abs," *Belfast Telegraph*, September 22, 2011, https://www.belfasttelegraph.co.uk/entertainment/film-tv/news/ryan-gosling-on-his-fake-abs/28661242.html.

19 Morwenna Ferrier, "'It's Just Easier to Dress Like Him Than Not': How the Ryan Gosling Look Took Over," *Guardian*, April 21, 2017, https://www.theguardian.com/fashion/2017/apr/21/ryan-gosling-look-dress-like-him.

20 Greven, *Ghost Faces*, 55.

21 Nancy Epton, *The Sound of Silence: Ryan Gosling, Expressionism and the Silent Hero in 21st Century Film* (London: Bloomsbury, 2024), 123–4.

22 "Literally Me Syndrome/Wow, This Is Literally Me—Wow, This Is Literally Me Origin," *Know Your Meme*, https://knowyourmeme.com/photos/1472164-literally-me-syndrome-wow-this-is-literally-me.

23 Faris Firoozye, "'Literally Me' Characters: A Take on Modern Pop Culture," *The Oxford Blue*, February 10, 2023, https://theoxfordblue.co.uk/literally-me-characters/.

24 Malcolm Croft, *I'm Just Ryan: The Little Guide to Ryan Gosling* (London: Headline, 2024), 77.

25 Armando Quesada Webb, "'Literally me': Why do so many straight guys love Ryan Gosling?" *El Pais Lifestyle*, November 23, 2023, https://english.elpais.com/lifestyle/2023-11-03/literally-me-why-do-so-many-straight-guys-love-ryan-gosling.html.

26 Quesada Webb, "'Literally me.'"

27 Nick Johnstone, *The Biography: Ryan Gosling, Hollywood's Finest* (London: John Blake, 2013), 9.

28 Meka Beresford, "Ryan Gosling: 'I'm 49 percent woman,'" *Pink News*, June 3, 2016, https://www.thepinknews.com/2016/06/03/ryan-gosling-im-49-woman/.

29 Croft, *I'm Just Ryan*, 87.

30 Joanna Benecke, *100 Reasons to Love Ryan Gosling* (Medford, NJ: Plexus Books, 2013).

31 Benecke, *100 Reasons.*

32 Benecke*, 100 Reasons.*

33 "Ken--How Ryan Gosling Lives and How Much He Earns," MixShow Star Newx, September 24, 2023, YouTube video, https://www.youtube.com/watch?v=ILHLtlNH48w.

34 Diana Pearl, "14 Hot Hollywood Male Feminists That Will Set Your Heart Aflame," *People*, April 20, 2017, https://people.com/celebrity/celebrity-men-who-are-feminists/.

35 "Ryan Gosling Does 'Hey Girl,'" *MTV After Hours* hosted by Josh Horowitz, November 12, 2014, YouTube video, 1:47, https://www.youtube.com/watch?v=hawvCTJCjOU.

36 Danielle Henderson, *Feminist Ryan Gosling: Feminist Theory from Your Favorite Sensitive Movie Dude* (Philadelphia: Running Press, 2012), 71.

37 Henderson, *Feminist Ryan Gosling*, 69.

38 Shelley Cobb, "Is this what a feminist looks like? Male celebrity feminists and the postfeminist politics of 'equality,'" *Celebrity Studies* 6, no .1 (2015): 138.

39 Cobb, "Is this what a feminist looks like?," 136.

40 Although neither character is portrayed as homosexual, the power dynamics between high school classmates Richard Haywood (Gosling) and Justin Pendleton (Michael Pitt) in the psychological drama *Murder by Numbers* (dir. Barbet Schroeder, 2002) arguably contains sexual undertones.

41 "Ryan Gosling talks about the queer influences on Ken," *b-gay.com*, https://b-gay.com/ryan-gosling-talks-about-the-queer-influences-on-ken/.

42 Ryan Gosling quoted in "Ryan Gosling talks."

43 Dan Savage, "Ken Comes Out," *The Reader*, July 22, 1993, https://chicagoreader.com/news-politics/ken-comes-out/.

44 Shannon Carlin, "The History Behind Barbie's Ken," *time.com*, 2023, https://time.com/6296386/barbie-ken-history/.

45 Mei Rude, "Ryan Gosling Is Serving Body-ody-ody as Ken in New *Barbie* Still," *out.com*, June 15, 2022.

46 Setoodeh, "Ryan Gosling on Nearly Turning Down Ken."

Barbie, Feminism, and Consumerism: An Incoherent Combination

1 Noël Burch, "Double speak: De l'ambiguïté tendancielle du cinéma hollywoodien," *Réseaux* 99 (2000): 99–130, https://www.persee.fr/doc/reso_0751-7971_2000_

num_18_99_2197. Editor's note: all material published solely in French was translated by Alistair Fox, unless otherwise indicated. When a published English-language version was available, this version was cited.

2 Robin Wood, "Chapter Four: The Incoherent Text: Narrative in the 70s," *Hollywood from Vietnam to Reagan* (New York: Columbia University Press, 1986), 41–62.

3 Sandra Onana, "'Aupres de ma blonde': *Barbie* de Greta Gerwig, la poupée ruse," *Libération*, July 18, 2023, https://www.liberation.fr/culture/cinema/barbie-de-greta-gerwig-la-poupee-ruse-20230718_OHYG2XFF6BH3JFQFPKVZQ23GVQ/.

4 Etienne Sorin, "Notre critique de *Barbie*: La poupée qui fait non," *Le Figaro*, July 19, 2023, https://www.lefigaro.fr/cinema/notre-critique-de-barbie-la-poupee-qui-fait-non-20230718.

5 Cécile Mury, "*Barbie*, un film pop et futé qui vend drôlement bien sa poupée," *Télérama*, July 19, 2023, https://www.telerama.fr/cinema/barbie-un-film-pop-et-fute-qui-vend-drolement-bien-sa-poupee-7027397.php.

6 Cyprien Caddeo, "*Barbie*, poupée dialectique," *L'Humanité*, July 20, 2023, https://www.humanite.fr/culture-et-savoir/cinema/barbie-poupee-dialectique.

7 Murielle Joudet, "*Barbie* Review: A Doll Soaked in Kitsch Mockery," *Le Monde,* July 20, 2023, https://www.lemonde.fr/en/culture/article/2023/07/20/barbie-a-doll-drowned-in-kitsch-mockery_6060003_30.html.

8 "Coppélia," a life-size mechanical doll, is a character in a story by E. T. Hoffman, later adapted as an eponymously titled ballet. [Editor's note.]

9 Charlotte Garson, "*Barbie*, la revente d'une blonde," *Cahiers du cinéma*, July 24, 2023, https://www.cahiersducinema.com/actualites/barbie_-la_revente_d_une_blonde/.

10 Marjolaine Boutet and Hélène Breda, "*Barbie*: Never has the female gaze imposed itself on hundreds of millions of viewers with such force," *Le Monde*, August 16, 2023. Note: Marjolian Boutet is the author of *Vampires: Au-delà du mythe* (Paris: Ellipses, 2011); Cold Case*: La mélodie du passé* (Paris: Presses universitaires de France, 2013); *Une village français: Une histoire de l'occupation. Saisons 1 à 7* (Paris: La Martinière, 2017). Hélène Breda is author of *Les Féminismes à l'ère d'Internet: Lutter entre anciens et nouveaux espaces médiatiques* (Paris: Éditions de l'INA, 2022).

11 Azélie Fayolle, "Une des forces de *Barbie* est de refonder la possibilité du premier degré," *Le Monde*, August 18, 2023, https://www.lemonde.fr/idees/article/2023/08/18/une-des-forces-de-barbie-est-de-refonder-la-possibilite-du-premier-degre_6185812_3232.html. Note: Azélie Fayolle is the author of *Des femmes et du style: Pour un* feminist gaze (Paris: Divergences, 2023).

12 Chiara Piazzesi, "*Barbie*: the younger generations are trying to use beauty culture to their advantage," *Le Monde*, August 26, 2023, https://www.lemonde.fr/en/opinion/article/2023/08/20/barbie-the-younger-generations-are-trying-to-use-beauty-culture-to-their-advantage_6100259_23.html. Note: Chiara Piazzesi is the author of *The Beauty Paradox: Femininity in the Age of Selfies* (Lanham, MD: Rowman & Littlefield, 2023).

13 Audrey Millet, "*Barbie:* This movie shows how capitalism and white-collar workers swallow up political and social demands," *Le Monde*, August 26, 2023, https://www.lemonde.fr/en/opinion/article/2023/08/26/barbie-this-movie-shows-how-capitalism-and-white-collar-workers-swallow-up-political-and-social-demands_6109562_23.html#.

14 Mona Chollet, *Beauté fatale: Les nouveaux visages d'une aliénation féminine* (Paris: La Découverte, 2012).

15 For a discussion of post-feminism from the perspective of a French scholar, see Céline Morin, *Les Héroïnes de séries américaines* (Tours: Presses universitaires François-Rabelais, 2017), https://doi.org/10.4000/books.pufr.9023.

16 Leslie Fielder, *Love and Death in the American Novel*, 2nd ed. (Dallas: Dalkey Archive Press, 1998), 24.

17 The scene evokes choreographers like Busby Berkeley associated with Classical Hollywood, who have been routinely copied and parodied. See, for example, the "Springtime for Hitler" sequence in *The Producers* (dir. Mel Brooks, 1968).

18 "Barbie," *scriptslug.com*, https://www.scriptslug.com/script/barbie-2023.

19 Eliana Dockterman, "Ruth Handler Is the Key to *Barbie*: What To Know About the Doll's Controversial Founder," *Time Magazine*, July 21, 2023, https://time.com/6293762/barbie-movie-ruth-handler/.

20 This ambivalence, as defined by Burch, manifested in what has been called "the woman's film" of the Hollywood era, led some scholars to argue that Hollywood cinema offered a vision of femininity (or more accurately a feminine subject) defined by masochism. See, for example, Mary Ann Doane, *The Desire to Desire: The Woman's Film of the 1940s* (Bloomington: Indiana University Press, 1987).

The Politics of "Always" and "Never": The Monologue Heard Around the World—Race, Class, and Gender in *Barbie*

1 Rebecca Rubin describes a *Barbie* "machine … that's sweeping the world." This machine constitutes an integrated production, distribution, and marketing strategy documented in a number of sources and accounts of the prerelease and postrelease of the film. See Rebecca Rubin, "Inside Barbie's Pink Publicity Machine: How Warner Bros. Pulled off the Marketing Campaign of the Year," *Variety,* July 23, 2023, https://variety.com/2023/film/box-office/barbie-marketing-campaign-explained-warner-bros-1235677922/.

2 For an excellent analysis of the film and brand as cultural "influencer," see Jul Parke, "Barbie isn't just a movie now— she's also a virtual social media influencer." *The Conversation*, July 18, 2023, https://theconversation.com/barbie-isnt-just-a-movie-star-now-shes-also-a-virtual-social-media-influencer-207885.

3 See, for example, Erik Kain, "The 'Barbie' Movie Isn't Feminist Propaganda, It's a Two-Hour Mattel Commercial," *Forbes*, August 5, 2023, https://www.forbes.com/sites/erikkain/2023/08/05/the-barbie-movie-isnt-feminist-propaganda-its-a-two-hour-mattel-commercial/.

4 For a highly engaging history of the abuses of the Hollywood moguls and the studio apparatus, see Karina Longworth, *Seduction: Sex, Lies, and Stardom in Howard Hughes's Hollywood* (New York: HarperCollins, 2018). For a fascinating analysis of the way in which actresses negotiated the strictures of patriarchy within the classical studio system, see Carmen Emily, *Independent Stardom: Freelance Women in the Hollywood Studio System* (Austin: University of Texas Press, 2016).

5 Films that interrogate patriarchy as a social and cultural organization include Jane Campion's *The Piano* (1993), Céline Sciamma's radiant *Portrait of a Lady on Fire* (2019), and the recent *Sight and Sound* "greatest films of all time" poll number 1, Chantal Ackerman's *Jeanne Dielman, 23 quai du Commerce, 1080 Bruxelles* (1975).

6 Bruce Isaacs, "Barbie Review," University of Sydney Instagram: Sydney_uni, July 27, 2023, https://www.instagram.com/sydney_uni/reel/CvL0F76Ov6a/.

7 I use the concept of intersectionality to refer to ways in which people are empowered and disempowered through the operation of institutions, regimes, and systems of oppression; this is primarily a Foucauldian reading on my part. But what is significant for me is that intersectional political theory seeks to expand and deepen easy and convenient models of identity politics. For a useful overview, see Angela R. Wilson, ed., *Situating Intersectionality: Politics, Policy, and Power* (New York: Palgrave Macmillan, 2013).

8 For Jameson's highly influential model of how capitalism structures thought, feeling, and action, see Frederic Jameson, *Postmodernism, or, The Cultural Logic of Late Capitalism* (Durham, NC: Duke University Press, 1992).

9 One of the most intriguing passages in the film and, I would argue, a second intrusion of the Lacanian real, occurs in the scene in which Barbie has what she refers to as a "real Proustian flashback." The memory represents the excess of the commodified product and its shelf life. In these sorts of references to other text scattered through the film, we see Gerwig's desire to construct an intellectual, and even literary, tapestry of ideas, themes, and philosophical concepts.

10 For her seminal formulation that brings existentialist thought to phenomenology, see Judith Butler, "Performative Acts and Gender Constitution: An Essay in Phenomenology and Feminist Theory," *Theatre Journal* 40, no. 4 (1988): 519–31. Butler writes: "[Gender] is an identity tenuously constituted in time—an identity instituted through a *stylized repetition of acts* ... This formulation moves the conception of gender off the ground of a substantial model of identity to one that requires a conception of a constituted *social temporality*" (pp. 519–20; italics in original).

11 Jean Baudrillard, *Simulacra and Simulation*, trans. Sheila Faria Glaser (Ann Arbor: University of Michigan Press, 1994).

12 See, for example, *The 40-Year-Old Virgin* (dir. Judd Apatow, 2005) and *Knocked-Up* (dir. Judd Apatow, 2007). For a superb reading of the way in which a postmodern aesthetic was constituted by irony and sincerity, see Jim Collins, "Genericity in the 90s: Eclectic Irony and the New Sincerity," in *Film Theory Goes to the Movies*, ed. Jim Collins, Ava Preacher Collins, and Hilary Radner (New York: Routledge, 1992), 242–64.

13 Adam Hodges, "'Yes, We Can' and the Power of Political Slogans," *Anthropology News* (2019), https://www.independent.co.uk/voices/trump-women-abortion-your-body-my-choice-b2644855.html.

14 For an excellent introduction to literary theory and the theory of the signifier, see Mathew R. Martin, *Psychoanalysis and Literary Theory: An Introduction* (London: Routledge, 2022).

15 Emma Clarke, "Your Body, Trump's Choice—America's war on women is about to get even worse," *Independent*, November 11, 2024, https://www.independent.co.uk/voices/trump-women-abortion-your-body-my-choice-b2644855.html.

16 Clare Duffy, "'Your body, my choice': Attacks on women surge on social medial following election," *CNN*, November 12, 2024, https://edition.cnn.com/2024/11/11/business/your-body-my-choice-movement-election/index.html.

17 See Debbie Ging, "Alphas, Betas, and Incels: Theorizing the Masculinities of the Manosphere," *Men and Masculinities* 22, no. 4 (2019): 638–57.

18 See Mark Bevir, "Foucault, Power, and Institutions," *Political Studies* 47 (1999): 345–59.

19 Andreas Reckwitz, *The End of Illusions: Politics, Economy, and Culture in Late Modernity* (Cambridge: Polity Press, 2021), 8.

20 For an excellent analysis of the way in which individual social media feeds integrate with advertising and influencer categories and discourse, see Martin J. Reidl, Josephine Lukito, and Samuel C. Woolley, "Political Influencers on Social Media: An Introduction," *Social Media + Society* 9/2 (2023): 1–9.

21 Intriguingly, Reckwitz describes the work of self-*making* as the "weariness of self-actualization": "[T]o an unprecedented extent, late modernity is a thoroughly psychologized culture that encourages individual self-reflection and self-transformation." Reckwitz, *The End of Ilusions*, 111.

22 Bella Arnold and Alejandra Gularte, "What Else is in Mattel's Toy Box?" *Vulture*, September 17, 2024, https://www.vulture.com/article/mattel-movies-upcoming.html.

Barbie, the Feminist Mattel Ad

1 McKenzie Wark, "*Détournement*: An Abuser's Guide," *Angelaki* 14, no. 1 (2009): 148.

2 Margot Robbie quoted in Eliana Dockterman, "How Barbie Came to Life," *Time*, June 27, 2023, https://time.com/6289864/barbie.time.cover.story/.

3 For example, the following commentators on *Barbie*'s feminism referred to the production, respectively, as "an overwritten hundred million-dollar Mattel commercial" and "an ad for Mattel." Chavisa Woods, "The Insidious Faux-Feminism of Barbie," *Full Stop*, August 7, 2023, https://www.full-stop.net/2023/08/07/features/essays/chavisa-woods/the-insidious-faux-feminism-of-barbie/; Tré Ventour-Griffiths, "'I Am Kenough': Guy DeBord, *Barbie*, and *The Society of the Spectacle*," *Medium*, September 7, 2023, https://treventour1995.medium.com/i-am-kenough-guy-debord-barbie-and-the-society-of-the-spectacle-bc4dfab17d5.

4 Roland Barthes, "Myth Today: The Inoculation," *Mythologies*, trans. Annette Lavers (New York: The Noonday Press / Farrar, Straus & Giroux, 25th printing, 1991), 151–2. See also White in this volume, 44. Originally published in French as: Roland Barthes, *Mythologies* (Paris: Éditions du Seuil, 1957).

5 Barthes, "Myth Today," 151.

6 Barthes, "Myth Today," 152.

7 Wark, "*Détournement*," 150.

8 Andi Zeisler, *We Were Feminists Once* (New York: Public Affairs, 2016).

9 Cheva Sandoval, *Methodology of the Oppressed* (Minneapolis: University of Minnesota Press, 2000), 118.

10 Barthes, "Myth Today," 151.

11 Sandoval, *Methodology of the Oppressed*, 118.

12 Barthes, "Myth Today," 151.

13 Barthes writes in 1957: "Les textes qui suivent on été écrits pendant environs deux ans, de 1954 à 1956, au gré de l'actualité" ["The texts that follow were written during about two years, from 1954 to 1956, to meet current demand," trans. Hilary Radner]. Roland Barthes, "Avant-propos," in *Mythologies*, 9.

14 Barthes, "Myth Today," 151.

15 Luc Boltanski and Eve Chiapello, *The New Spirit of Capitalism* (London: Verso, 2005). See Nancy Fraser's discussion of this source in relation to feminism in "Feminism, Capitalism and the Cunning of History," *New Left Review* 56 (2009): 97–117.

16 Wark, "*Détournement*," 150.

17 McKenzie Wark, *The Beach Beneath the Street: The Everyday Life and Glorious Times of the Situationist International*, (London: Verso, 2011); McKenzie Wark, *Fifty Years of Recuperation: The Situationist International 1957–2007* (New York: Princeton Architectural Press, 2008).

18 Guy Debord, "*Détournement* as Negation and Prelude," in *Situationist International Anthology*, ed. and trans. Ken Knabb. (Berkeley: Bureau of Public Secrets, 2006 [1959]); Guy Debord and Gil J. Wolman, *A User's Guide to Détournement* (Berkeley: Bureau of Public Secrets, 1956).

19 The Barbie Liberation Organization was created by Igor Vamos (a.k.a. Mike Bannano) of The Yes Men. The Yes Men practice "counterfeit *détournement*" (Wark, "*Détournement*," 149), which they term "identity correction," a practice of impersonating an entity such as a corporation or government in order to formally apologize for crimes that entity has committed but officially denies, thereby "correcting" the entity's public image and according due attention to crimes of the powerful. See The Yes Men, *The True Story of the End of the World Trade Organization* (London: Penguin, 2004). I gratefully acknowledge the Barbie Liberation Organization for granting access to their archive.

20 The Yes Men, *True Story*, 11.

21 Johanna Isaacson, "From Riot Grrrl to CrimethInc: A Lineage of Expressive Negation in Feminist Punk and Queercore," *Liminalities: A Journal of Performance Studies* 7, no. 4 (2011), http://liminalities.net/7-4/expressivenegation.pdf. More recent examples of feminist *détournement* include two-person art collective Soda Jerk's remix movies like *Terror Nullius* (dir. Soda Jerk, 2018), which recuts a wide breadth of Australian cinema classics into a new movie critiquing white settler colonialism through an intersectional feminist lens, and Anna Gensler's artful *détourning* of dick pics on Instagram: see Laura Vitis and Fairleigh Gilmour, "Dick Pics on Blast: A Woman's Resistance to Online Sexual Harassment Using Humour, Art and Instagram," *Crime, Media, Culture* 13, no. 3 (2017): 335–55.

22 See Guy Debord, *The Society of the Spectacle*, trans. Ken Knabb (Berkeley: Bureau of Public Secrets, 2014 [1967]) and Giorgio Agamben, "Difference and Repetition: On Guy Debord's Films," in *Guy Debord and the Situationist International: Texts and Documents*, ed. Tom McDonough (Cambridge, MA: MIT Press, 2002).

23 Wark, "*Détournement*," 150.

24 Wark, "*Détournement*," 145.

25 Fraser, "Feminism, Capitalism," 144.

26 Wark, "*Détournement*," 151.

27 Wark, "*Détournement*," 152.

28 See Angela McRobbie, *The Aftermath of Feminism: Gender, Culture and Social Change* (London: Sage, 2009) and Rosalind Gill, "Postfeminist Media Culture: Elements of a Sensibility," *European Journal of Cultural Studies* 10, no. 2 (2007): 147–66.

29 Linda Alcoff and Laura Gray, "Survivor Discourse: Transgression or Recuperation?," *Signs: Journal of Women in Culture and Society* 18, no. 2 (1993): 268.

30 Lisa Coulthard, Tanya Horeck, Barbara Klinger, and Kathleen McHugh, "Broken Bodies/Inquiring Minds: Women in Contemporary Transnational TV Crime Drama," *Television & New Media* 19, no. 6 (2018): 513.

31 Zeisler, *We Were Feminists Once*; Sarah Banet-Weiser, *Empowered: Popular Feminism and Popular Misogyny* (Durham, NC: Duke University Press, 2018); Anna Marie

Bautista, *Conspicuous Feminism on Television: Gender, Power, and #MeToo* (Lanham, MD: Lexington Books/Rowman & Littlefield, 2023).

32 Zeisler, *We Were Feminists Once*, 7.

33 On the #MeToo movement, see Tarana Burke, *Unbound: My Story of Liberation and the Birth of the Me Too Movement* (London: Headline, 2021).

34 Claudia Mitchell and Jacqueline Reid-Walsh, "And I Want to Thank You Barbie: Barbie as a Site for Cultural Interrogation," *The Review of Education/Pedagogy/Cultural Studies* 17, no. 2 (1995): 143–55.

35 Karen Orr Vered and Christèle Maizonniaux, "Barbie and the Straight-to-DVD Movie: Pink Post-Feminist Pedagogy," *Feminist Media Studies* 17, no. 2 (2017): 200.

36 For example, in West Virginia a bill sought to "ban the sale of Barbie dolls because they 'place an undue importance on physical beauty to the detriment of [girls'] intellectual and emotional development.'" See Orr Vered and Maizonniaux, "Barbie and the Straight-to-DVD Movie," 200.

37 Orr Vered and Maizonniaux, "Barbie and the Straight-to-DVD Movie," 201.

38 Orr Vered and Maizonniaux, "Barbie and the Straight-to-DVD Movie," 200–1.

39 Eliana Dockterman, "How Barbie Came to Life," *Time*, June 27, 2023, https://time.com/6289864/barbie.time.cover.story/.

40 Dockterman, "How Barbie Came to Life."

41 Abbey White, "Why 'Barbie' Creatives and Mattel Execs Struggle to Agree on Whether the Film Is Feminist," *The Hollywood Reporter*, June 27, 2023, https://www.hollywoodreporter.com/movies/movie-news/barbie-team-mattel-executives-barbie-movie-feminist-1235524678/.

42 Jack Sharf, "Mattel President flew to London to argue with Margot Robbie and Greta Gerwig over an off-brand 'Barbie' scene," *Variety,* June 27, 2023, https://variety.com/2023/film/news/mattel-ceo-argued-margot-robbie-barbie-scene-off-brand-1235655398/.

43 Kyle Buchanan, "Greta Gerwig on the Blockbuster 'Barbie' Opening (and How She Got Away with It)," *New York Times*, June 27, 2023, https://www.nytimes.com/2023/07/25/movies/greta-gerwig-barbie-movie.html.

44 Sharf, "Mattel President Flew."

45 Dockterman, "How Barbie Came to Life."

46 Adam Hanieh, "Petrochemical Empire. The Geo-Politics of Fossil-Fueled Production," *New Left Review* 130 (2021): 25–51.

47 Buchanan, "Greta Gerwig on the Blockbuster 'Barbie.'"

48 Mattel, Inc., "2023 Proxy Statement and Notice of Annual Meeting of Stockholders" (El Segundo, CA: Mattel, Inc., 2023), 8, https://s201.q4cdn.com/696436908/files/doc_financials/2022/ar/Mattel-2023-Proxy-Statement-Bookmarked.pdf.

49 "Workers in Misery: An Investigation into Two Toy Factories," *chinalaborwatch.org*, December 3, 2020, https://chinalaborwatch.org/workers-in-misery-an-investigation-into-two-toy-factories/.

50 "The Hypocrisy of Barbie's Feminism—Labor Conditions of Working Class Women in a Mattel Factory in China," *chinalaborwatch.org*, October 18, 2024, https://chinalaborwatch.org/the-hypocrisy-of-barbies-feminism-labor-conditions-of-working-class-women-in-a-mattel-factory-in-china/.

51 Alcoff and Gray, "Survivor Discourse," 282.

52 Barbie Liberation Organization, "Ecowarrior Barbie," *barbieliberation.org*, https://www.barbieliberation.org/mycelia.

53 See Nardine Saad, "Daryl Hannah announced a plastic-free Barbie, but it was actually a hoax—here's what happened," *Los Angeles Times*, August 3, 2023, https://www.latimes.com/entertainment-arts/movies/story/2023-08-02/daryl-hannahs-ecowarrior-barbie-mattel-hoax#:~:text=The%20elaborate%20prank%20also%20involved,bogus%20media%20contact%20e%2Dmail.

Plastic, Kitsch: Ecologies of Barbie Land

1 Mél Hogan, "Artificial Intelligence is a Hot Mess," in *Training the Archive*, ed. Inke Arns, Eva Birkenstock, Dominik Bönisch, and Francis Hunger (Köln: König, 2024), 33–54, https://www.academia.edu/113935440/AI_is_a_Hot_Mess_2024.

2 Jennifer Dawn Whitney, "Beauty Made Plastic: Constructions of a Western Feminine Ideal," *Word and Text: A Journal of Literary Studies and Linguistics* 3, no. 2 (2013): 119–32, citing Sander L. Gilman, *Making the Body Beautiful: A Cultural History of Aesthetic Surgery* (Princeton: Princeton University Press, 1999).

3 See Fredric Jameson, "Postmodernism, or the Cultural Logic of Late Capitalism," *New Left Review* 146 (1984): 53–92; Linda Hutcheon, *A Poetics of Postmodernism* (London: Routledge, 1988).

4 OECD (Organisation for Economic Co-operation and Development), *Global Plastics Outlook: Economic Drivers, Environmental Impacts, and Policy Options* (Paris: OECD Publishing, 2022), https://doi.org/10.1787/de747aef-en.

5 National Research Council, *Polymer Science and Engineering: The Shifting Research Frontiers* (Washington, DC: The National Academies Press, 1994), 65, https://doi.org/10.17226/2307.

6 EIA (U.S. Energy Information Administration), "How much oil is used to make plastic?," Frequently Asked Questions, last modified July 10, 2024, https://www.eia.gov/tools/faqs/faq.php?id=34&t=6.

7 Nick Couldry and Ulises A. Mejias, *The Costs of Connection: How Data is Colonizing Human Life and Appropriating It for Capitalism* (Stanford: Stanford University Press, 2019).

8 Eva Boesenberg, "Saving the Planet with Barbie? Ecological Perspectives on a Plastic Doll," *M/C Journal* 27, no. 3 (2024), https://www.journal.media-culture.org.au/index.php/mcjournal/article/view/3069.

9 Heather B. Trigg and Stephen A. Mrozowski, "Dominion and Improvement: The Moral Ecologies of Colonial encounters," *Journal of Social Archaeology* 4: 23 (2024): 246–65, https://doi.org/10.1177/14696053241268.

10 Amelia Tait, "Let's Not Forget the Real Star of *Barbie*: Shameless Product Placement," *Guardian*, August 11, 2023, https://www.theguardian.com/commentisfree/2023/aug/10/barbie-shameless-product-placement-film-adverts-global-cinema.

11 Amelia Tait, "Let's Not Forget."

12 Nicole Sudhindra, "Barbie and Bratz: The Feud Continues," *WIPO Magazine*, August 2020, https://www.wipo.int/wipo_magazine/en/2011/04/article_0006.html.

13 Anirban Gupta-Nigam, "Plastic Flowers: Overlooking Resource Scarcity in Postwar America," *Theory, Culture & Society* 37, no. 6 (2020): 128.

14 Richard Dyer, *Heavenly Bodies: Film Stars and Society,* 2nd ed. (London: Macmillan, 2004).

15 UNEP (United Nations Environment Programme), *Turning off the Tap. How the World Can End Plastic Pollution and Create a Circular Economy* (Nairobi: UNEP, 2023), https://wedocs.unep.org/bitstream/handle/20.500.11822/42277/Plastic_pollution.pdf?sequence=3.

16 Patrick Wolfe, "Settler Colonialism and the Elimination of the Native," *Journal of Genocide Research* 8, no. 4 (2006): 387–409.

17 E. P. Thompson, "Time, Work-Discipline and Industrial Capitalism," *Past and Present* 38 (1967): 95.

18 Alain Badiou with Nicolas Truong, *In Praise of Love*, trans. Peter Bush (London: Serpent's Tail, 2012).

19 For a different history, see Jerry Oppenheimer, *Toy Monster: The Big, Bad World of Mattel* (Hoboken, NJ: John Wiley & Sons, 2009), 13–16.

20 Slavoj Žižek, *Less than Nothing: Hegel and the Shadow of Dialectical Materialism* (London: Verso, 2012), https://search.ebscohost.com/login.aspx?direct=true&scope=site&db=nlebk&db=nlabk&AN=729941.

21 Žižek, *Less Than Nothing*, 367.

22 Trisia Farrelly, Sy Taffel, and Ian Shaw, eds., *Plastic Legacies: Pollution, Persistence, and Politics* (Edmonton: Athabasca University Press, 2021).

23 Mary Arensberg, ed., *The American Sublime* (Albany: SUNY Press, 1986).

24 Heather Davis, *Plastic Matter* (Durham, NC: Duke University Press, 2022).

25 Tom Perkins, "Coffee, Eggs and White Rice Linked to Higher Levels of PFAS in Human Body," *Guardian*, July 4, 2024, https://www.theguardian.com/environment/article/2024/jul/04/pfas-toxic-forever-chemicals-food.

26 Bruno Latour, *We Have Never Been Modern*, trans. Catherine Porter (Cambridge, MA: Harvard University Press, 1993), 10–11.

27 Catherine Malabou, *The Future of Hegel: Plasticity, Temporality, and Dialectic*, trans. Lisbeth During (New York: Routledge, 2005); Catherine Malabou, *Ontology of the Accident: An Essay on Destructive Plasticity*, trans. Carolyn Shread (Cambridge: Polity Press, 2012).

28 Alberto Toscano, "Plasticity, Capital, and the Dialectic," in *Plastic Materialities: Politics, Legality, and Metamorphosis in the work of Catherine Malabou*, ed. Brenna Bhandar and Jonathan Coldberg-Hiller (Durham, NC: Duke University Press), 91–110; Justin Clemens, "The Age of Plastic; or, Catherine Malabou on the Hegelian Futures Market," *Cosmos and History: The Journal of Natural and Social Philosophy* 6, no. 1 (2010): 153–62.

29 Catherine Malabou, *What Should We Do with Our Brain?*, trans. Sebastian Rand (New York: Fordham University Press, 2008), 82.

30 Sy Taffel, 'Technofossils of the Anthropocene: Media, Geology and Plastics', *Cultural Politics* 12, no. 3 (2016): 360.

31 Seán Cubitt, "Virtual Screens and the Human Gaze," in *Virtual Production: What Is Real?* ed. Sian Mitchell, Colin Perry, Sean Redmond, and Lienors Torre (London: Routledge, 2025).

32 Mike Davis, *Ecology of Fear: Los Angeles and the Imagination of Disaster* (London: Picador, 1998).

33 Malabou, *What Should We Do with Our Brain?*, 82.

34 Taffel, "Technofossils of the Anthropocene," 360.

35 Clement Greenberg, "Avant-Garde and Kitsch," in *Art and Culture: Critical Essays* (Boston: Beacon Press, 1961), 10.

36 Klaus Theweleit, *Male Fantasies: Volume One – Women, Floods, Bodies, History*, trans. Stephen Conway (Cambridge: Polity Press, 1987).

37 Clement Greenberg, "Avant-Garde and Kitsch," 10.

38 Terry Smith, *What Is Contemporary Art?* (Chicago: University of Chicago Press, 2009).

39 Theodor W. Adorno, *Aesthetic Theory*, ed. Gretel Adorno and Rolf Tiedemann, trans. Robert Hullot-Kentor (London: Athlone Press, 1997).

40 Tomas Kulka, *Kitsch and Art* (University Park, PA: Pennsylvania State University Press, 1996), 111.

41 Linda Hutcheon, *A Poetics of Postmodernism* (London: Routledge, 1988), 11.

42 "*Realist* means: laying bare society's causal network," Bertolt Brecht in "The Popular and the Realistic," *Brecht on Theatre*, ed. and trans. John Willett (New York: Hill & Wang, 1964), 109.

43 Bernard Stiegler, *Technics and Time 2: Disorientation*, trans. Stephen Barker (Stanford: Stanford University Press, 2009), 163.

44 Bertolt Brecht in "A Short Organum for the Theatre," *Brecht on Theatre*, ed. and trans. Willett, 181.

Greta Gerwig: Biography and Filmography

1 Vikram Murthi, "A Requiem for Mumblecore: Looking Back at the Last Time Movies Were Allowed to Be Small," *Indiewire*, August 14, 2024, www.indiewire.com/criticism/movies/mumblecore-requiem-funny-ha-ha-andrew-bujalski-joe-swanberg-greta-gerwig-1235036281/.

2 All cited release dates and film budgets are sourced from *The Numbers*, https://www.the-numbers.com/.

3 Mark Olsen, "The Accidental 'It' Girl," *Los Angeles Times*, July 26, 2008, https://www.latimes.com/archives/la-xpm-2008-jul-26-et-greta26-story.html.

4 Guy Adams, "Greta Gerwig: The queen of low-budget cinema is breaking into the mainstream with her role in *Arthur*," *Independent*, April 16, 2011, https://www.independent.co.uk/arts-entertainment/films/features/greta-gerwig-the-queen-of-lowbudget-cinema-is-breaking-into-the-mainstream-with-her-role-in-arthur-2267216.html.

5 Tatiana Siegel, "The first couple of film: Greta Gerwig and Noah Baumbach open up on their personal and professional partnership," *The Hollywood Reporter*, December 13, 2019, https://www.hollywoodreporter.com/movies/movie-features/greta-gerwig-noah-baumbach-are-making-history-oscars-season-1261857/.

6 Gerwig began writing *Lady Bird* in 2013. Aisha Harris, "Greta Gerwig on Lady Bird, John Hughes, and Being 'Ready' to Step Behind the Camera," *Slate*, December 8, 2017, https://slate.com/culture/2017/12/greta-gerwig-on-em-lady-bird-em-john-hughes-and-being-ready-to-step-behind-the-camera.html.

7 Esther Zuckerman, "How Greta Gerwig Turned the Personal 'Lady Bird' into a Perfect Movie," *Rolling Stone*, November 6, 2017, https://www.rollingstone.com/tv-movies/tv-movie-features/how-greta-gerwig-turned-the-personal-lady-bird-into-a-perfect-movie-126300/

8 Neil Iyer, "The Demise of Mid-Budget Cinema," *Independent Magazine*, October 22, 2022, https://independent-magazine.org/2022/10/22/the-demise-of-mid-budget-cinema/.

9 Brent Lang, "Greta Gerwig's 'Narnia' adaptation for Netflix gets Imax release," *Variety*, January 17, 2025, https://variety.com/2025/film/news/greta-gerwig-narnia-adaptation-netflix-imax-release-date-1236277005/.

10 "He doesn't tend to write American characters, but Mike Leigh continues to be my favorite." Greta Gerwig speaking to host Kirsty Lang in "Greta Gerwig, Opportunities for disabled actors, National Short Story Award," *Front Row* podcast, February 14, 2018, https://www.bbc.co.uk/programmes/b09r3nsz.

Barbie (dir. Greta Gerwig, 2023): Summary in Three Acts

1 All dialogue and quoted descriptions, unless otherwise indicated, from Greta Gerwig and Noah Baumbach, "Barbie," *Deadline*, https://deadline.com/wp-content/uploads/2024/02/Barbie-Read-The-Screenplay.pdf.

Select Bibliography

Adorno, Theodor W. *Aesthetic Theory*. Edited by Gretel Adorno and Rolf Tiedemann. Translated by Robert Hullot-Kentor. London: Athlone Press, 1997.

Agamben, Giorgio. "Difference and Repetition: On Guy Debord's Films." In *Guy Debord and the Situationist International: Texts and Documents*, edited by Tom McDonough, 313–20. Cambridge, MA: MIT Press, 2002.

Ahmed, Sara. *Queer Phenomenology*. Durham, NC: Duke University Press, 2006.

Akalın, Ayşe. "'We Don't Want to Die': Diffuse Feminism against Femicide in Turkey." *Third World Quarterly* (October 2024): 1–17. doi:10.1080/01436597.2024.2413847.

Alcoff, Linda, and Laura Gray. "Survivor Discourse: Transgression or Recuperation?" *Signs: Journal of Women in Culture and Society* 18, no. 2 (1993): 260–90.

Alexander, Cate, and Camille Intson. "Bimbos and Bombs: The Barbenheimer Phenomena." *Imaginations: Journal of Cross-Cultural Image Studies* (March 2024): 1–13.

Arensberg, Mary, ed. *The American Sublime*. Albany: SUNY Press, 1986.

Badiou, Alain, with Nicolas Truong. *In Praise of Love*. Translated by Peter Bush. London: Serpent's Tail, 2012.

Badley, Linda, Claire Perkins, and Michele Schreiber. "Introduction." In *Indie Reframed: Women's Filmmaking and Contemporary American Independent Cinema*, edited by Linda Badley et al., 2–3. Edinburgh: Edinburgh University Press, 2016.

Banet-Weiser, Sarah. *Empowered: Popular Feminism and Popular Misogyny*. Durham, NC: Duke University Press, 2018.

Barthes, Roland. *Mythologies*. Translated by Annette Lavers. New York: The Noonday Press / Farrar, Straus & Giroux [25th printing, 1991]. Originally published in French as: Roland Barthes, *Mythologies*. Paris: Éditions du Seuil, 1957.

Basinger, Jeanine. *A Woman's View: How Hollywood Spoke to Women, 1930–1960*. New York: Knopf, 1993.

Baudrillard, Jean. *Simulacra and Simulation*. Translated by Sheila Faria Glaser. Ann Arbor: University of Michigan Press, 1994.

Bautista, Anna Marie. *Conspicuous Feminism on Television: Gender, Power, and #MeToo*. London: Rowman & Littlefield, 2023.

Bayar, Tuğba. "Turkey's Withdrawal from Istanbul Convention: International Human Rights Regime vis à vis Authoritarian Survival." *Turkish Studies* 25, no. 1 (2023): 22–42. doi:10.1080/14683849.2023.2262721.

Behlil, Melis. "Turkey: Transnational Dimensions of a Large National Film Industry." In *Contemporary Balkan Cinema: Transnational Exchanges and Global Circuits*, edited by Lydia Papadimitriou and Ana Grgić. Edinburgh: Edinburgh University Press, 2020.

Benecke, Joanna. *100 Reasons to Love Ryan Gosling*. New York: Plexus Books, 2013.

Benson-Allot, Caetlin. "Greta Gerwig's Girlhood Trilogy." *Film Quarterly* 77, no. 2 (2023): 67–72.

Berber, John. *Ways of Seeing*. London: BBC / Penguin, 1972.

Berlant, Lauren. *Cruel Optimism*. Durham, NC: Duke University Press, 2011.

Bevir, Mark. "Foucault, Power, and Institutions." *Political Studies* 47 (1999): 345–59.

Biguenet, John. "Double Takes: The Role of Allusion in Cinema." In *Play It Again Sam: Retakes on Remakes*, edited by Andrew Horton and Stuart Y. McDougal. Los Angeles: UCLA Press, 1998.

Boltanski, Luc, and Eve Chiapello. *The New Spirit of Capitalism*. London: Verso, 2005.

Boorstin, Daniel J. *The Image: A Guide to Pseudo-Events in America*. New York: Atheneum, 1962.

Bourriaud, Nicolas. *Postproduction: Culture as Screenplay: How Art Reprograms the World*. New York: Lukas & Sternberg, 2002.

Boutet, Marjolaine. *Vampires: Au-delà du mythe*. Paris: Ellipses, 2011.

Boutet, Marjolaine. Cold Case: *La mélodie du passé*. Paris: Presses universitaires de France, 2013.

Boutet, Marjolaine *Un village français: Une histoire de l'occupation. Saisons 1 à 7*. Paris: La Martinière, 2017.

Boyce Kay, Jilly. *Gender, Media and Voice: Communicative Injustice and Public Speech*. Cham: Springer, 2020.

Bradbury-Rance, Clara. "Butch Barbie." *Feminist Media Studies* (July 25, 2024): 1–5.

Brecht, Bertolt. *Brecht on Theatre*. Edited and translated by John Willett. New York: Hill & Wang, 1964.

Breda, Hélène. *Les Féminismes à l'ère d'Internet: Lutter entre anciens et nouveaux espaces médiatiques. Paris*: Editions de l'INA, 2022.

Brunsdon, Charlotte. *Screen Tastes: Soap Opera to Satellite Dishes*. New York: Routledge, 1996.

Burch, Noël. "Double Speak: De l'ambiguïté tendancielle du cinéma hollywoodien." *Réseaux* 99 (2000) : 99–130. https://www.persee.fr/doc/reso_0751-7971_2000_num_18_99_2197.

Burke, Tarana. *Unbound: My Story of Liberation and the Birth of the Me Too Movement*. London: Headline, 2021.

Butler, Judith. *Gender Trouble: Feminism and the Subversion of Identity*. New York: Routledge, 1990.

Butler, Judith. "Performative Acts and Gender Constitution." *Theatre Journal* 40, no. 4 (December 1988): 519–31.

Butler, Judith. *Undoing Gender*. New York/London: Routledge, 2004.

Byrnes, Alicia. "Surface *and* Depth: Ambivalence as Postfeminist Ideal in *Barbie*." *Feminist Media Studies* (July 17, 2024): 1–7.

Chollet, Mona. *Beauté fatale: Les nouveaux visages d'une aliénation féminine*. Paris: La Découverte, 2012.

Clemens, Justin. "The Age of Plastic; or, Catherine Malabou on the Hegelian Futures Market." *Cosmos and History: The Journal of Natural and Social Philosophy* 6, no. 1 (2010): 153–62.

Cobb, Shelley. "Is this What a Feminist Looks Like? Male Celebrity Feminists and the Postfeminist Politics of 'Equality.'" *Celebrity Studies* 6, no. 1 (2015): 136–9.

Collins, Jim. "Genericity in the 90s: Eclectic Irony and the New Sincerity." In *Film Theory Goes to the Movies*, edited by Jim Collins, Ava Preacher Collins, and Hilary Radner, 242–64. New York: Routledge, 1992.

Corrigan, Timothy. "The Commerce of Auteurism: A Voice without Authority." *New German Critique* 49 (Winter 1990): 50.

Couldry, Nick, and Ulises A. Mejias. *The Costs of Connection: How Data Is Colonizing Human Life and Appropriating It for Capitalism*. Stanford: Stanford University Press, 2019.

Coulthard, Lisa, Tanya Horeck, Barbara Klinger, and Kathleen McHugh. "Broken Bodies/ Inquiring Minds: Women in Contemporary Transnational TV Crime Drama." *Television & New Media* 19, no. 6 (2018): 507–14.

Craik, Jennifer. *The Face of Fashion: Cultural Studies in Fashion*. New York: Routledge, 1994.

Croft, Malcolm. *I'm Just Ryan: The Little Guide to Ryan Gosling*. London: Headline, 2024.

Cubitt, Seán. "Virtual Screens and the Human Gaze." In *The Screens of Virtual Production: What Is Real?* edited by Sian Mitchell, Colin Perry, Sean Redmond, and Lienors Torre, 211–24. London: Routledge, 2025.

Cunningham, Stuart, and David Randolph Craig. *Social Media Entertainment: The New Intersection of Hollywood and Silicon Valley*. New York: New York University Press, 2019.

Davis, Fred. *Fashion, Culture and Identity*. Chicago: University of Chicago Press, 1992.

Davis, Heather. *Plastic Matter*. Durham, NC: Duke University Press, 2022.

Davis, Mike. *Ecology of Fear: Los Angeles and the Imagination of Disaster*. London: Picador, 1998.

de Villiers, Nicholas. "Glancing, Cruising, Staring: Queer Ways of Looking." *Bright Lights Film Journal*. August 1, 2007. https://brightlightsfilm.com/glancing-cruising-staring-queer-ways-looking/.

DeAngelis, Michael. "Soft and Hard: Accessible Masculinity, Celebrity, and Post-Millennial Cuteness." In *The Aesthetics and Affects of Cuteness*, edited by Joshua Paul Dale, Joyce Goggin, Julia Leyda, Anthony P. McIntyre, and Diane Negra, 194–215. New York: Routledge, 2017.

Debord, Guy. "*Détournement* as Negation and Prelude." In *Situationist International Anthology*, translated by Ken Knabb. Reprint, Oakland: PM Press, 2024. First published in 1959.

Debord, Guy. *The Society of the Spectacle*. Translated and annotated by Ken Knabb. Berkeley: Bureau of Public Secrets, 2014. First published in 1967.

Debord, Guy, and Gil J. Wolman. "A User's Guide to *Détournement*." In *Situationist International Anthology*, translated by Ken Knabb. Reprint, Oakland: PM Press, 2024. First published in 1956.

Diner, Cagla, and Şule Toktaş. "Waves of Feminism in Turkey: Kemalist, Islamist and, Kurdish Women's Movements in an Era of Globalization." *Journal of Balkan and Near Eastern Studies* 12, no. 1 (2010): 41–57. doi:10.1080/19448950903507388.

Doane, Mary Ann. *The Desire to Desire the Women's Film of the 1940s*. Bloomington Indiana University Press, 1987.

Dole, Carol M. "The Return of Pink: Legally Blonde, Third-Wave Feminism, and Having It All." *Chick Flicks: Contemporary Women at the Movies*, edited by Suzanne Ferriss and Mallory Young, 58–78. New York: Routledge, 2008.

Doty, Alexander. *Flaming Classics: Queering the Film Canon*. New York: Routledge, 2000.

Doty, Alexander. *Making Things Perfectly Queer: Interpreting Mass Culture*. Minneapolis: University of Minnesota Press, 1993.

Dyer, Richard. *Heavenly Bodies: Film Stars and Society*. 2nd ed. London: Macmillan, 2004.

Eckert, Charles. "The Carole Lombard in Macy's Window." *Quarterly Review of Film Studies* 3, no. 1 (1978): 1–21. doi:10.1080/10509207809391376.

Edelman, Lee. *No Future: Queer Theory and the Death Drive*. Durham, NC: Duke University Press, 2004.

Emily, Carmen. *Independent Stardom: Freelance Women in the Hollywood Studio System*. Austin: University of Texas Press, 2016.

Entwistle, Joanne. *The Fashioned Body: Fashion, Dress and Modern Social Theory*. 2nd ed. London: Polity Press, 2015.

Epton, Nancy. *The Sound of Silence: Ryan Gosling, Expressionism and the Silent Hero in 21st Century Film*. New York: Bloomsbury, 2024.

Evans, Caroline. "The Enchanted Spectacle." *Fashion Theory* 5, no. 3 (August 2001): 271–310. https://doi.org/10.2752/136270401778960865.

Farrelly, Trisia, Sy Taffel, and Ian Shaw, eds. *Plastic Legacies: Pollution, Persistence, and Politics*. Edmonton: Athabasca University Press, 2021.

Fielder, Leslie. *Love and Death in the American Novel*. 2nd ed. Dallas: Dalkey Archive Press, 1998.

Fleury, John, Bryan Hikari Hartzheim, and Stephen Mamber, eds. *The Franchise Era: Managing Media in the Digital Economy*. Edinburgh: Edinburgh University Press, 2019.

Ford, Jessica. "Women's Indie Television: The Intimate Feminism of Women-Centric Dramedies." *Feminist Media Studies* 19, no. 7 (2019): 928–43.

Fraser, Nancy. "Feminism, Capitalism and the Cunning of History." *New Left Review* 56 (2009): 97–117.

Freeman, Elizabeth. "Queer Belongings: Kinship Theory and Queer Theory." In *A Companion to Lesbian, Gay, Bisexual, Transgender, and Queer Studies*, edited by George Haggerty and Molly McGerry, 293–313. Malden, MA: Blackwell Publishing, 2007.

Garber, Marjorie. "Introduction." In *Vested Interests: Cross-Dressing and Cultural Anxiety*, 1–3. New York: Routledge, 1992.

Garson, Charlotte. "*Barbie*, la revente d'une blonde." *Cahiers du cinéma*, July 24, 2023. https://www.cahiersducinema.com/actualites/barbie_-la_revente_d_une_blonde/.

Gill, Rosalind. "From Sexual Objectification to Sexual Subjectification: The Resexualisation of Women's Bodies in the Media." *Feminist Media Studies* 3, no. 1 (2003): 100–6.

Gill, Rosalind. "Postfeminist Media Culture: Elements of a Sensibility." *European Journal of Cultural Studies* 10, no. 2 (2007): 147–66.

Gill, Rosalind. "Post-Post-Feminism? New Feminist Visibilities in Postfeminist Times." *Feminist Media Studies* 16, no. 4 (June 23, 2016): 610–30. https://doi.org/10.1080/14680 777.2016.1193293.

Gillis, Stacy. "A Proposal in Plastic: Jane Austen in Barbie Land." *Feminist Theory* 25, no. 4 (2024): 580–86.

Gilman, Sander L. *Making the Body Beautiful: A Cultural History of Aesthetic Surgery.* Princeton: Princeton University Press, 1999.

Ging, Debbie. "Alphas, Betas, and Incels: Theorizing the Masculinities of the Manosphere." *Men and Masculinities* 22, no. 4 (2019): 638–57.

Grasso, Silvia. *Filosofia di Barbie.* Genoa: Il Melangolo, 2024.

Greenberg, Clement. "Avant-Garde and Kitsch." In *Art and Culture: Critical Essays*, 3–21. Boston: Beacon Press, 1961.

Greenblatt, Stephen. *Renaissance Self-Fashioning: From More to Shakespeare.* Chicago: University of Chicago Press, 2005.

Greven, David. *Ghost Faces: Hollywood and Post-Millennial Masculinity.* Albany: SUNY Press, 2016.

Gundle, Stephen. *Glamour: A History.* Oxford: Oxford University Press, 2009.

Güneş, Ayşe, and Ezikoğlu Çağlar. "Legal and Political Challenges of Gender Equality and Crimes against Women in Turkey: The Question of Istanbul Convention." *Women & Criminal Justice* 33, no. 1 (2022): 14–27. doi:10.1080/08974454.2022.2040695.

Gupta-Nigam, Anirban. "Plastic Flowers: Overlooking Resource Scarcity in Postwar America." *Theory, Culture & Society* 37, no. 6 (2020): 111–33.

Halberstam, Jack. *In a Queer Time and Place: Transgender Bodies, Subcultural Lives.* New York: New York University Press, 2005.

Halberstam, Jack. *The Queer Art of Failure.* Durham, NC: Duke University Press, 2011.

Hall, Stuart James. "Love Must Imagine the World: Quantum Mechanics in *Barbie*." *Feminist Theory* 25, no. 4 (2024): 516–20.

Halperin, David. *Saint Foucault: Towards a Gay Hagiography.* Oxford: Oxford University Press, 1995.

Hanieh, Adam. "Petrochemical Empire. The Geo-Politics of Fossil-Fuelled Production." *New Left Review* 130 (2021): 25–51.

Heidegger, Martin. *Being and Time.* Translated by John Macquarrie and Edward Robinson. New York: Harper & Row Publishers, 1962.

Henderson, Danielle. *Feminist Ryan Gosling: Feminist Theory from Your Favorite Sensitive Movie Dude.* Philadelphia: Running Press, 2012.

Henderson, Lisa. *Love and Money: Queers, Class and Cultural Production.* New York: New York University Press, 2013.

Hilal, Peker-Dura. "The Social Construction of Masculinity on New Media: Ekşi Sözlük and Interpretative Repertoires." *Nesne Dergisi* 9, no. 21 (2021): 511–33.

Hodges, Adam. "'Yes, We Can' and the Power of Political Slogans." *Anthropology News*, 2019. http://works.bepress.com/adamhodges/105/.

Hülagü, Funda. "Anti-Feminism in Turkey: A Critical Political Economy Perspective." *Gender: Zeitschrift für Geschlecht, Kultur und Gesellschaft* 6 (2021): 25–41. http://dx.doi.org/10.25595/2290.

Hutcheon, Linda. *A Poetics of Postmodernism.* London: Routledge, 1988.

Hutcheon, Linda. *Irony's Edge: The Theory and Politics of Irony.* London: Routledge, 1995.

Isaacson, Johanna. "From Riot Grrrl to CrimethInc: A Lineage of Expressive Negation in Feminist Punk and Queercore." *Liminalities: A Journal of Performance Studies* 7, no. 4 (2011): 1–18. http://liminalities.net/7-4/expressivenegation.pdf.

Izod, John. *Hollywood and the Box Office, 1895–1986*. Basingstoke: Macmillan, 1988.

Jagose, Annamarie. *Queer Theory: An Introduction*. New York: New York University Press, 1996.

Jameson, Fredric. *Postmodernism, or the Cultural Logic of Late Capitalism*. Durham, NC: Duke University Press, 1992.

Jeffords, Susan. *Hard Bodies: Hollywood Masculinity in the Reagan Era*. New Brunswick, NJ: Rutgers University Press, 1994.

Johnstone, Nick. *The Biography: Ryan Gosling, Hollywood's Finest*. London: John Blake, 2013.

Kancı, Tuba, Buşra Çelik, Yavuz Bülent Bekki, and Umutcan Tarcan. "The Anti-Gender Movement in Turkey: An Analysis of Its Reciprocal Aspects." *Turkish Studies* 24, no. 5 (2023): 882–904. doi:10.1080/14683849.2022.2164189.

Kandiyoti, Deniz. "Locating the Politics of Gender: Patriarchy, Neo-Liberal Governance and Violence in Turkey." *Research and Policy on Turkey* 1, no. 2 (2016): 103–18. doi:10.1080/23760818.2016.1201242.

Keeling, Kara. *Queer Times, Black Futures*. New York: New York University Press, 2019.

Kendrick, James. "What Is the Criterion? The Criterion Collection as an Archive of Film as Culture." *Journal of Film and Video* 53, nos. 2/3 (2001): 124–39.

Kessler, Kelly. *Destabilizing the Hollywood Musical*. London: Palgrave Macmillan, 2010.

Kimmel, Michael, and Lisa Wade. "Ask a Feminist: Michael Kimmel and Lisa Wade Discuss Toxic Masculinity." *Signs: Journal of Women in Culture and Society* 44, no. 1 (2018): 233–54.

King, Claire Sisco, and Isaac West. "This Could Be the Place: Queer Acceptance in *Lars and the Real Girl*." *QED: A Journal of GLBTQ Worldmaking* 1, no. 3 (Fall 2014): 59–84.

Kohnen, Melanie. *Queer Representation, Visibility, and Race in American Film and Television: Screening the Closet*. New York/London: Routledge, 2015.

Kulka, Tomas. *Kitsch and Art*. University Park: Pennsylvania State University Press, 1996.

Laebens, Melis G., and Aykut Öztürk. "Partisanship and Autocratization: Polarization, Power Asymmetry, and Partisan Social Identities in Turkey." *Comparative Political Studies* 54, no. 2 (2021): 245–79. https://doi.org/10.1177/0010414020926199.

Landy, Marcia, and Amy Villarejo. *Queen Christina*. London: British Film Institute, 1995.

Latour, Bruno. *We Have Never Been Modern*. Translated by Catherine Porter. Cambridge, MA: Harvard University Press, 1993.

Lezotte, Chris. "Pink Power: The Barbie Car and Female Automobility." *The Journal of American Culture* 46, no. 3 (2023): 197–208.

Longworth, Karina. *Seduction: Sex, Lies, and Stardom in Howard Hughes's Hollywood*. New York: Harper Collins, 2018.

Lundén, Elizabeth Castaldo. *Fashion on the Red Carpet: A History of the Oscars, Fashion, and Globalisation*. Edinburgh: Edinburgh University Press, 2021.

Lyons, James, and Yannis Tzioumakis, eds. *Indie TV: Industry, Aesthetics and Medium Specificity*. Abingdon: Routledge, 2023.

MacKinnon, Kenneth. *Love, Tears, and the Male Spectator*. Vancouver: Fairleigh Dickinson University Press, 2002.

Malabou, Catherine. *The Future of Hegel: Plasticity, Temporality and Dialectic*. Translated by Lisbeth During. New York: Routledge, 2005.

Malabou, Catherine. *What Should We Do with Our Brain?* Translated by Sebastian Rand. New York: Fordham University Press, 2008.

Malabou, Catherine. *Ontology of the Accident: An Essay on Destructive Plasticity*. Translated by Carolyn Shread. Cambridge: Polity Press, 2012.

Martin, Mathew R. *Psychoanalysis and Literary Theory: An Introduction*. London: Routledge, 2022.

Massanari, Adrienne L., and Shira Chess. "Attack of the 50-Foot Social Justice Warrior: The Discursive Construction of SJW Memes as the Monstrous Feminine." *Feminist Media Studies* 18, no. 4 (2018): 525–42. doi:10.1080/14680777.2018.1447333.

Mayne, Judith. "Female Authorship Reconsidered. The Case of Dorothy Arzner." In *Auteurs and Authorship: A Film Reader*, edited by Barry Keith Grant, 265–6. Malden, MA: Blackwell Publishing, 2008.

McQuiston, Kate. "Some Assembly Required: Hybrid Scores in Moonrise Kingdom and The Grand Budapest Hotel." In *The Routledge Companion to Screen Music and Sound*, edited by Miguel Mera, Ronald Sadoff, and Ben Winters, 477–94. London: Routledge, 2017.

McRobbie, Angela. *The Aftermath of Feminism: Gender, Culture and Social Change*. London: Sage, 2009..

McRobbie, Angela. "Notes on the Perfect: Competitive Femininity in Neoliberal Times." *Australian Feminist Studies* 30, no. 83 (2015): 3–20..

McRobbie, Angela. *Feminism and the Politics of Resilience: Essays on Media, Gender and the End of Welfare*. Cambridge: Polity Press, 2020.

Mears, Ashley. "Discipline of the Catwalk." *Ethnography* 9, no. 4 (December 2008): 429–56. https://doi.org/10.1177/1466138108096985.

Miller, Nancy K. *The Heroine's Text: Readings in the French and English Novel, 1722-1782*. New York: Columbia University Press, 1980.

Mitchell, Audrey, ed. "Forum: Barbenheimer." *Australasian Journal of American Studies* 43, no. 1 (2024): 119–50. https://www.jstor.org/stable/48787093.

Mitchell, Claudia, and Jacqueline Reid-Walsh. "And I Want to Thank You Barbie: Barbie as a Site for Cultural Interrogation." *The Review of Education/Pedagogy/Cultural Studies* 17, no. 2 (1995): 143–55.

Morin, Céline. *Les Héroïnes de séries américaines*. Tours: Presses universitaires François-Rabelais, 2017. https://doi.org/10.4000/books.pufr.9023.

Mulvey, Laura. "Visual Pleasure and Narrative Cinema." *Screen* 16, no. 3 (1973): 6–18.

Muñoz, José Esteban. *Cruising Utopia: The Then and There of Queer Futurity*. New York: New York University Press, 2009.

Mutter, Zoe. "Adventures in Barbie Land." *British Cinematographer* 119 (September/October 2023): 42–9.

National Research Council. *Polymer Science and Engineering: The Shifting Research Frontiers*. Washington, DC: The National Academies Press, 1994. https://doi.org/10.17226/2307.

Negra, Diane. *What a Girl Wants: Fantasizing the Reclamation of Self in Postfeminism*. London: Routledge, 2009.

Newman, Michael Z. *Indie: An American Film Culture*. New York: Columbia University Press, 2011.

Nygaard, Taylor, and Jorie Lagerwey. *Horrible White People: Gender, Genre, and Television's Precarious Whiteness*. New York: New York University Press, 2020.

Oppenheimer, Jerry. *Toy Monster: The Big, Bad World of Mattel*. Hoboken, NJ: John Wiley & Sons, 2009.

Pease, Bob. "The Rise of Angry White Men: Resisting Populist Masculinity and the Backlash against Gender Equality." In *The Challenge of Right-Wing Nationalist Populism for Social Work: A Human Rights Approach*, edited by Carolyn Noble and Goetz Frank Ottmann, 198–205. London: Routledge, 2021.

Perkins, Claire. *American Smart Cinema*. Edinburgh: Edinburgh University Press, 2012.

Perkins, Claire. "My Effortless Brilliance: Women's Mumblecore." In *Indie Reframed: Women's Filmmaking and Contemporary American Independent Cinema*, edited by Linda Badley, Claire Perkins, and Michele Schreiber, 138–53. Edinburgh: Edinburgh University Press, 2016.

Perkins, Claire, and Michele Schreiber. "Independent Women: From Film to Television." *Feminist Media Studies* 19, no. 7 (2019): 919–27.

Piazzesi, Chiara. *The Beauty Paradox: Femininity in the Age of Selfies*. Lanham, MD: Rowman & Littlefield, 2023.

Polhemus, Ted. *Street Style: From Sidewalk to Catwalk*. London: Thames & Hudson, 1994.

Radner, Hilary. *Neo-Feminist Cinema: Girly Films, Chick Flicks, and Consumer Culture*. New York/London: Routledge, 2010.

Radner, Hilary. "Creating Female Audiences: The Decline of the 'Girly' Heroine and the Return of the Formidable 'Femme.'" *Communicazioni sociali* 33 (2014): 357–67. https://www.vitaepensiero.it/autore-hilary-radner-196327.html.

Radner, Hilary. *The New Woman's Film: Femme-Centric Movies for Smart Chicks*. New York: Routledge, 2017.

Radner, Hilary. "Une renaissance féministe?: Le cinéma populaire contemporain et la culture de consommation." Translated by Geneviève Sellier. *genre & écran*. January 5, 2018. https://www.genre-ecran.net/?Une-renaissance-feministe.

Radner, Radner. "Barbenheimer: An Unholy Alliance?," in "Forum: Barbenheimer," edited by Audrey Mitchell, *Australasian Journal of American Studies* 43, no. 1 (2024a): 132–5. https://www.jstor.org/stable/48787093.

Hilary Radner, "Response to Geneviève Sellier," "Forum: Barbenheimer," edited by Audrey Mitchell, *Australasian Journal of American Studies* 43, no. 1 (2024b): 138–9. https://www.jstor.org/stable/48787093.

Radner, Hilary, and Rebecca Stringer, eds. *Feminism at the Movies: Understanding Gender in Contemporary Popular Cinema*. New York: Routledge, 2011.

Rand, Erica. *Barbie's Queer Accessories*. Durham, NC: Duke University Press, 1996.

Reckwitz, Andreas. *The End of Illusions: Politics, Economy, and Culture in Late Modernity*. Cambridge: Polity Press, 2021.

Reeves, Richard V. *Of Boys and Men: Why the Modern Male Is Struggling, Why It Matters, and What to Do about It*. Washington, DC: Brookings Institution Press, 2022.

Reidl, Martin J., Josephine Lukito, and Samuel C. Woolley. "Political Influencers on Social Media: An Introduction." *Social Media + Society* 9, no. 2 (2023): 1–9.

Rottenberg, Catherine. *The Rise of Neoliberal Feminism*. New York: Oxford University Press, 2018.

Rubin, Gayle. "Thinking Sex." In *The Gay and Lesbian Studies Reader*, edited by Michelle Aina Barale, Henry Abelove, and David M. Halperin, 3–44. New York: Routledge, 1993.

Ruti, Mari. *Feminist Film Theory and* Pretty Woman. New York: Bloomsbury, 2016.

San Filippo, Maria. *The B Word: Bisexuality in Contemporary Film and Television*. Bloomington: Indiana University Press, 2013.

Sandoval, Chela. *Methodology of the Oppressed*. Minneapolis: University of Minnesota Press, 2000.

Schatz, Thomas. "New Hollywood, New Millennium." In *Film Theory and Contemporary Hollywood Movies*, edited by Warren Buckland, 19–46. London: Routledge, 2009.

Sconce, Jeffrey. "Irony, Nihilism and the New American 'Smart' Film." *Screen* 43, no. 4 (2002): 349–69.

Sedgwick, Eve. *Epistemology of the Closet*. Berkeley: University of California Press, 1990.

Sellier, Geneviève. "*Barbie*: Une opération commerciale de blanchiment féministe." *le genre & l'écran*, July 30, 2023. https://www.genre-ecran.net/?barbie. Translated into English as: Sellier, Geneviève. "*Barbie*: A Marketing Exercise in Laundering Feminism." In "Forum: Barbenheimer," edited by Audrey Mitchell, *Australasian Journal of American Studies* 43, no. 1 (2024): 135–7. https://www.jstor.org/stable/48787093.

Simmel, Georg. "Fashion." *International Quarterly* 10, no. 1 (October 1904): 130–55. Reprinted in *American Journal of Sociology* 62, no. 6 (May 1957): 541–58.

Sinwell, Sarah. *Indie Cinema Online*. New Brunswick, NJ: Rutgers University Press, 2020.

Smith, Terry. *What Is Contemporary Art?* Chicago: University of Chicago Press, 2009.

Sosa, Joseph Jay. "Backlash." *Feminist Anthropology* 3, no. 2 (2022): 198–205. https://doi.org/10.1002/fea2.12087.

Spencer, Carol. *Dressing Barbie: A Celebration of the Clothes That Made America's Favorite Doll, and the Incredible Woman Behind Them*. New York: Harper Design, 2019.

Staiger, Janet. "The Package-Unit System: Unit Management after 1955." In *The Classical Hollywood Cinema: Film Style & Mode of Production to 1960*, edited by David Bordwell et al., 571–79. London: Routledge & Kegan Paul, 1985.

Stamp, Shelley. *Movie-Struck Girls: Women and Motion Picture Culture after the Nickelodeon*. Princeton: Princeton University Press, 2000.

Stanfill, Mel. "Where the Femslashers Are: Media on the Lesbian Continuum." *Transformative Works and Cultures*. Special Issue, *Queer Female Fandom* 24 (2017). https://doi.org/10.3983/twc.2017.0959.

Steinbock, Eliza. *Shimmering Images: Trans Cinema, Embodiment, and the Aesthetics of Change*. Durham, NC: Duke University Press, 2019.

Stiegler, Bernard. *Technics and Time 2: Disorientation*. Translated by Stephen Barker. Stanford: Stanford University Press, 2009.

Taffel, Sy. "Technofossils of the Anthropocene: Media, Geology and Plastics." *Cultural Politics* 12, no. 3 (2016): 355–75.

Tasker, Yvonne. "Vision and Visibility: Women Filmmakers, Contemporary Authorship, and Feminist Film Studies." In *Reclaiming the Archive: Feminism and Film History*, edited by Vicki Callahan, 219–26. Detroit: Wayne State University Press, 2010.

Theweleit, Klaus. *Male Fantasies: Volume One—Women, Floods, Bodies, History*. Translated by Stephen Conway. Cambridge: Polity Press, 1987.

Thompson, E. P. "Time, Work-Discipline and Industrial Capitalism." *Past and Present* 38, no.1 (December 1967): 56–97.

Toscano, Alberto. "Plasticity, Capital, and the Dialectic." *Plastic Materialities: Politics, Legality, and Metamorphosis in the Work of Catherine Malabou*, edited by Brenna Bhandar and Jonathan Coldberg-Hiller, 91–110. Durham, NC: Duke University Press, 2015.

Turner, Luke. *Men at War: Loving, Lusting, Fighting, Remembering 1939–1945*. London: Weidenfeld & Nicolson, 2024.

Tzioumakis, Yannis. "After the 'Great Studio Pullback of '08': Late Indiewood and American Independent Film Theatrical Distribution in the Age of Streaming (2008–2019)." *Media Industries* 10, no. 1 (2023): 1–28.

UNEP (United Nations Environment Program). *Turning off the Tap. How the World Can End Plastic Pollution and Create a Circular Economy*. Nairobi: UNEP, 2023.

Uzun-Weidner, Nil, and Aksu Bora. "Women's and Feminist Movements." In *Authoritarianism and Resistance in Turkey: Conversations on Democratic and Social Challenges*, edited by Esra Özyürek, Gaye Özpınar, and Emrah Altındiş, 117–23. Cham: Springer, 2018.

Vered, Karen Orr, and Christèle Maizonniaux. "Barbie and the Straight-to-DVD Movie: Pink Post-Feminist Pedagogy." *Feminist Media Studies* 17, no. 2 (2017): 198–214.

Verevis, Constantine. "New Millennial Remakes." In *Media of Serial Narrative*, edited by Frank Kelleter. Columbus: Ohio State University Press, 2017.

Verhoeven, Deb. *Jane Campion*. New York: Routledge, 2009.

Vincent, Ben, Sonja Erikainen, and Ruth Pearce, eds. *TERF Wars: Feminism and the Fight for Transgender Futures*. London: Sage, 2020.

Vitis, Laura, and Fairleigh Gilmour. "Dick Pics on Blast: A Woman's Resistance to Online Sexual Harassment, Using Humour, Art and Instagram." *Crime, Media, Culture* 13, no. 3 (2017): 335–55.

Wardak, Thomas James. "Author Functions, Auteur Fictions, Understanding Authorship in Conglomerate Hollywood Commerce, Culture, and Narrative." PhD Thesis, University of Sheffield, 2017.

Wark, McKenzie. *Fifty Years of Recuperation: The Situationist International 1957–2007*. New York: The Temple Hoyne Buell Center and Princeton Architectural Press, 2008.

Wark, McKenzie. "*Détournement*: An Abuser's Guide." *Angelaki* 14, no. 1 (2009): 145–53.

Wark, McKenzie. *The Beach Beneath the Street: The Everyday Life and Glorious Times of the Situationist International*. London: Verso, 2011.

Warner, Michael. "Introduction." In *Fear of a Queer Planet: Queer Politics and Social Theory*, vii–xxxi. Minneapolis: University of Minnesota Press, 1993.

Whitesell, Lloyd. "Expressive Thresholds and Anomalous Utterances." in *The Oxford Handbook of the Hollywood Musical*, edited by Dominic McHugh, 7–22. New York: Oxford University Press, 2022.

Wilkins, Kim. *American Eccentric Cinema*. New York: Bloomsbury, 2019.

Wilson, Angela R, ed. *Situating Intersectionality: Politics, Policy, and Power*. New York: Palgrave Macmillan, 2013.

Winters, Della J., Courtney A. Grimm, and Raveena Bola. "'I'm Here to See My Gynaecologist': Reproductive Justice and the Deleuzian Becoming of Barbie." *Feminist Theory* 25, no. 4 (2024): 665–8.

Wolfe, Patrick. "Settler Colonialism and the Elimination of the Native." *Journal of Genocide Research* 8, no. 4 (December 2006): 387–409.

Wood, Robin. "The Incoherent Text: Narrative in the 70s." Ch. 4 in *Hollywood from Vietnam to Reagan*, 41–62. New York: Columbia University Press, 1986.

Wright Wexman, Virginia, ed. *Film and Authorship*. New Brunswick, NJ: Rutgers University Press, 2002.

Yes Men, The. *The True Story of the End of the World Trade Organisation*. London: Penguin, 2004.

Zeisler, Andi. *We Were Feminists Once: From Riot Grrrl to Cover Girlr, the Buying and Selling of a Political Movement*. New York: Public Affairs, 2016.

Žižek, Slavoj. *Less Than Nothing: Hegel and the Shadow of Dialectical Materialism*. London: Verso, 2012.

Index